LEGENDARY LOCALS

OF

COLUMBUS

INDIANA

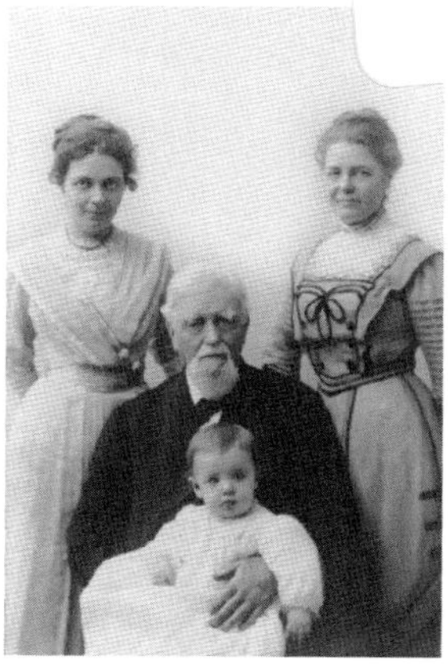

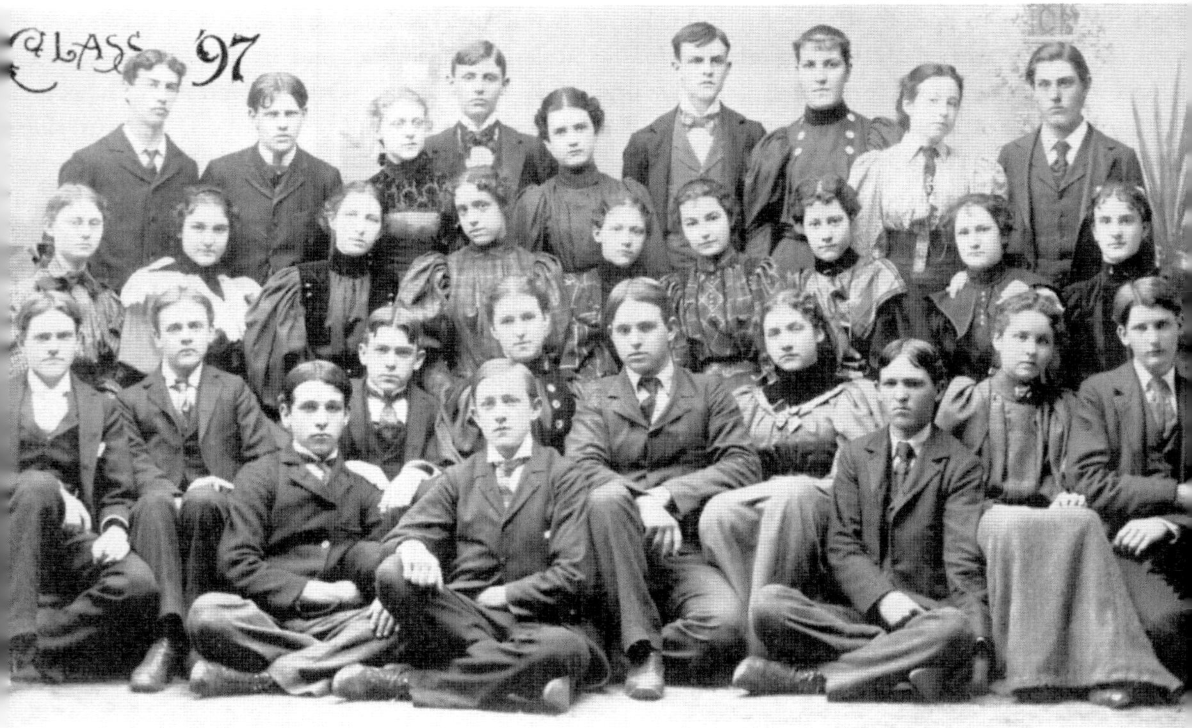

Class of 1897

The Columbus High School class of 1897 included many members of prominent families, such as class president Joseph Irwin Jr., class vice president Joseph Sweeney, Beulah Brown (page 96), Will Schwartzkopf, and George Pence (page 108). (BCHS Collection.)

Page 1: Irwin-Sweeney-Miller Family

Four generations of the Irwin-Sweeney-Miller family are pictured. Joseph Ireland Irwin holds his great-grandson J. Irwin Miller. Standing on the right is Joseph Irwin's daughter Linnie Irwin Sweeney. On the left is his granddaughter Nettie Sweeney Miller, mother of J. Irwin Miller. (Irwin-Sweeney-Miller Family Collection, IHS.)

LEGENDARY LOCALS

OF

COLUMBUS

INDIANA

TAMARA STONE IORIO

LEGENDARY LOCALS

ISBN 978-1-4671-0088-5

Legendary Locals is an imprint of Arcadia Publishing
Charleston, South Carolina

Printed in the United States of America

Library of Congress Control Number: 2013933918

For all general information, please contact Arcadia Publishing:
Telephone 843-853-2070
Fax 843-853-0044
E-mail sales@arcadiapublishing.com
For customer service and orders:
Toll-Free 1-888-313-2665

Visit us on the Internet at www.arcadiapublishing.com

Dedication
To all the people who make Columbus, Indiana, a truly remarkable place to live.
To Chris, Julia, Colvin, Lukas, and Leo, who make it all worthwhile.

On the Front Cover: Clockwise from top left:
Shirley Lyster (Courtesy of Kim Stover; see page 69), J. Irwin Miller (Courtesy of Cummins, Inc.; see pages 20–21), Gen. John Tipton (BCHS Collection; see page 10), Rev. William Laws (Courtesy of Marty Ahlemeyer; see page 52), Prentess Smith (Courtesy of Smith family; see page 98), Beulah Brown Fletcher (BCHS Collection; see page 96).

On the Back Cover: From left to right:
Clessie Cummins (Courtesy of Cummins, Inc.; see page 30), Reeves brothers (BCHS Collection; see page 26).

CONTENTS

ACKNOWLEDGMENTS

I am indebted to many people who helped make this book a reality. First, I could not have shared these stories about remarkable individuals without the many people who gave their time to share memories of themselves or of their family and friends. Without exception, everyone was gracious and encouraging, and their trust in me to tell their stories motivated me greatly. Second, the Bartholomew County Historical Society made the book possible by allowing permission to use its collection of pictures and portraits. I am grateful to executive director Julie Hughes for her knowledge of local history, suggestions about worthy subjects, and her repeated help in locating various images. Nick Speth and Ben Schulte also gave their time to help me find and scan images. It is my honor to donate the author's portion of the book's proceeds to the Bartholomew County Historical Society.

Because any book about remarkable people is limited by the author's ability to identify those people, I was particularly conscious of omissions. Including 145 individuals allows many but not nearly all the worthy people to be highlighted. Thus, the book is a sampling of and not a complete list of the interesting and influential people from Columbus. The chapter distinctions are also arbitrary, as most individuals could fit into several categories.

I must thank the following people, all with knowledge of local history and of the community, to whom I repeatedly turned with questions: Melinda Engelking, Ellen Brunner, Linda Glick Forster, Candy Carr, Ann Knobloch, Barbara Johnson (at the Yellow Trail Museum), and Gordan Lake (at the Atterbury-Bakalar Air Museum.)

I could not have completed this project without the unwavering support from my family, especially my husband, Chris.

Throughout the process of creating the book, I thoroughly enjoyed learning more about the history of my hometown through the people who made it what it is. Before I started, I thought I appreciated Columbus. Now that I am finished, I really understand just how special a place is Columbus, Indiana.

Courtesy line abbreviations include the following: Bartholomew County Historical Society (BCHS), Indiana Historical Society (IHS), and Daughters of the American Revolution (DAR).

INTRODUCTION

Columbus, Indiana, is a small town unlike most small towns. Its beginnings were ordinary, but its story is not. Founded in 1821 in south central Indiana, Columbus was designated the county seat for Bartholomew County, which was founded that same year. The town was briefly named Tiptona in honor of John Tipton, who had surveyed the area the prior year and built a cabin near present-day downtown at the confluence of the Driftwood and Flatrock Rivers, but within a few weeks, the name was changed to Columbus. While it was primarily an agricultural region, businesses quickly sprang up in the new town, and river traffic was very important in the early days before the first railroad arrived in 1844.

An influx of pioneer families, including the Irwins, Crumps, Doups, Marrs, and Perrys, arrived around the time of the county's founding and formed the foundation of the growing community. Many families established farms all over the county, and some of these families remain in the area today. Others settled in town and started businesses to meet the needs of local citizens and to make a life for themselves and their families in the young town.

By the mid-19th century, industry was growing in Columbus. Mills of various types were located all over Columbus and around the county. By the mid-1800s, the Mooney family had moved its large tannery to the downtown area, and the Brown family founded the *Columbus Republican* (forerunner to today's local newspaper, the *Republic*) in 1872. New businesses continued to spring up around the turn of the 20th century, including the Reeves family's Reeves and Co. and Reeves Pulley Company. M.O. Reeves was an inventor and important pioneer in the development of early automobiles.

Outside Columbus, other areas of Bartholomew County developed as well. In southeastern Bartholomew County, Sandcreek Township was the oldest township, organized in May 1821 and home to the town of Azalia, which was known for its Quaker congregations. Azalia was also home to stops on the Underground Railroad during the 19th century. In the northeast corner of the county, Haw Creek Township included both Hartsville and Hope. Hartsville had a well-respected college during the second part of the 19th century. Hartsville College brought Milton and Susan Wright, parents of aviation pioneers Orville and Wilbur, to the area for a time before they settled in Dayton, Ohio. Martin Hauser founded the town of Hope, Indiana, in 1830. Hauser and several other Moravian families traveled from North Carolina to found a new Moravian church and settlement, and the town has been home to the Hope Moravian Church for more than 175 years.

Joseph Ireland Irwin was the patriarch of the Irwin-Sweeney-Miller family, which, perhaps more than any other, left its mark on Columbus. The family was heavily involved in many business ventures, including Irwin's Bank, which became Irwin Union Bank and survived until 2009. In 1919, Joseph Irwin's son W.G. Irwin cofounded Cummins with Clessie Cummins, who was working as W.G.'s chauffeur. Joseph Irwin's great-grandson J. Irwin Miller chaired the company for many years, and today, Cummins, Inc., remains the city's largest employer. Generations of the Irwin-Sweeney-Miller family have also been great supporters of the arts and of historic preservation, and family members were active in the community and supported many philanthropic causes in Columbus and beyond.

When the Tabernacle Christian Church (now First Christian Church) needed a new building in the late 1930s, J. Irwin Miller began to consider the idea of experimenting with modern architecture for the building. The resulting 1942 building designed by Eliel Saarinen was the first example of fine modern architecture in Columbus and the start of an unusual and unlikely story. Miller believed that the built environment enhances a community, and he established the Cummins Foundation to pay the architect's fees for any public building designed by a select list of accomplished architects, paving the way for Columbus to develop into a showplace of modern architecture.

As chairman of Cummins for many years, J. Irwin Miller believed his duty was not only to make Cummins successful but also to make Columbus successful. In 1964, he said the following:

> We would like to see this community come to be . . . the very best community of its size in the country. We would like to see it become the city in which the smartest, the ablest, the best young families anywhere would like to live; a community open in every respect to persons of every race, color, and opinion; one that makes them feel welcome and at home here; a community that offers their children the best education; a community of outspoken churches, genuine cultural interests; exciting opportunities for recreation and a community whose citizens are themselves well paid and who will not tolerate poverty for others, or slums in their midst . . .

Although his influence on Columbus was larger than many, J. Irwin Miller is but one example of the many interesting, influential, and legendary individuals who have made and are making Columbus the unique place it is today.

CHAPTER ONE

Building the City

Many of Columbus's early citizens left lasting imprints on their town. Some established farms, many of which remained in their families for years to come. From the early pioneer settlers to business and civic leaders of the 20th and 21st centuries, people have built Columbus.

Joseph and Mary Cox and their family were the earliest pioneer settlers when they bought a large tract of land in 1819, before the county's founding. They built their home and a gristmill near Haw Creek, and Rocky Ford Road is named for the shallow place in the creek where first wagons and then automobiles crossed the water for decades before a bridge was built. Among other early pioneers were Ransom Perry, Francis Crump, and George Doup, and descendants of these families still live in the area almost 200 years later.

Some early citizens, such as Revolutionary War veteran and abolitionist Joseph Hart, left legacies of service and strong convictions. Hart came to Bartholomew County to escape slave-friendly areas in the South, and the local DAR chapter is named in his honor.

In a city that today is celebrated for its modern architecture, many of Columbus's iconic, historic buildings were designed and built in the 19th and early 20th centuries. John Storey's 19th-century home serves today as the Columbus Area Visitors Center, and Charles Baker's early-20th-century law office is part of the vibrant downtown scene on Washington Street. Although world-renowned architects have worked in Columbus since the 1940s, local architect Charles Sparrell designed many of Columbus's important buildings in the 1880s and 1890s. Several of these buildings survive today, including old city hall, First United Methodist Church, the old post office at Sixth and Washington Streets (now Viewpoint Books), the Maple Grove/Garfield School (now Bartholomew Consolidated School Corporation Administration), the Prall House (Fifth Street and Lafayette Avenue), and the Overstreet House (Washington and Eleventh Streets).

The Brown family's lasting legacy has been among the most important for Columbus. Isaac T. Brown and his family started a weekly newspaper, which later became a daily paper. Although the paper changed names, it not only survives today but also remains in the Brown family.

In the 20th century, Taylor Brothers Construction was responsible for many important building projects around town. Twin brothers Luke and Foss Taylor started a construction business in 1932, and in 1946, Luke's sons Virgil and Dean formed Taylor Brothers with their father. Dean was an architect and worked with the restoration of many historic buildings, such as the Prall House and the BCHS Building on Third Street. Virgil was an original member of the River Rats, the group dedicated to cleaning up and then maintaining Mill Race Park. Rex Breeden and his company also shaped the face of Columbus; Breeden's company led the way for many of the residential and commercial real estate projects that increased options for housing and commerce. It is hard to imagine Columbus without the many development projects achieved by Breeden's company.

Columbus was built by many people who showed vision and determination for a better community.

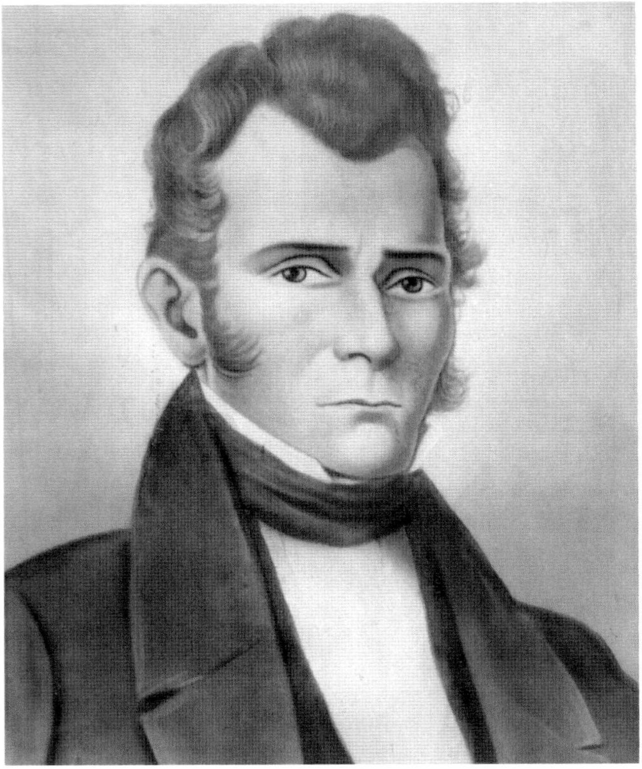

Gen. John Tipton

Considered the founder of Bartholomew County, Gen. John Tipton came to the area in 1820 and pronounced it a good place to live with "good land, good water, and good timber." He later built a cabin near the confluence of the Driftwood and Flatrock Rivers where Mill Race Park is today. When Bartholomew County was founded in 1821, the state legislature briefly named the town "Tiptona" in Tipton's honor but changed it to "Columbus" 36 days later. (BCHS Collection.)

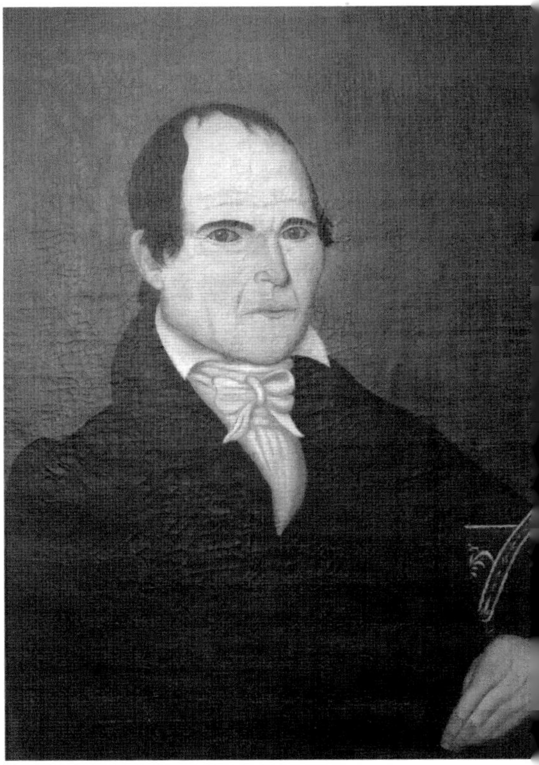

Gen. Joseph Bartholomew

Gen. Joseph Bartholomew fought with Gen. John Tipton in the Battle of Tippecanoe in 1811, where Bartholomew was severely wounded. The battle pitted soldiers led by future president William Henry Harrison against Native Americans living in an area of Indiana Territory north of present-day Lafayette. When Bartholomew County was founded in 1821, General Tipton suggested the county be named after his friend and fellow fighter. (BCHS Collection.)

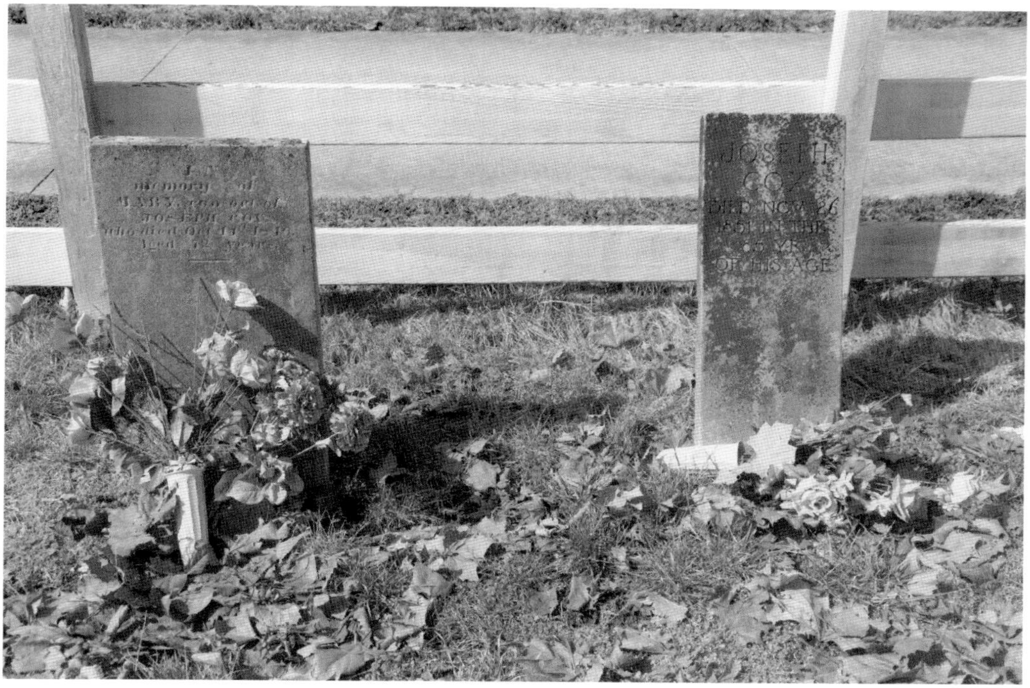

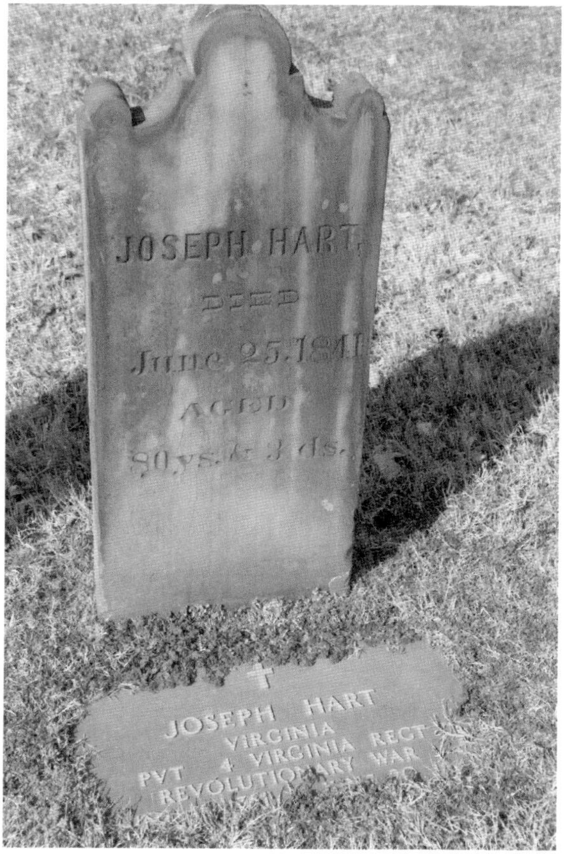

Joseph and Mary Cox
The Cox family was the first pioneer family to settle in Bartholomew County. Joseph and Mary came with their 10 children and their children's families and bought 1,300 acres of land in 1819. Cox built the family's first cabin on Haw Creek near today's Rocky Ford Road. He cleared the first county road in Bartholomew County and built a gristmill. Joseph and Mary's graves can still be found along Middle Road. (Photograph by author.)

Joseph Hart
The local DAR chapter is named after Joseph Hart, a Revolutionary War veteran who was injured in battle in South Carolina. After the war, he moved from Virginia to Tennessee, desiring to live in an area untainted by slavery. When slave-holding families moved into Eastern Tennessee, Hart moved his family to the wilderness of Bartholomew County in 1821 to escape what he considered a sin against man and God. Hart is buried in Garland Brook Cemetery. (Photograph by author.)

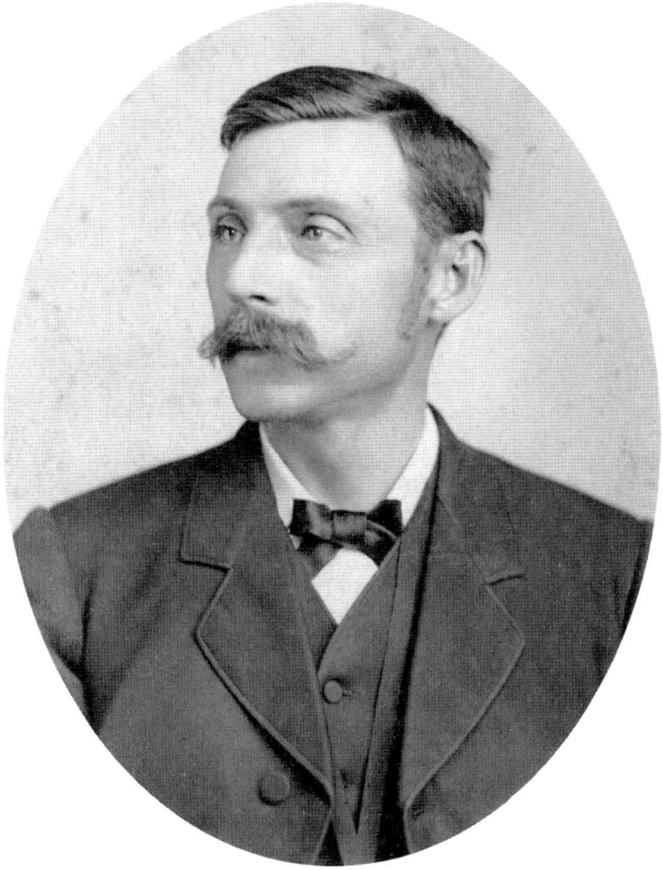

Isaac T. Brown

Isaac T. Brown and a business partner founded the *Weekly Republican* newspaper in 1872. A few months later, the partner sold his interest to Brown's brother, Chalmers Brown. Their father, Isaac M. Brown, became editor of the paper, making it truly a family business. Both Isaac M. and Isaac T. were veterans of the Civil War, although Isaac T. enlisted three times. He first attempted to enlist in 1863 into his father's Indiana regiment without giving an age, but he was rejected, possibly because he was only 15. Early in 1864, he enlisted again and claimed to be 19 (when he was in fact 16). He served in this unit for several months before being discharged and then enlisted again in 1865 for several months near the end of the war. Isaac T. learned the printing trade from his father before and after their military service, as Isaac M. had worked at newspapers in Vigo and Sullivan Counties. In 1872, Isaac T. and his wife relocated to Columbus. After five years of producing a weekly paper, a daily paper was added, and the *Daily Evening Republican* was born. For several years, both weekly and daily papers were published. The Brown family published in two other locations before moving to the building on the northeast corner of Washington and Fifth Streets. This building sat at an angle to the intersection because the train tracks ran diagonally across Washington Street here. In addition to his newspaper work, Isaac T. was appointed postmaster of Columbus in 1881, a prestigious appointment that came directly from Pres. James Garfield; he held the position for four years. In 1894, the Browns sold the paper for $9,000 and moved to Texas for a few years, where they ran a paper in San Antonio. The *Evening Republican* did not fare very well under its new owners, and Isaac T. Brown was eventually convinced to return to Columbus and to buy back the paper for the bargain price of $3,325. He continued to run the paper until his death in 1917. More than 130 years after the Browns founded a daily newspaper in the city, Columbus's daily newspaper, the *Republic*, is still owned by members of the Brown family. (BCHS Collection.)

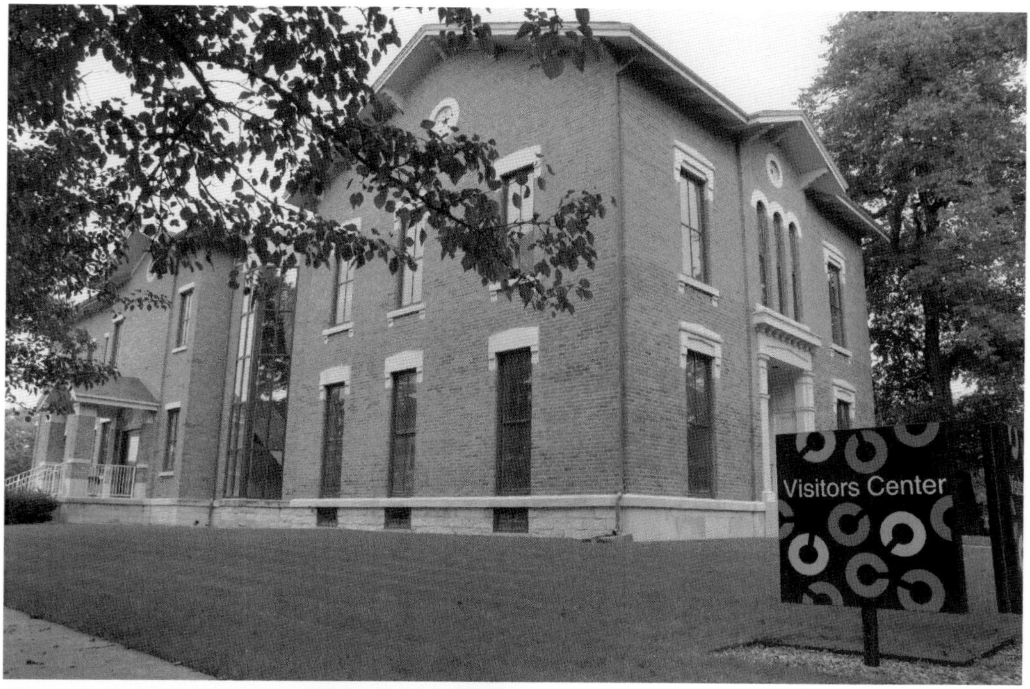

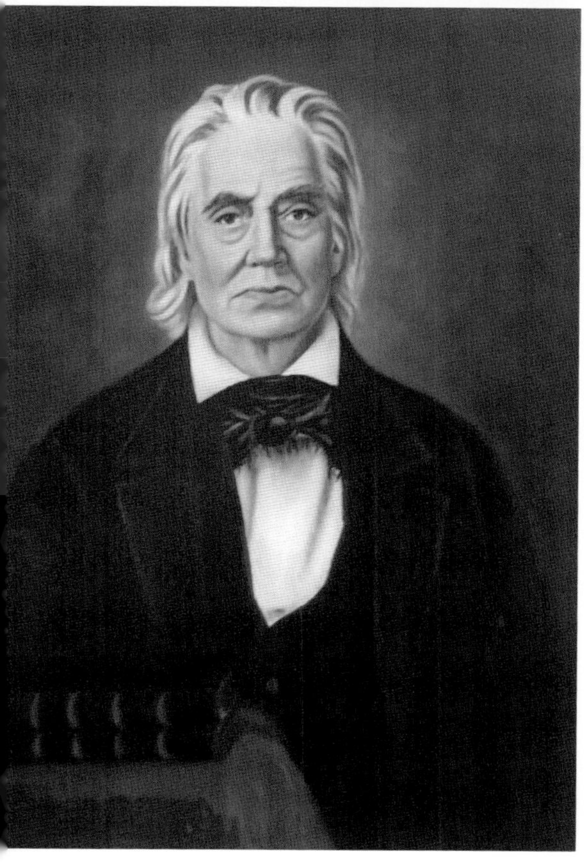

John V. Storey
John Storey was a successful Columbus businessman who came to town from his birthplace of Jennings County in 1853. Originally a saddle maker, he also owned a drugstore, ran a flour mill, and was an original investor in First National Bank. In the 1860s, Storey and his wife built a house at 506 Fifth Street, which today is the Columbus Area Visitors Center. (Photograph by author.)

Ransom Perry
After Bartholomew County was initially surveyed in 1819, a flood of interested men began purchasing property, with Ransom Perry among the earliest settlers. Perry and his family would inhabit several historic homes in the county, starting with the brick home he built in 1835 at 2900 Washington Street. Perry's son James and his wife, Amanda, built another brick home, which still stands just north of the New Hope Christian Church; James and Amanda helped establish New Hope Christian Church. Ransom Perry's great-granddaughter Blanche married Henry Breeding. (BCHS Collection.)

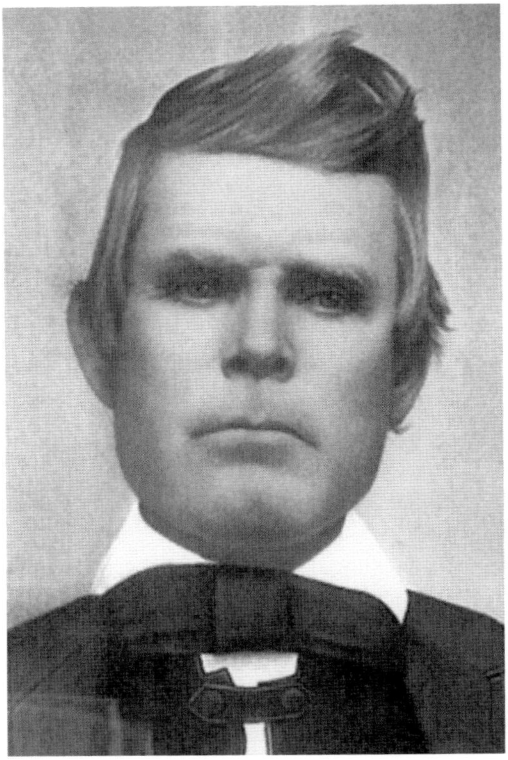

Francis J. Crump

Francis J. Crump arrived in Bartholomew County with the wave of early pioneers who came in 1821. A cabinetmaker, he made money initially constructing coffins during a malarial outbreak. Crump gradually found success buying and selling real estate and, in 1874, he was thought to be the wealthiest man in Columbus. In 1865, Crump was one of 10 original shareholders of First National Bank and the first vice president. (Courtesy of Joy Deckard.)

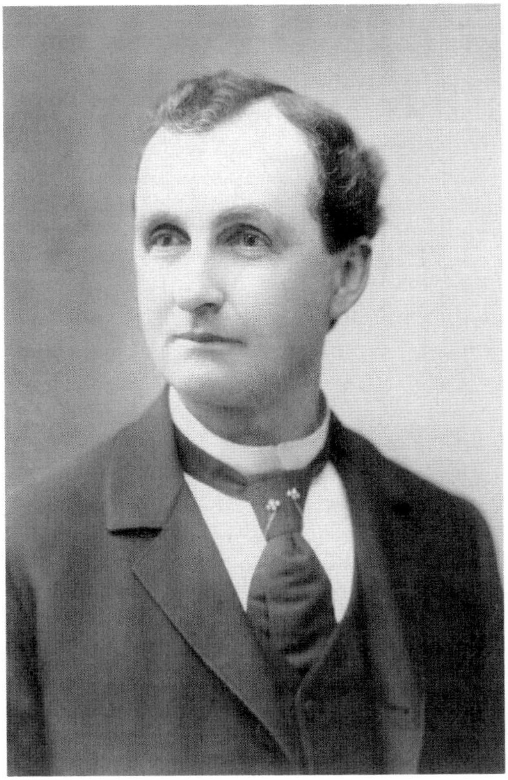

Charles Sparrell

Before Columbus became known for its many modern buildings designed by famous architects, Charles Sparrell left his own mark on Columbus, designing numerous buildings in the 1880s and 1890s. Sparrell was born in Boston but came to Columbus around 1881. He started as a foreman in a lumber company and then began a prolific period during which he designed many buildings, including the Crump Theatre, old city hall, the IOOF Building on Washington Street, and McKinley School (now apartments). (BCHS Collection.)

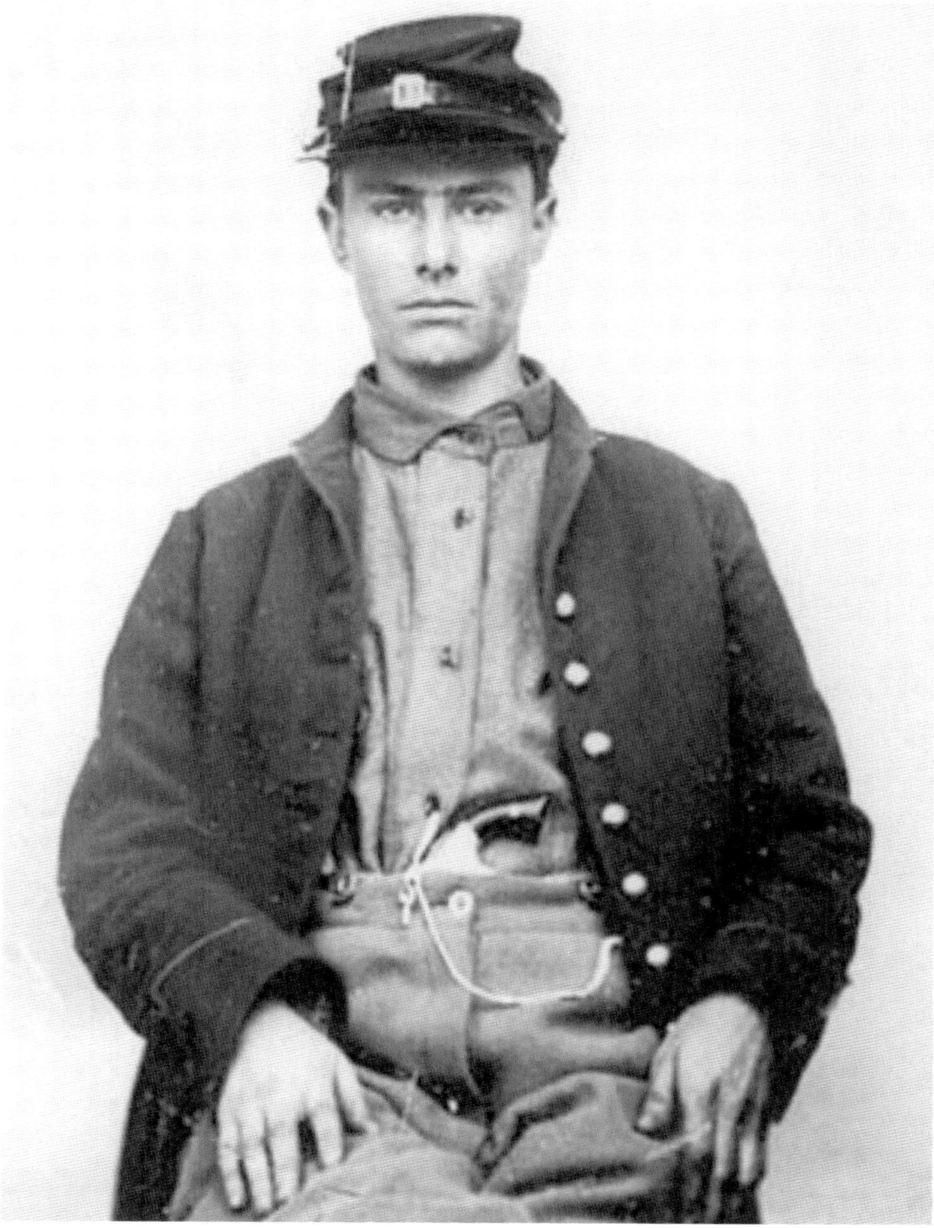

John Crump

The son of Francis Crump, John S. Crump left a lasting mark on Columbus. Crump enlisted as a teenager and spent time with the 22nd Indiana Regiment during the Civil War before being discharged due to illness. He eventually returned to Columbus and became a successful businessman and city leader. In 1889, he opened a theater on Third Street, which still stands today. Across the street from the theater, he built the very fine Belvedere Hotel, which stood until 1967. Crump followed this up by starting the city's first streetcar system in 1890, first powered by mules and then eventually electrified. He also built a powerhouse to provide electricity to his home and to his streetcar system. During his lifetime, Crump was awarded a medal from Columbus citizens as the person who had contributed most to the city. (Courtesy of Joan Weinantz collection.)

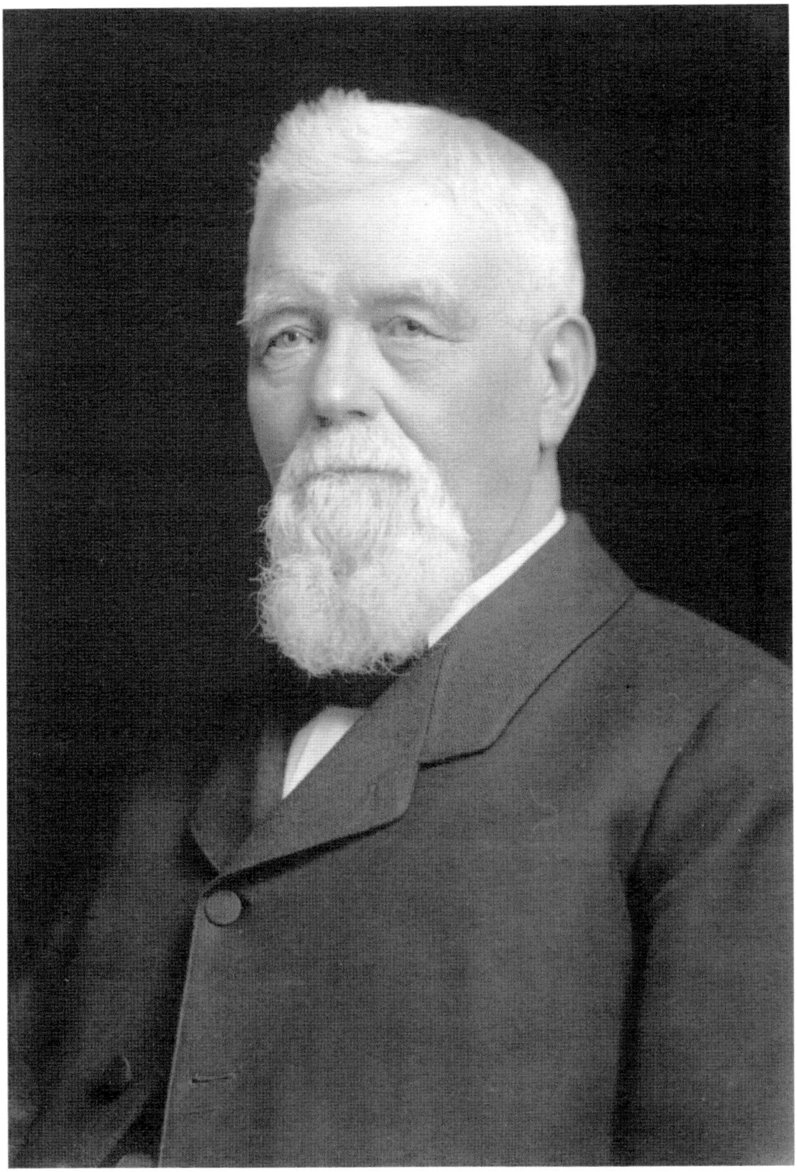

Joseph Ireland Irwin

Joseph Irwin was one of Columbus's most influential early citizens and the patriarch of the prominent Irwin-Sweeney-Miller family. Irwin was born in 1824 outside of Columbus and worked on his father's farm before taking a job in 1846 in a dry goods store in town. According to local lore, Irwin walked the four miles between his home and the store twice daily to save his money and, by 1850, he had enough money to buy the store. Because Irwin's store contained the largest safe in town, Columbus citizens began bringing their money to the store for safekeeping, and gradually Irwin developed a thriving banking business. In 1871, he opened a bank on the northeast corner of Third and Washington Streets called Irwin's Bank, over which he presided until his death. Irwin was a shrewd businessman and realized the importance of transportation. He built miles of roads leading in and out of town and erected the first telephone line in the state. With his son W.G. Irwin, he also invested in the interurban railway and other businesses. (Irwin-Sweeney-Miller Family Collection, IHS.)

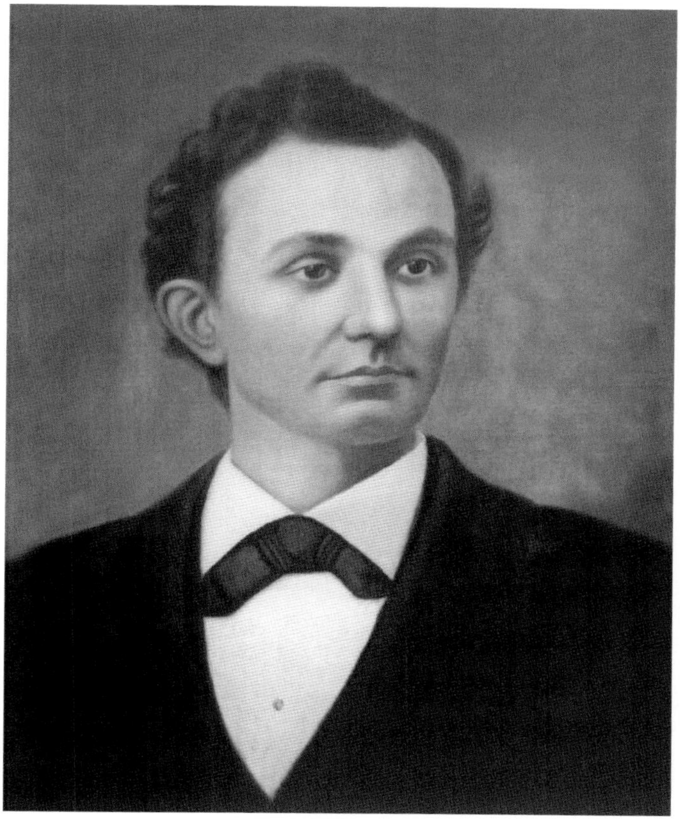

Zachary Taylor Sweeney

Z.T. Sweeney was a member of one of Columbus's most prominent late-19th-century families whose influence went far beyond his community. Born in Kentucky and educated at what is now DePauw University, Sweeney initially considered entering the field of law before being called to ministry. In 1871, he preached in Columbus and was immediately asked to assume the role of pastor of the Tabernacle Church (now First Christian Church), a post he accepted and held until 1898. During this time, he led the congregation in constructing a new building, which stood where today's public library stands. In 1875, Sweeney married Linnie Irwin, daughter of businessman Joseph Irwin, whose home was directly across the street from the Tabernacle building. The Sweeneys had three children—a son who died in a swimming accident at age 20 and two daughters, Elsie Sweeney (page 79) and Nettie Sweeney Miller. Sweeney's grandson was J. Irwin Miller (page 20–21). Besides his local pastorate, Sweeney was active in church, state, and international affairs. Pres. Benjamin Harrison appointed him consul-general to Turkey in 1889, and he and his family spent three years living in Constantinople, where he worked to establish better relations between Turkey and the United States. Later, Sweeney was chair of the Commission on Foreign Relations of the Christian Church, which required him to travel to Russia to lay groundwork for possible church missionary work in the future. Sweeney gave frequent speeches to churches and universities, and he was a prolific writer of articles and books. One of his books, *Under Ten Flags*, reflects his love of art and architecture, as it describes in vivid detail with many illustrations his travels through the Mediterranean. Like many other protestant leaders of the time, Sweeney believed that wealthy nations' increasing power in the world was attributable to God's grace and benevolence and that these nations had a responsibility to use their power to benefit all people and nations. After retiring from ministry, Sweeney served as Indiana Commissioner of Fisheries and Game for 14 years. He was a trustee of Butler University and a founder of Butler School of Religion (now Christian Theological Seminary), where the Sweeney Chapel is named is his honor. (Courtesy of First Christian Church.)

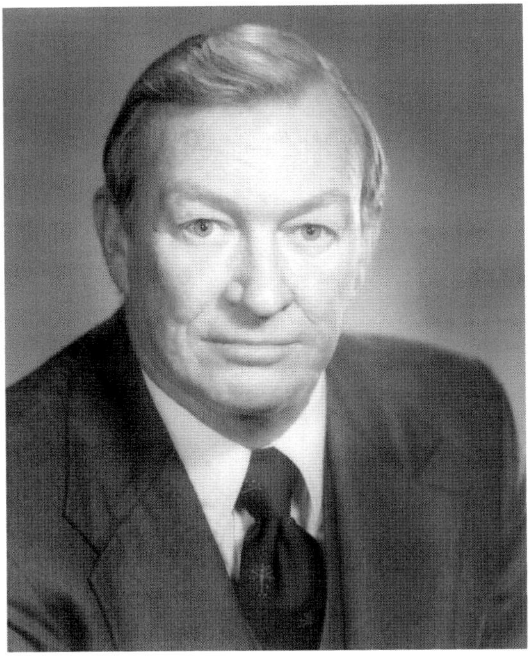

Ray Marr Jr.
Ray Marr was a sixth-generation Bartholomew County farmer and World War II veteran. Marr was also a state legislator, county commissioner, and member of the Bartholomew County Plan Commission. He was involved in the construction of the county jail and was a member of the Mayor's Downtown Task Force. He and his wife, Lou, were champions of historic preservation, restoring the Marr family farmhouse, now in the National Register of Historic Places, and several buildings downtown. (Courtesy of the *Republic*.)

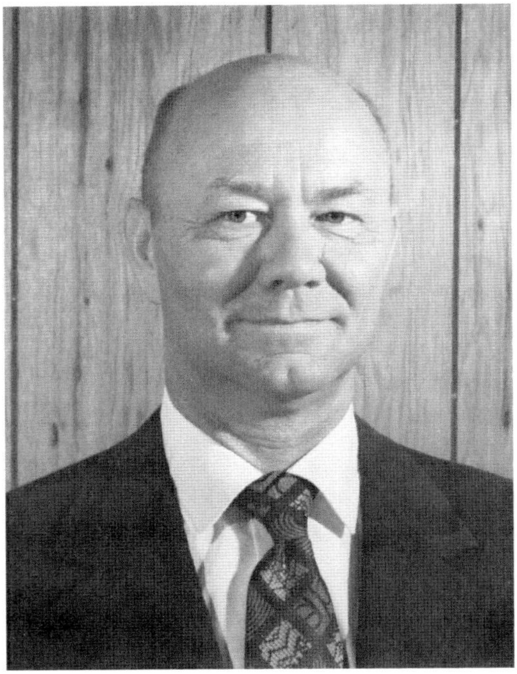

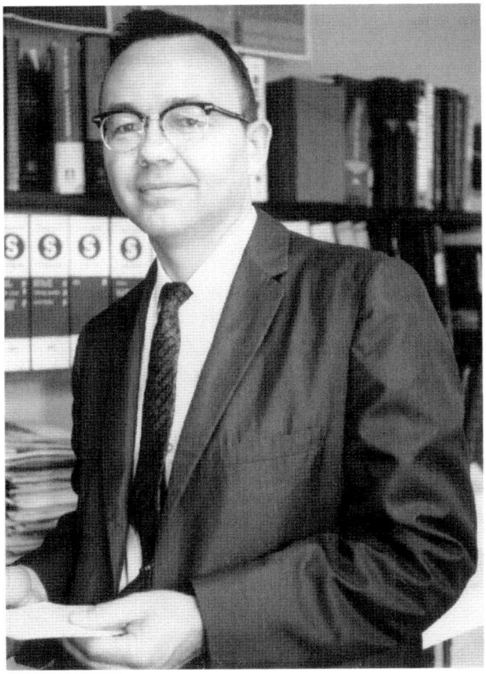

Virgil and Dean Taylor
Virgil and Dean Taylor founded Taylor Brothers Construction in 1946 with their father, Luke Taylor. Taylor Brothers was involved in building many Columbus buildings in the late 20th century—including the post office and Castalia—and restoring others, such as the courthouse. Virgil (left) was also an original River Rat instrumental in bringing a covered bridge to Mill Race Park. Dean was the associate architect for Fodrea School. (Left, courtesy of Taylor Brothers Construction; right, courtesy of Taylor family.)

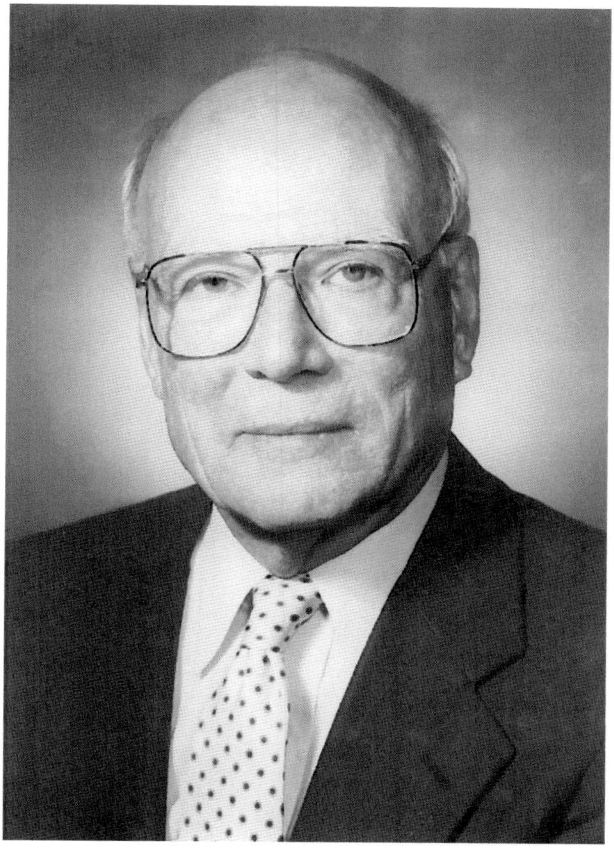

Robert N. Brown

The fourth-generation member of the Brown family to publish a newspaper in Columbus, Robert N. Brown (1920–2004) was also a veteran of two wars, an engineer, and an inventor. Born in May 1920, he was the second child born in the new Bartholomew County Hospital (now Columbus Regional Hospital) on Seventeenth Street. He earned an engineering degree from Purdue University and served in both World War II and the Korean War before joining his father in the newspaper business in Columbus, where he became publisher in 1964. Throughout his career, Brown looked for new ways to grow the business and increase efficiency. He bought several small papers and started a new newspaper in Johnson County, Indiana, which eventually bought out its competition. The newspaper building he designed in Franklin was revolutionary, and people came from all over the nation to view the new offset printing technology. He also patented two newspaper-printing devices he invented. Brown was publisher in 1967 when the *Evening Republican* became the *Republic* in order to project a picture of political independence. The vibrant downtown Columbus of today might never have developed if Brown had not led the way by commissioning the newspaper's new building in a redevelopment zone. This modern glass building on Second Street has received several architectural awards and was named a National Historic Landmark in 2012. Brown was also involved in several industry organizations and was named to the Indiana Journalism Hall of Fame in 1976. Throughout his career, he was heavily involved in the Columbus community, serving on the boards of many organizations, including the Boys Club and the chamber of commerce. He led the fundraising for Heritage Fund's $3-million endowment and served for many years on the hospital's board of trustees during several hospital expansions. Another lasting contribution to the community is the Robert and Betty Brown Awards for Vocal Excellence that Brown and his wife started in 1984 (along with an instrumental award started a few years later), which have provided thousands of dollars in scholarship aid to local students. (Courtesy of the *Republic*.)

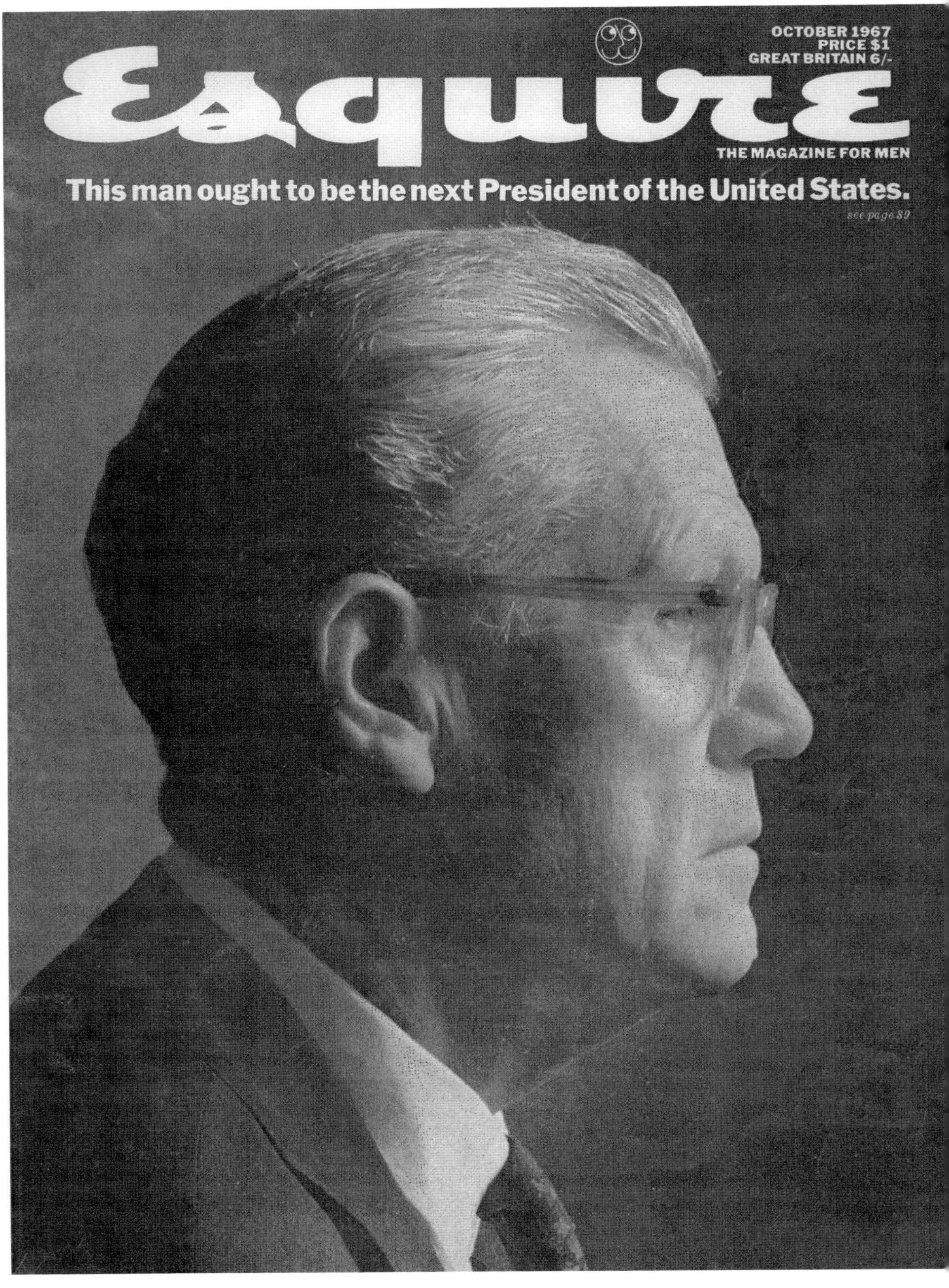
OCTOBER 1967
PRICE $1
GREAT BRITAIN 6/-
Esquire
THE MAGAZINE FOR MEN
This man ought to be the next President of the United States.
see page 89

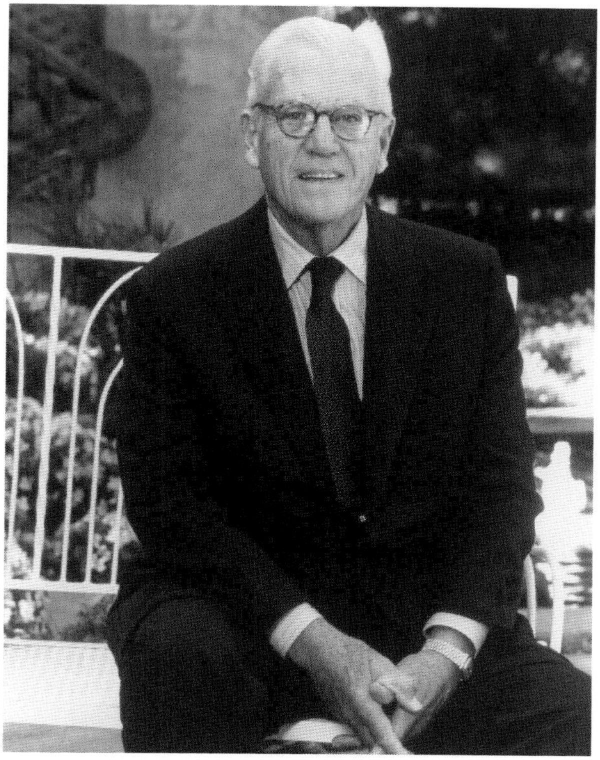

J. Irwin Miller

J. Irwin Miller was an industrialist, businessman, philanthropist, and visionary, who was active in many civic causes and was a member of one of the most prominent families in Columbus. His great-grandfather Joseph Irwin was the founder of Irwin's Bank in 1871, and his great-uncle was cofounder of the Fortune 500 company Cummins, Inc., which is still headquartered in Columbus. J. Irwin Miller was a World War II veteran who worked at Cummins from 1934 to 1977, serving as chairman from 1951 to 1977. Miller's contributions to Columbus and beyond extend far past his time with the city's largest employer. He established the Irwin-Sweeney-Miller Foundation with several family members, which gave millions to various causes in Columbus for more than 50 years. Miller was the first lay person to serve as president of the National Council of Churches and chaired its Commission on Religion and Race, which played a major role in the Civil Rights Movement and helped organize the March on Washington. He once said, "The most important service to others is service to those who are not like yourself," and his actions reflected this. Locally, he supported the efforts of city leaders to pass an open housing ordinance in the early 1960s and, nationally, he headed delegations that met with US presidents John F. Kennedy and Lyndon B. Johnson to advocate for the Civil Rights Act of 1964. In October 1967, Miller was featured on the cover of *Esquire* magazine with the following headline: "This man ought to be the next president of the United States." One of Miller's most-lasting achievements in his hometown was his patronage of modern architecture. In 1954, he established the Cummins Foundation, which offered to pay the architect's fees for any public buildings designed by a select group of well-known architects. World-renowned architects who later designed buildings in Columbus included Eliel Saarinen, Eero Saarinen, Cesar Pelli, I.M. Pei, and Harry Weese. This program directly led to Columbus's prominence in the world of architecture, including being named the sixth most important city for architectural innovation in the United States by the American Institute of Architects in 1991. The Miller home in Columbus, designed by Eero Saarinen in the 1950s, was named a National Historic Landmark in 2000. After the deaths of J. Irwin Miller in 2005 and his wife, Xenia, in 2008, members of the family donated the home to the Indianapolis Museum of Art. (Left, designed by and courtesy of George Lois; above, courtesy of Cummins, Inc.)

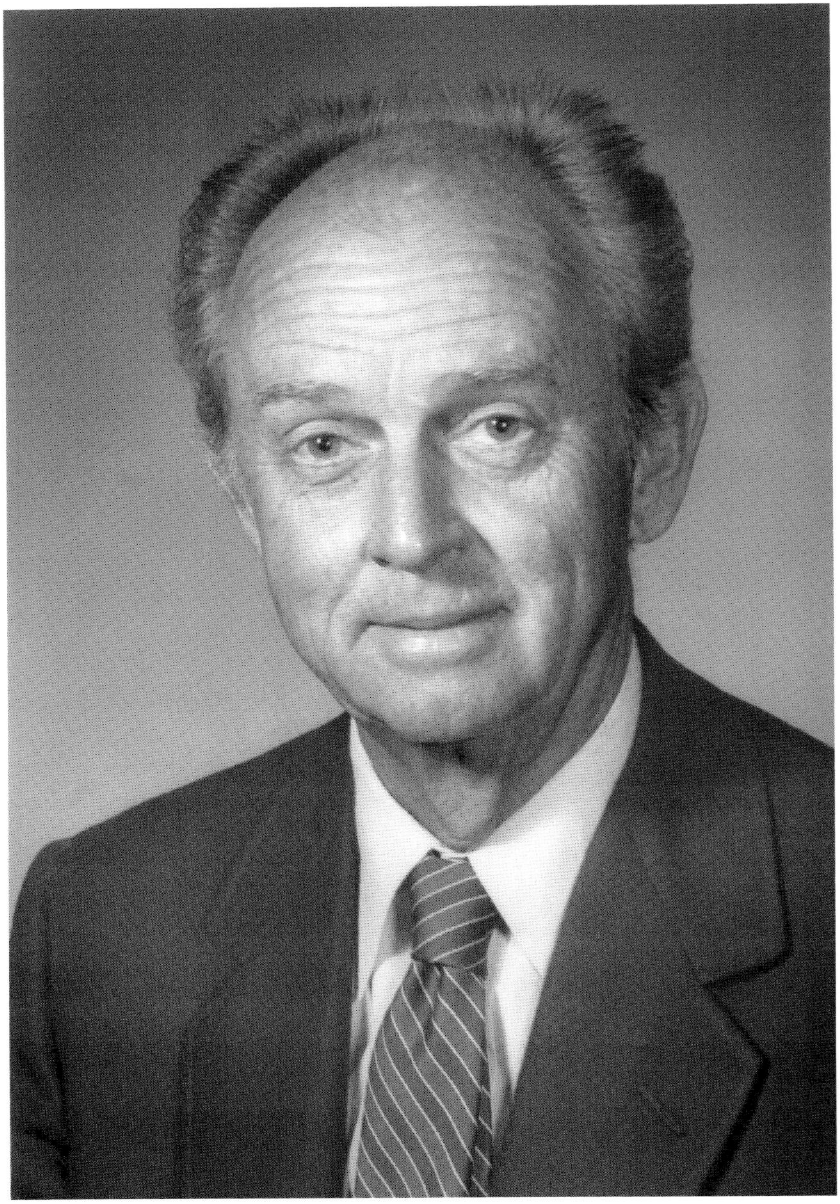

Rex Breeden
In 1951, Rex Breeden and a partner started Breeden Realtors. In the early 1960s, the company played an important role in opening the real estate market to all by helping black families find homes to buy or rent, for which Breeden and his agents received anonymous threats by some who feared their property values would decrease. Later, Breeden expanded from selling homes into development. Breeden was responsible for many residential neighborhoods, including Indian Hills, Parkside Addition, Flatrock Park North, Sandy Hook, Broadmoor, and many others. Important commercial projects for which Breeden was responsible included the Interstate 65 and State Road 46 junction and Woodside Industrial Park. Today, Woodside continues to grow and includes companies employing more than 5,000 workers. Rex Breeden also was involved in many community causes including the United Way and Heritage Fund, and he served as president of the Indiana State University Board of Trustees. (Courtesy of Rex Breeden.)

CHAPTER TWO

Leading in Business and Industry

Columbus has been filled with entrepreneurs and creative and driven business people since the city's earliest days.

Joseph Irwin was one of the town's earliest entrepreneurs, starting a dry goods business that developed into a banking enterprise that lasted for more than 150 years after citizens began bringing their money to the safe in Irwin's store. Irwin and his son W.G. Irwin later invested in multiple business ventures, including the interurban electric railroad, which was a very popular means of travel carrying people all over Indiana in the early 1900s.

The Crumps, including Francis J. and his son John S., were also examples of successful early businessmen. The Crump family had a large farm that extended west of Washington Street and north of Eleventh Street and owned land all over the county. Their business ventures included First National Bank, the Crump Brickworks, a powerhouse, a streetcar system, and a theater as well.

Around the turn of the 20th century, important Columbus industry included the Reeves family's Reeves and Co. and Reeves Pulley Company; Edmund Mooney and sons' Mooney's Tannery; and W.H. Lincoln and George Lucas's Orinoco Furniture and its spin-off, the Lincoln Chair Company. All of these companies had international reputations and did business far beyond Columbus.

The first half of the 20th century saw Clessie Cummins and W.G. Irwin begin the successful engine maker Cummins; Q.G. Noblitt and Frank Sparks found what later became Arvin; and B.F. Hamilton and sons start what became Cosco. These three companies continued to grow until near the end of the 20th century. At one time, Columbus had the unusual distinction of being a small town that was home to the headquarters of two Fortune 500 companies (Cummins and Arvin) before mergers and buyouts changed the business landscape.

Multiple small family businesses also enriched the scene in Columbus. Zaharakos was a family-owned ice cream parlor and restaurant for more than 100 years before it was purchased and restored by Tony Moravec. Stadler Packing Company and Pentzer Printing were other early family enterprises that were eventually bought by others. Kroot Corporation, Dell Brothers, and the *Republic*, however, remain with third, fourth, or fifth generations of the same families.

From the 1950s to 1980s, more local businesses began and later found success, including Johnson Enterprises, Brand's, Columbus Container, IMPACT Forge, and Elwood Staffing to name just a few. All of these companies still had a presence in Columbus in 2013.

Since the very beginning, business leaders in Columbus developed a culture of community involvement. An early example of this was businessman John Storey, an entrepreneur who had owned a saddlery, drugstore, and mill. Storey was serving a term as treasurer of the local school board in 1871 when the bank that held the schools' funds failed. He sought a judge's order to prevent any payouts to anyone else before the schools were repaid, and he covered the salaries of local teachers for two terms with his own money. Since then, Columbus business leaders have been involved in numerous civic and community organizations, and many regularly have looked for ways to share their knowledge, experience, and resources with the community.

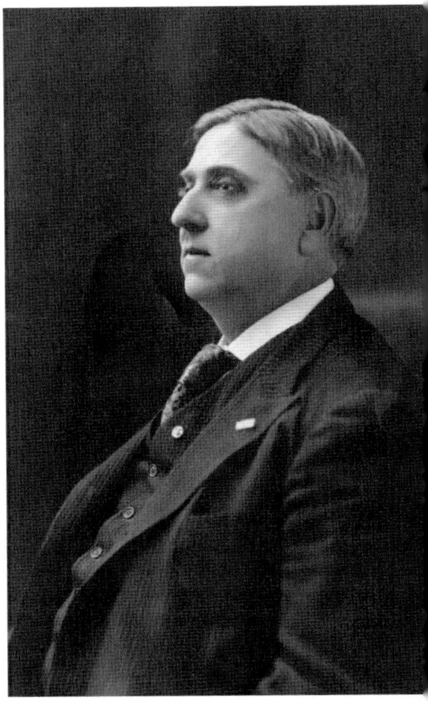

William A. Mooney

Edmund Mooney and his son William W. Mooney established a tannery in Ninevah Township in 1837. In order to be closer to the rail lines, they moved to the future Mill Race Park area in 1863. William A. Mooney entered the partnership of the family business in 1886, and a few years later, the business was thought to be the largest tannery in the world. Mooney's Tannery closed in 1962, and the building was demolished in 1963. (BCHS Collection.)

William H. Lincoln

Some of the finest furniture made in the United States in the early 20th century was made in Columbus, Indiana. The Orinoco Furniture Company, bought by William Harvey Lincoln (seated in the center) and his brother-in-law in the early 1890s, was one of the city's largest employers with 600 employees and was known for finely crafted European-style furniture. The Lincoln Chair Company was spun off in 1913 to make pieces to complement Orinoco Furniture. Business became difficult after the Great Depression and W.H. Lincoln's death in 1935, and both companies were gone by 1940. (Courtesy of Rhonda Bolner.)

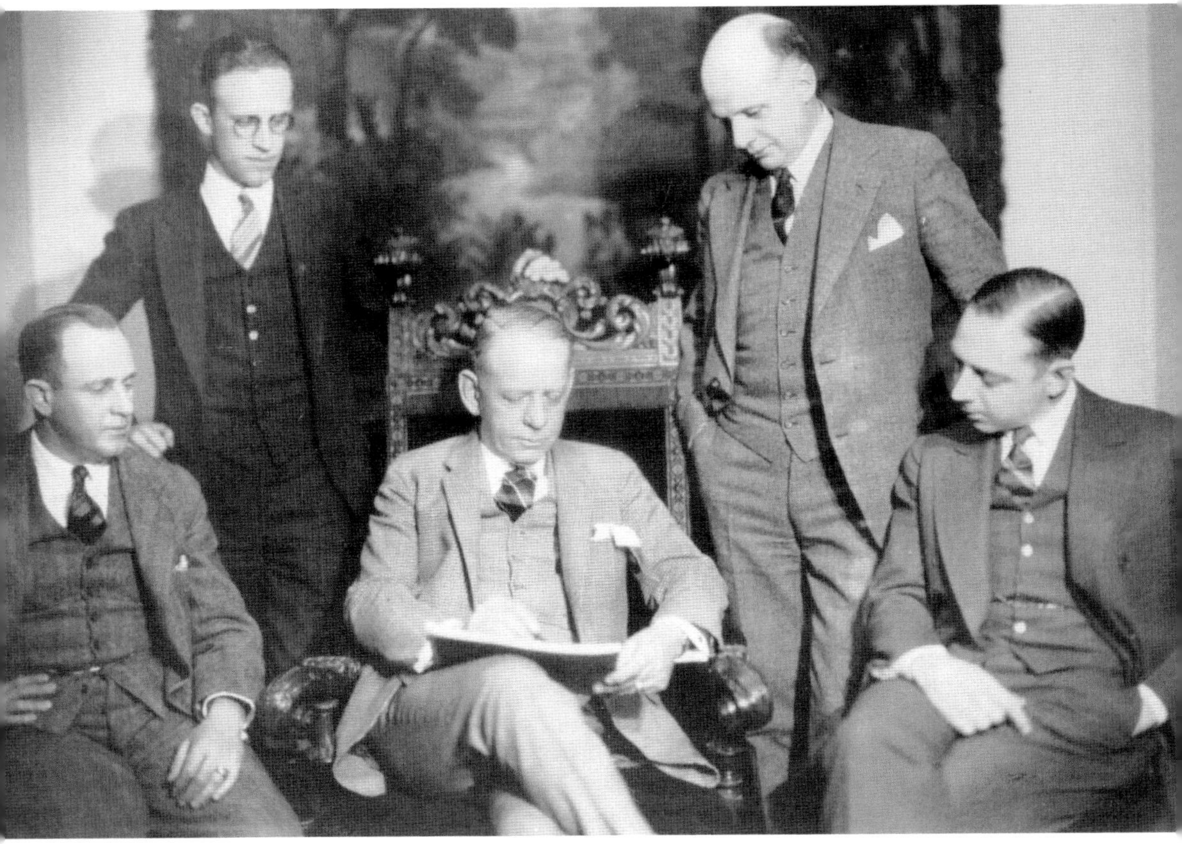

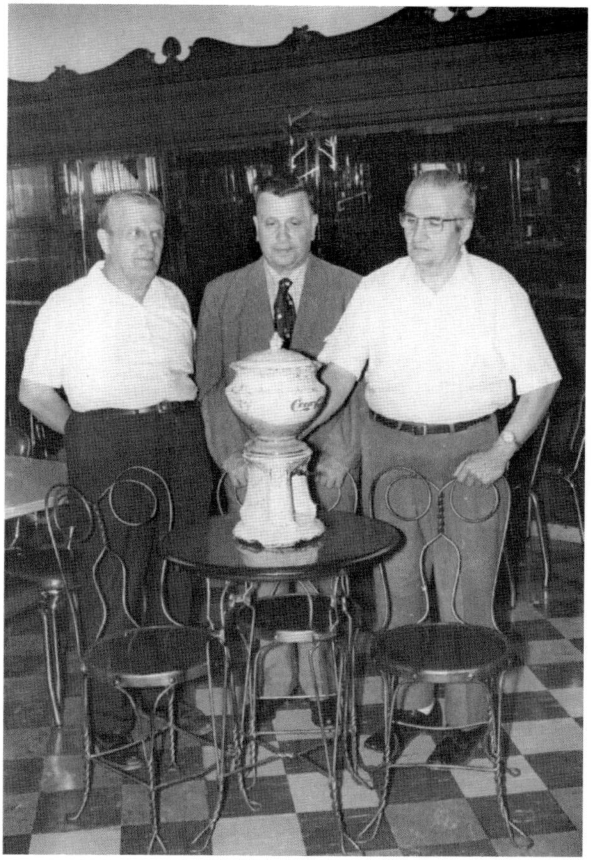

Zaharako Brothers

In 1900, brothers James, Lewie, and Pete Zaharako opened Zaharako's (note the initial spelling included an apostrophe) candy store on Washington Street. Later, the store became an ice cream parlor and soda shop, and it was the social center of Columbus for young people in town for much of the first half of the 20th century. James Zaharako's five sons (three of whom are pictured, from left to right, Manuel, Pete, and Lewie) inherited the business after his death in 1945. A third generation of the family members operated the restaurant until the early 2000s. (BCHS Collection.)

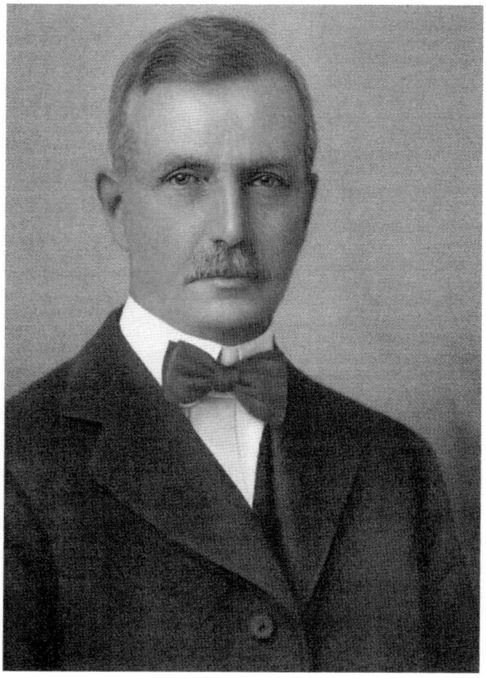

Charles S. Baker

Charles Baker erected the building at 433 Washington Street in 1910 and used the second floor for his law office. A corporate attorney for Irwin's Bank, Reeves Pulley, Mooney's Tannery, and the railroad, Baker later became judge, and he and his wife, Lulu Brevoort Baker, lived on Fifth Street across from the Irwin house. Baker died a few weeks after his 100th birthday in 1956. The building on Washington Street currently houses Baker's Fine Gifts, run by Baker's great-grandson Jeff Baker. (Courtesy of Jeff Baker.)

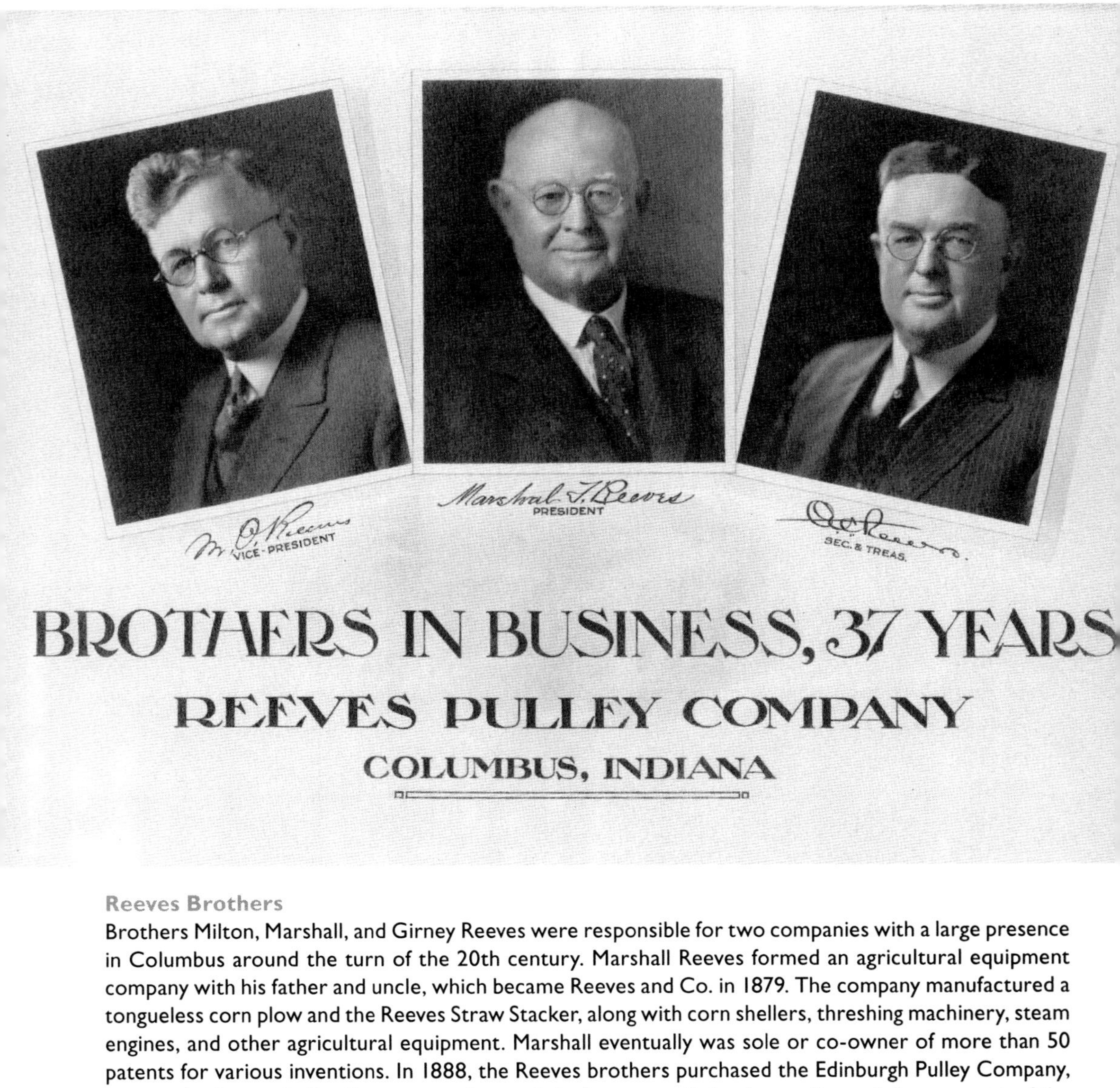

Reeves Brothers

Brothers Milton, Marshall, and Girney Reeves were responsible for two companies with a large presence in Columbus around the turn of the 20th century. Marshall Reeves formed an agricultural equipment company with his father and uncle, which became Reeves and Co. in 1879. The company manufactured a tongueless corn plow and the Reeves Straw Stacker, along with corn shellers, threshing machinery, steam engines, and other agricultural equipment. Marshall eventually was sole or co-owner of more than 50 patents for various inventions. In 1888, the Reeves brothers purchased the Edinburgh Pulley Company, renamed it Reeves Pulley Company and moved the factory to Columbus on Seventh Street north of the Reeves and Co. factory for the manufacture of split-wood pulleys. In most late-19th-century factories, steam engines supplied the power, with the engines turning overhead shafts attached to pulleys, and belts connecting the pulleys to necessary machinery. Wood pulleys were lighter and stronger than cast-iron pulleys, which were too heavy and prone to shattering, and the Reeves split-wood pulleys were considered among the best on the market. (BCHS Collection.)

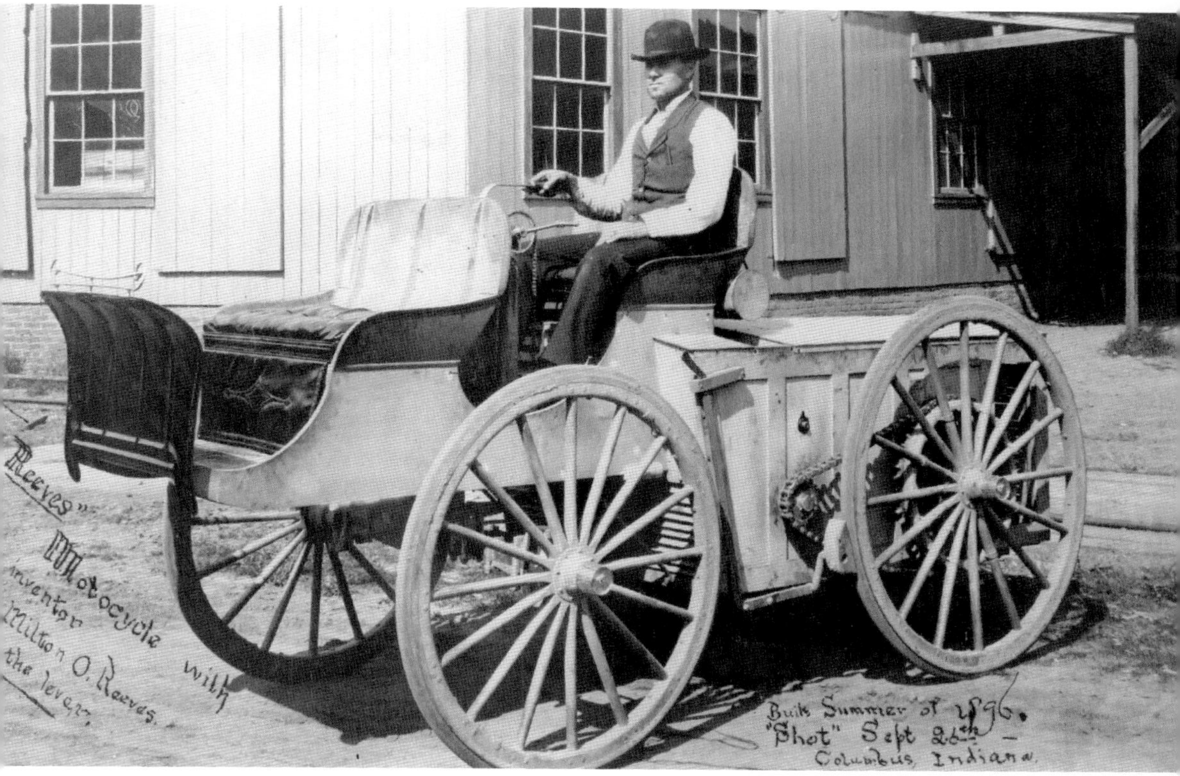

Milton O. Reeves

M.O. Reeves was an industrialist, inventor, and philanthropist who was involved with the family businesses but also was a pioneer in the early automobile field. Born in Rush County in 1864, Reeves held more than 100 patents at his death in 1925. Early in his career, Reeves worked in a sawmill and noticed the structural limitations in the pulleys employed there. After much experimentation, he created a variable speed transmission that helped adjust the speed of a pulley at a workstation, which also would be important in his later experiments in early automobiles. Reeves's first attempt at an automobile—thought to be the fourth or fifth American automobile—came in 1896 when he successfully tested his variable speed transmission in his "motocycle" (pictured). Reeves considered his vehicle superior to Henry Ford's, which had a single-speed transmission. The engine was very loud, which meant the risk of scaring horses sharing the road, and Reeves later created what is thought to be the first automotive muffler. Although most early automobiles contained four wheels, Reeves decided to experiment with the idea that more wheels might make a smoother ride. In 1911, he created the "Octo-Auto" with four axles and eight wheels. The large vehicle, which measured more than 20 feet long and carried four people, attracted public attention but was not a commercial success. Reeves tried again with the six-wheeled Sexto-Auto, but the $4,500 price tag may have been part of the reason that this vehicle also failed to sell. While M.O. Reeves did not achieve great success as an automobile inventor, he was well respected as a genius in the scientific and engineering worlds, speaking at numerous engineering societies and possessing a large private library of scientific works. Reeves also served as a bank president for over 20 years and had numerous community interests. (BCHS Collection.)

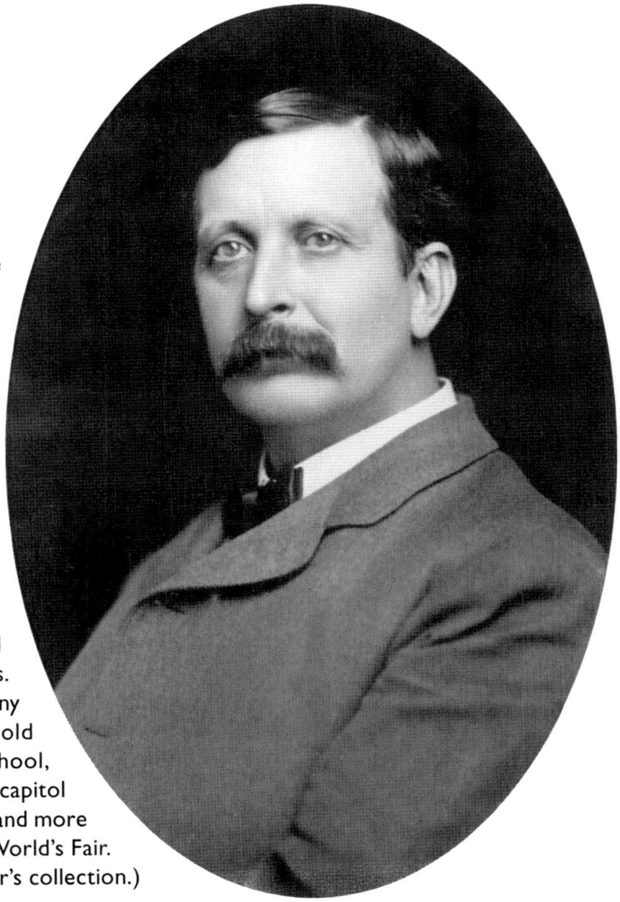

George Caldwell

At the turn of the 20th century, George Caldwell was among Columbus's most famous citizens. Besides serving as mayor from 1898 to 1902, Caldwell was a partner in Caldwell and Drake Iron Works, which was one of the largest contracting firms in the country at the time. The most unique building erected by Caldwell and Drake was the West Baden Springs Hotel in southern Indiana from 1901 to 1902. At its completion, it was the largest dome in the world, larger than the US Capitol and St. Peter's Basilica, and in 1974, the hotel was placed in the National Register of Historic Places. Caldwell and Drake also constructed many buildings in Columbus, including the old waterworks and the 1904 Central School, and around the country, including state capitol buildings in Arkansas and West Virginia and more than 20 buildings at the 1904 St. Louis World's Fair. (Above, BCHS Collection; below, author's collection.)

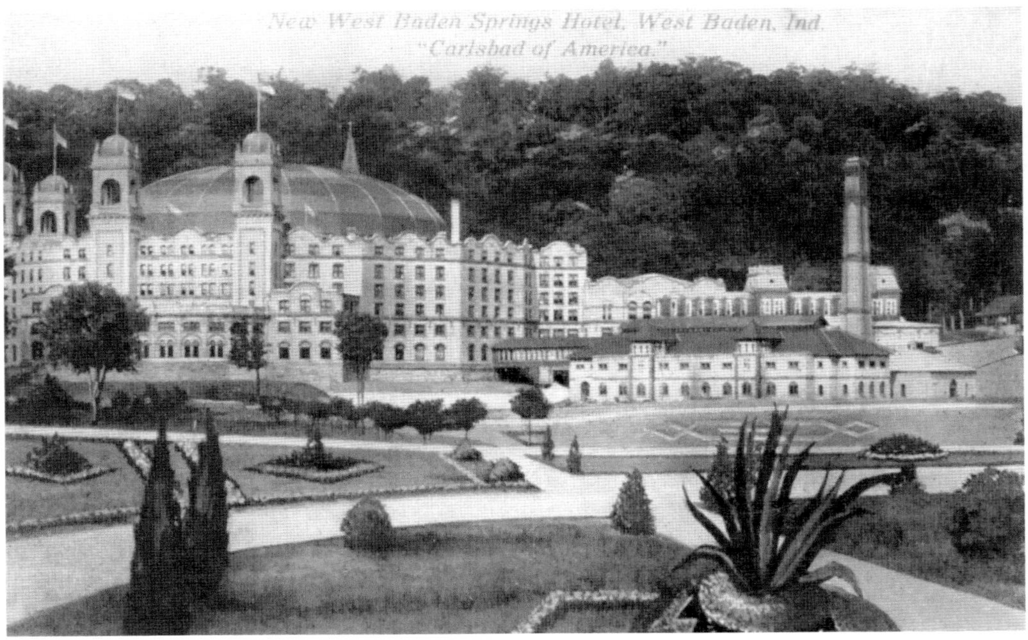

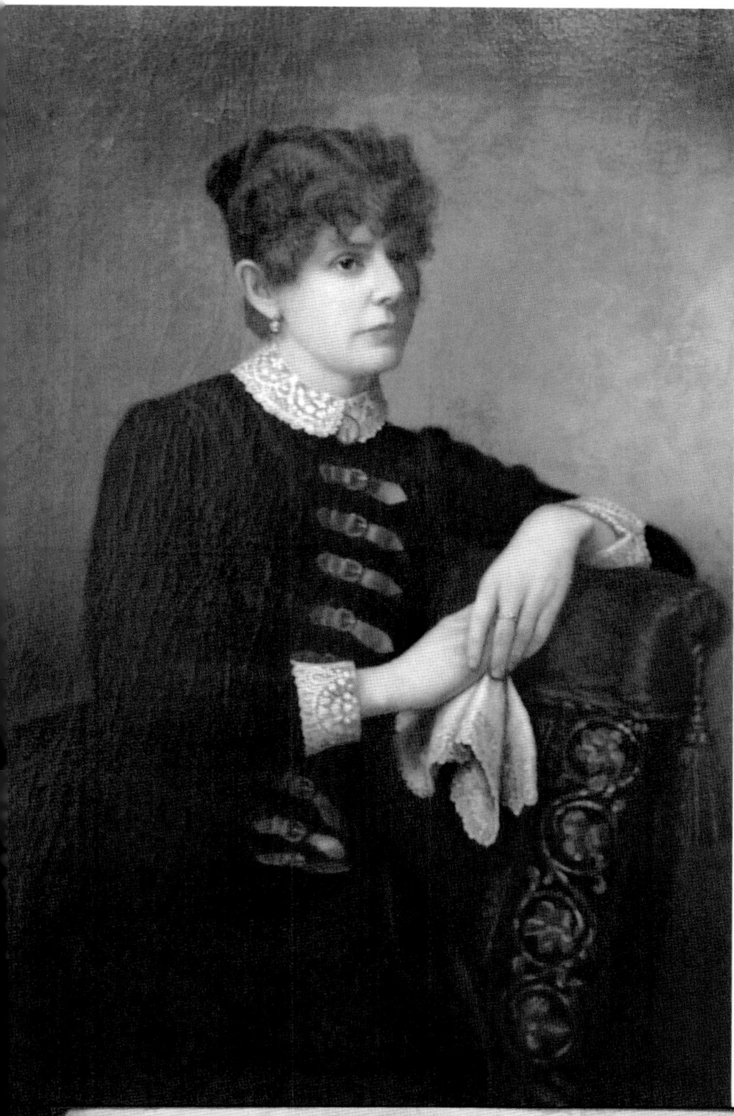

Elizabeth Crump Lucas
Elizabeth Crump Lucas was a member of two of the most prominent early Columbus families. The youngest daughter of Francis J. Crump (page 14), she married Capt. William Lucas, a veteran of the Civil War who was involved in many business ventures in Columbus. They lived in a beautiful home at Washington and Ninth Streets that was demolished in the 1950s. One of many members of her family involved with First National Bank, Elizabeth became known as one of the most prominent businesswomen in Indiana, as she was director of the bank for more than 20 years. In 1927, she became president of the bank, making her the first female bank president in Indiana. Prior to centralized banking, banks issued their own currency, and this 1929 banknote for $50 includes both the bank's name and Elizabeth Lucas's signature. (Left, courtesy of Julie McCawley and Rhonda Bolner; below, author's collection.)

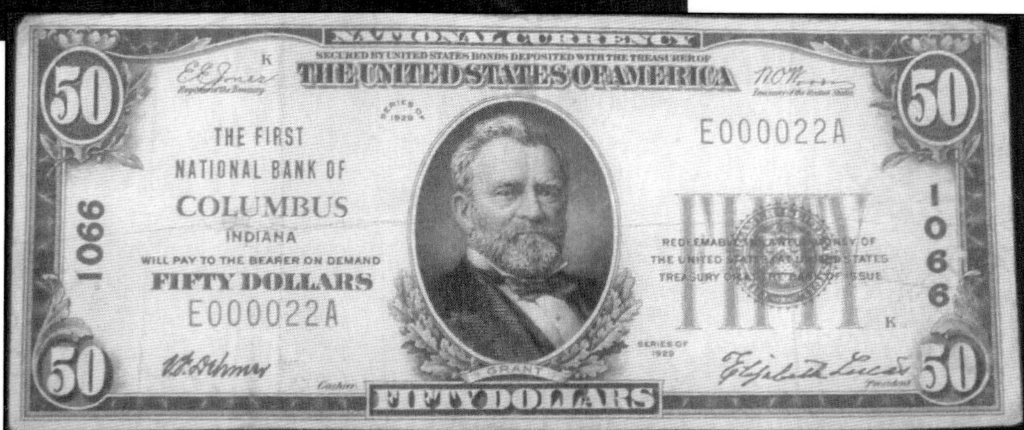

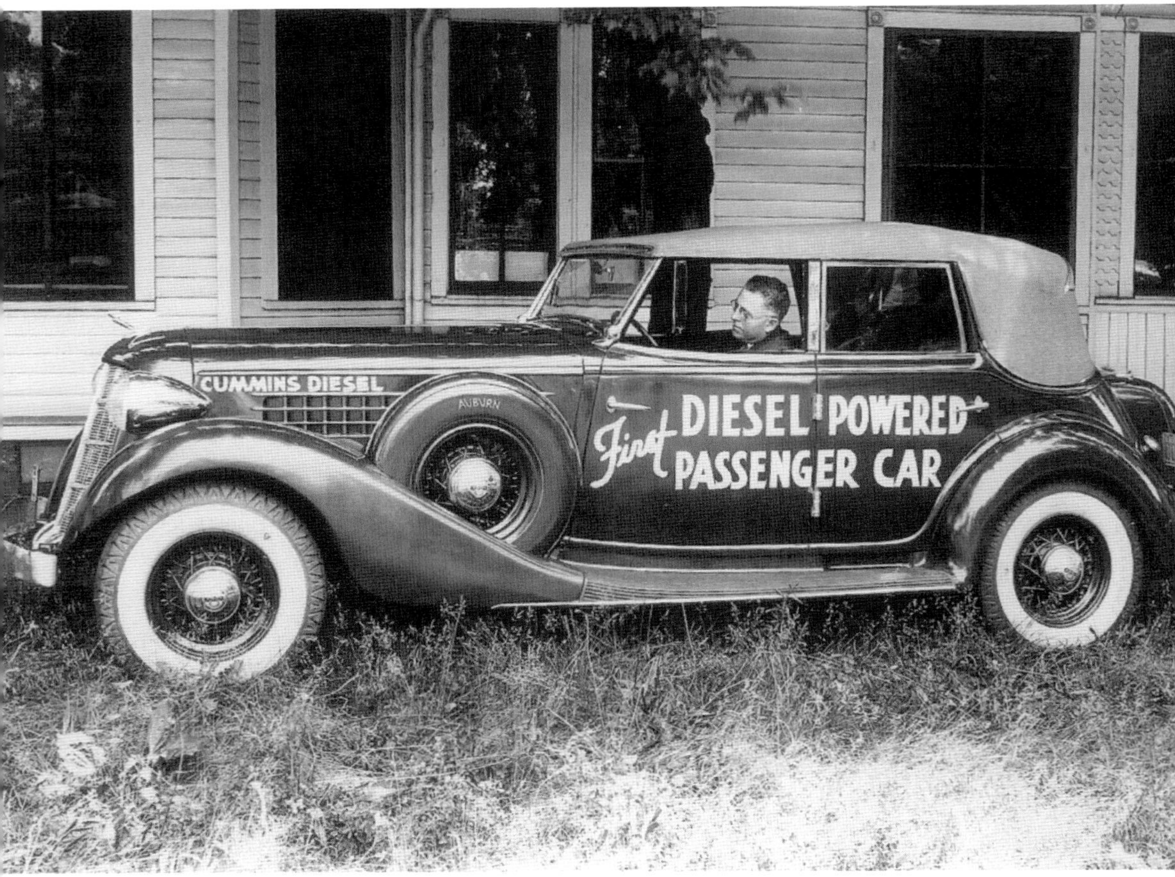

Clessie Cummins

Clessie Lyle Cummins (1888–1968) was the cofounder of Cummins Engine Company with W.G. Irwin, a banker for whom Cummins worked as a chauffeur and mechanic. Cummins grew up on a farm in Indiana, and his formal schooling ended after the eighth grade. He taught himself about engines and spent his whole adult life working to make engines better. After moving to Columbus in the early part of the 20th century, Cummins worked for several different machine and automobile companies, including Reeves and Co., before being hired by W.G. Irwin as a chauffeur. Cummins almost did not get the job with Irwin because Irwin was afraid that the young Cummins was not strong enough to crank the engine of his Packard. Although he had driven other automobiles, he had never driven a Packard (in a time when all automobiles were very different) but somehow was able to start the engine and to successfully take Irwin for a ride around town. After working for Irwin for more than a decade and continuing to tinker with engines during this time, Clessie Cummins founded Cummins in 1919 with Irwin's financial backing. The first engine was a six-horsepower engine designed for use on a farm. Over the next 10 years, the company was not financially successful and was in danger of losing its funding until Clessie came up with the idea to put one of his diesel engines in a used Packard and take W.G. Irwin for a ride. Irwin was motivated to pour more cash into the business, and Cummins eventually took off. Over the years, Clessie Cummins continued to work on ways to make engines better, and he owned 33 US patents. In 1931, Cummins entered the Indianapolis 500 and made news for completing the race without a pit stop. Today, the company has become Cummins, Inc., a Fortune 500 company with sales all over the world. Its headquarters are still located in Columbus, where Cummins today employs more than 4,000. Clessie Cummins left the company he founded in 1955 and moved to California, where he continued to work on automobile and engine innovations until his death in 1968. (Courtesy of Cummins, Inc.)

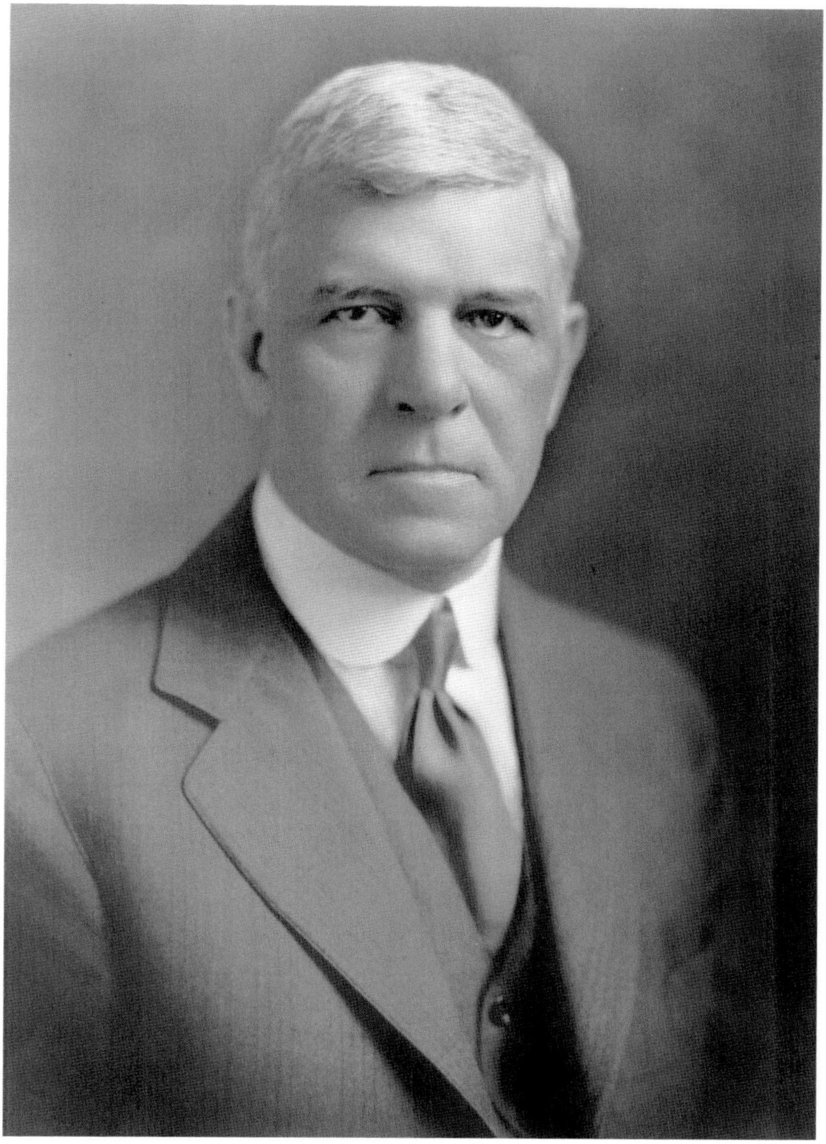

W.G. Irwin

W.G. Irwin (1866–1943) was a man of diverse business interests. The son of Joseph Irwin (page 16), W.G. Irwin worked in his father's bank while in school and, eventually, took it over after his father's death. He and his father purchased the Union Starch company and invested in the interurban rail system in southern Indiana, and Irwin eventually served as president of the electric railroad. His most-lasting business investment was his financial support of his chauffeur, Clessie Cummins, who was designing and creating diesel engines in the Irwin family garage. Together, Irwin and Cummins founded Cummins Engine Company, and Irwin later served as chairman of the board. Irwin was very active in national Republican Party politics and in civic affairs and was president of the US Chamber of Commerce in 1936. Personally, he was an active member of the Tabernacle Church and donated large sums to support the construction of what is now First Christian Church. He also enjoyed gardening and helped design the famous sunken garden at the Irwin family home on Fifth Street, eventually allowing public tours of the gardens. (BCHS Collection.)

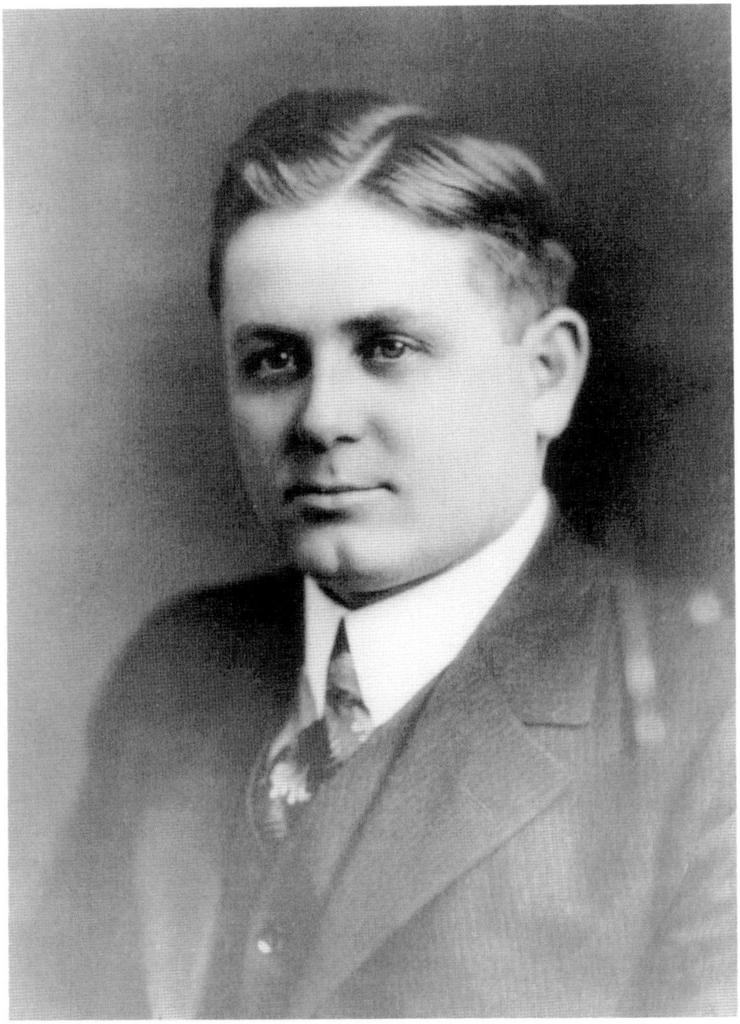

Q.G. Noblitt

Q.G. Noblitt was born southwest of Columbus in 1882 and grew up working on a farm and tinkering with farm machinery. He moved into town at age 17 to work as a bike mechanic and, a year later, went to work at Reeves Pulley for $2 per week. After three years, Noblitt moved to Indianapolis to look for new opportunities and he worked in a variety of jobs in the emerging automobile industry. In 1919, he founded the Indianapolis Air Pump Company with Frank Sparks and Albert G. Redmond. Beginning with tire pumps, the company, which was renamed first Noblitt-Starks Industries and then, in 1950, Arvin Industries, eventually manufactured a variety of automotive parts and household goods, including radios and metal furniture. In 1930, the company moved to Columbus, and Noblitt began to devote more of his time and money to community causes. In 1935, Noblitt donated 70 acres of land west of town to create Youth Camp, along with a financial donation to develop the property. He built two new grade schools out in the county to replace the crumbling schools he and his wife had attended. In addition, Noblitt was interested in water and soil conservation and was a pioneer in the development of man-made lakes in southern Indiana, developing Harrison Lakes and Noblitt Falls (now called the Lagoons) and starting the planning for Grandview Lake. In 1949, the Columbus Chamber of Commerce named him the person who had done the most for the Columbus community. Noblitt died in 1954, and his heirs donated the land that became Noblitt Park in his honor. (BCHS Collection.)

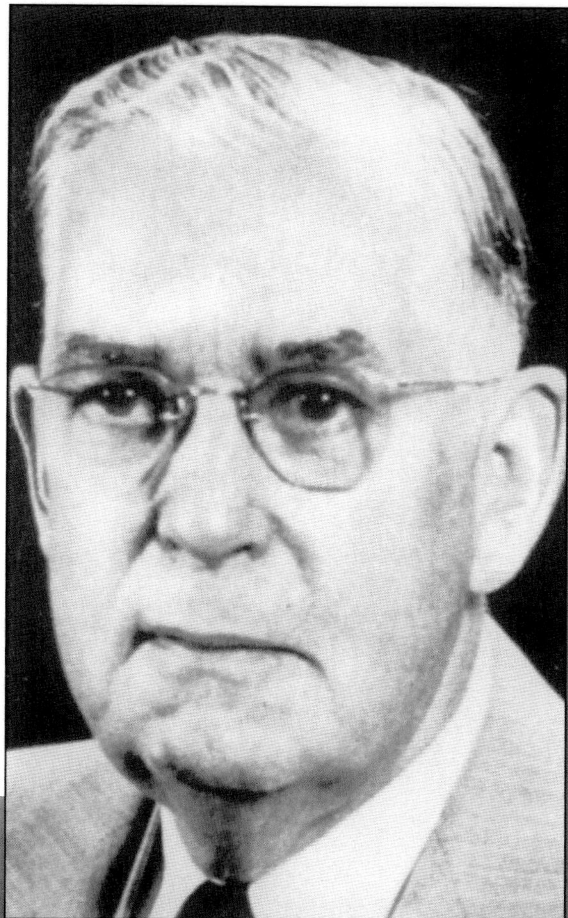

B.F. Hamilton
In 1935, B.F. Hamilton and his sons Clarence and Earl formed a company, which became Hamilton Cosco. Cosco developed into one of the premier makers of baby equipment and today is part of Dorel Juvenile Group. In 1960, the Hamilton family donated to Columbus an open ice rink, which was later enclosed and is now called Hamilton Center. B.F. Hamilton was known for giving gifts to private colleges, and the Hamilton Library at Franklin College is named in his honor. (BCHS Collection.)

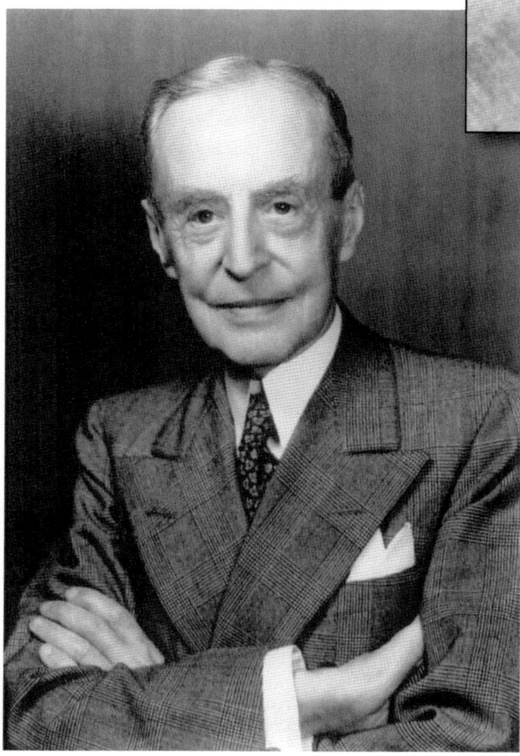

William Donner
Although Will Donner moved to Pittsburgh at age 30 to make his fortune in the steel business, he never forgot his hometown. In 1916, he donated 32 acres to become Donner Park, and he later added the pool and community center within the park. Donner cofounded Union Steel, but after his son Joseph died of cancer at age 29, he became a prominent international philanthropist. He made a large donation to the Bartholomew County Hospital to provide a complete clinical laboratory, x-ray equipment, and salaries for the first pathologist and radiologist in town, and he supported numerous other charitable organizations around the US and Canada. (Courtesy of Donner Canadian Foundation.)

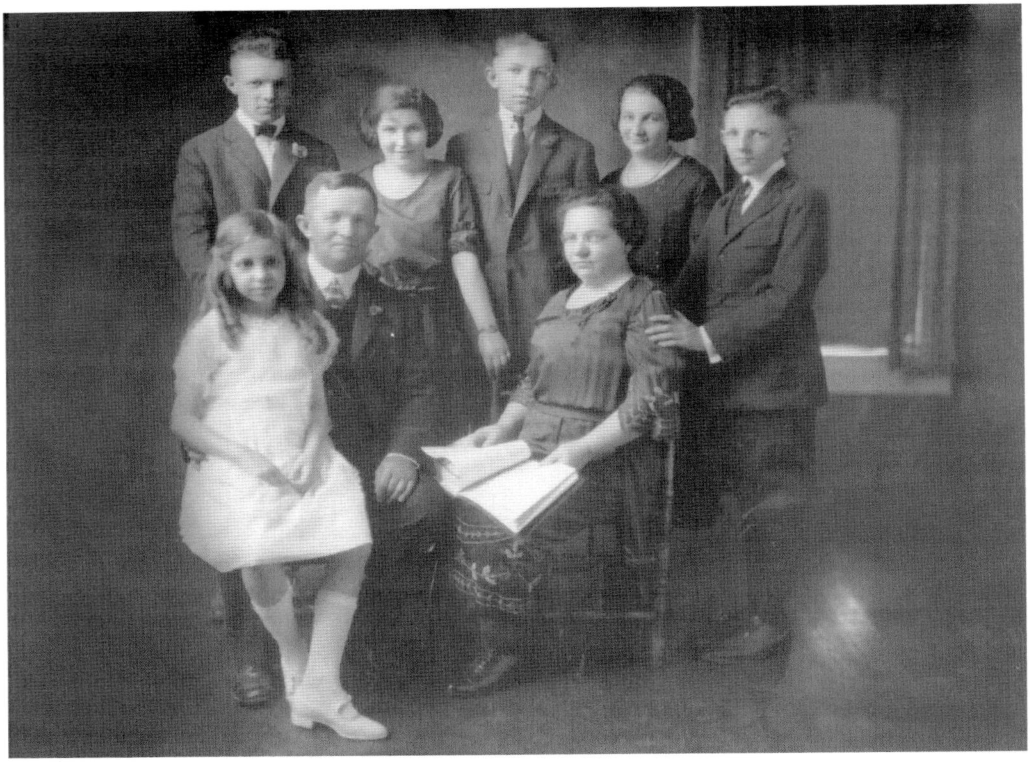

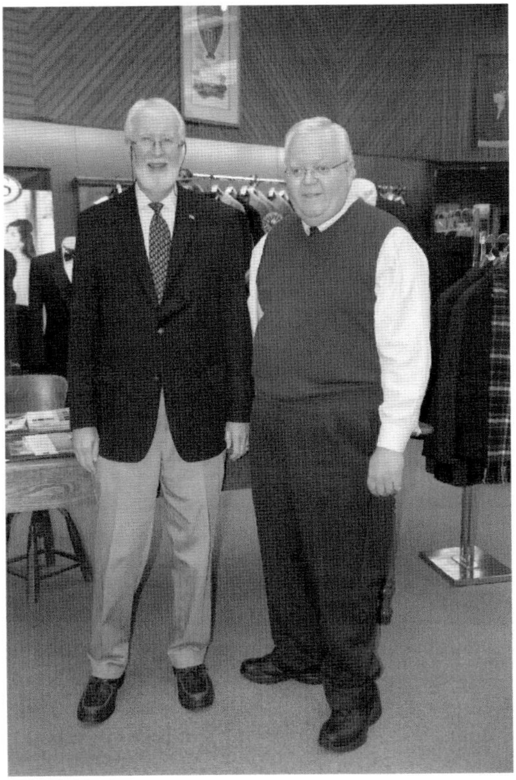

Kroot Family
Polish immigrant Joseph Kroot (pictured with his wife and children) started a salvage business in Edinburgh in 1900. He moved the business to Columbus in 1907, and the business has built a reputation as a family-owned scrap yard over the ensuing years. In 1965, the company moved to its current location on State Street under the ownership of Joseph's grandsons Joe and Arthur. In 1995, Josh Kroot became the fourth generation of the family to own the company. (Courtesy of Arthur Kroot.)

Dell Brothers
Charles Dell and his two brothers, Nicholas and William Dell, bought a clothing store on Washington Street in 1916 and named it Dell Brothers. Today, Dell Brothers men's store remains in the same building and is run by a new generation of Dell brothers, Charles's grandsons Tom (left) and Mike (right) Dell. (Photograph by author.)

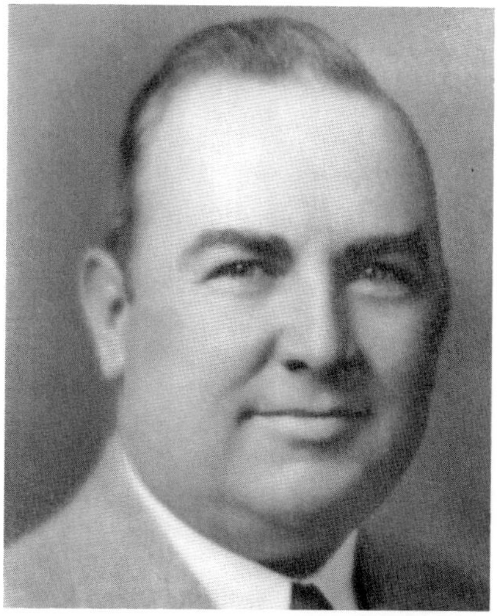

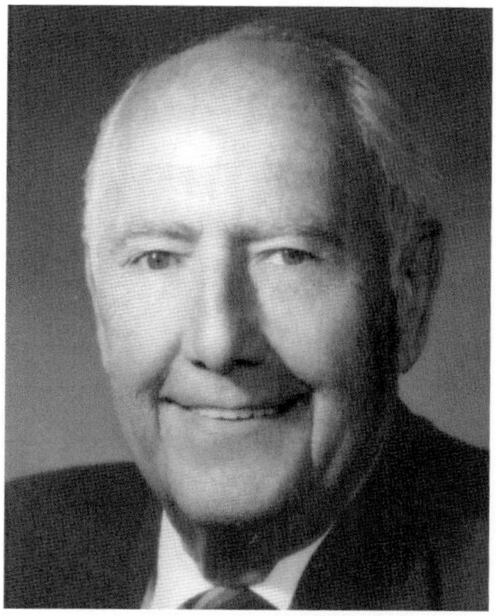

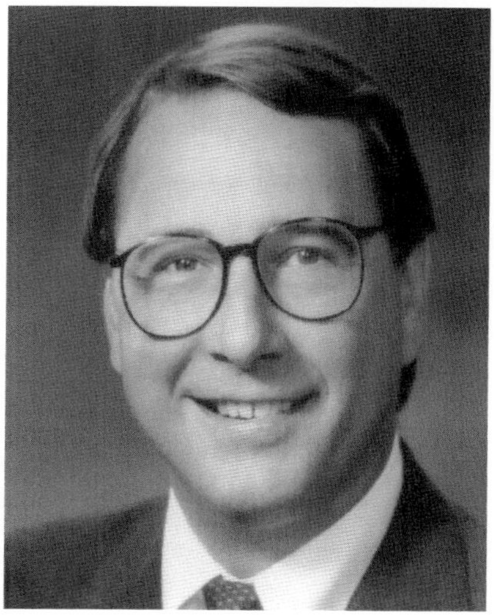

Schumaker Family
The son of German immigrants, Albert E. "Junie" Schumaker (top) was born in Columbus in 1891. In 1912, he bought a bottling company that became the Coca-Cola bottling franchise for several surrounding counties in 1916. Junie was active in the Kiwanis Club and the county fair board. Junie's son A.H. "Ab" Schumaker (middle) bought the business from his father in 1956 and carried on the tradition of involvement in local affairs when he served five terms on the city council and was influential in the development of Ivy Tech Community College. Today, Ab's son A.H. "Hutch" Schumaker (bottom) runs the family business, which ended bottling in the 1990s but continues to serve as a Coca-Cola distributor. Hutch has continued his family's tradition of local involvement, volunteering for hospice and Big Brothers and serving as a trustee of the Foundation for Youth and Columbus Regional Hospital. He led the effort to save the Crump Theatre in 2002 and was involved in the restoration of Zaharakos. In a remarkable example of the family tradition of service, all three Schumaker men served as board chairman of the Columbus Chamber of Commerce—Junie in 1932, Ab in 1963, and Hutch in 1998. (Courtesy of Hutch Schumaker.)

Lowell Engelking

Lowell Engelking had a great respect for education—something he was denied in his own life. Engelking came from a humble background and left high school to accept a job as a patternmaker apprentice. He came to Columbus in 1934 to work for a one-man pattern shop, which he bought out in the mid-1940s, paying it off over many years. The company became known as Engelking Patterns and made many metal pieces for the military through several conflicts. He was too old for military service during World War II but wanted to make an additional contribution, so he volunteered to be the chairman of the local Draft Board, a thankless position he held for 30 years. As Engelking's fortunes improved, he was always looking for ways to give back to the community. In the 1950s, Engelking and Dr. E.W. Williams (his future brother-in-law) led the discussion about the need for mental health services in Columbus. They became the cofounders of Quinco, the first mental health service in the area. Engelking loaned Quinco office space at his pattern company so the organization did not have to pay rent. In addition, Engelking always felt strongly about supporting youth in the community. When there was concern about development near Columbus Youth Camp west of town, Engelking donated 40 acres of his land in 1958 to enlarge and protect the property. Officials at the high school would sometimes call Engelking to say that a poor student needed new clothing or shoes because they knew he would make sure that student quietly received what was needed. One of his most-lasting contributions to Columbus came later when, in 1977, Engelking gave the $25,000 donation of seed money that started Heritage Fund, a community charitable foundation. Since then, Heritage Fund has grown both in financial assets and importance to the community and, by 2011, had assets of $45 million, which fund numerous scholarships and support various community initiatives and needs. Engelking died in 1978, leaving a vast legacy of civic involvement that continues to benefit Columbus today. (Courtesy of Melinda Engelking.)

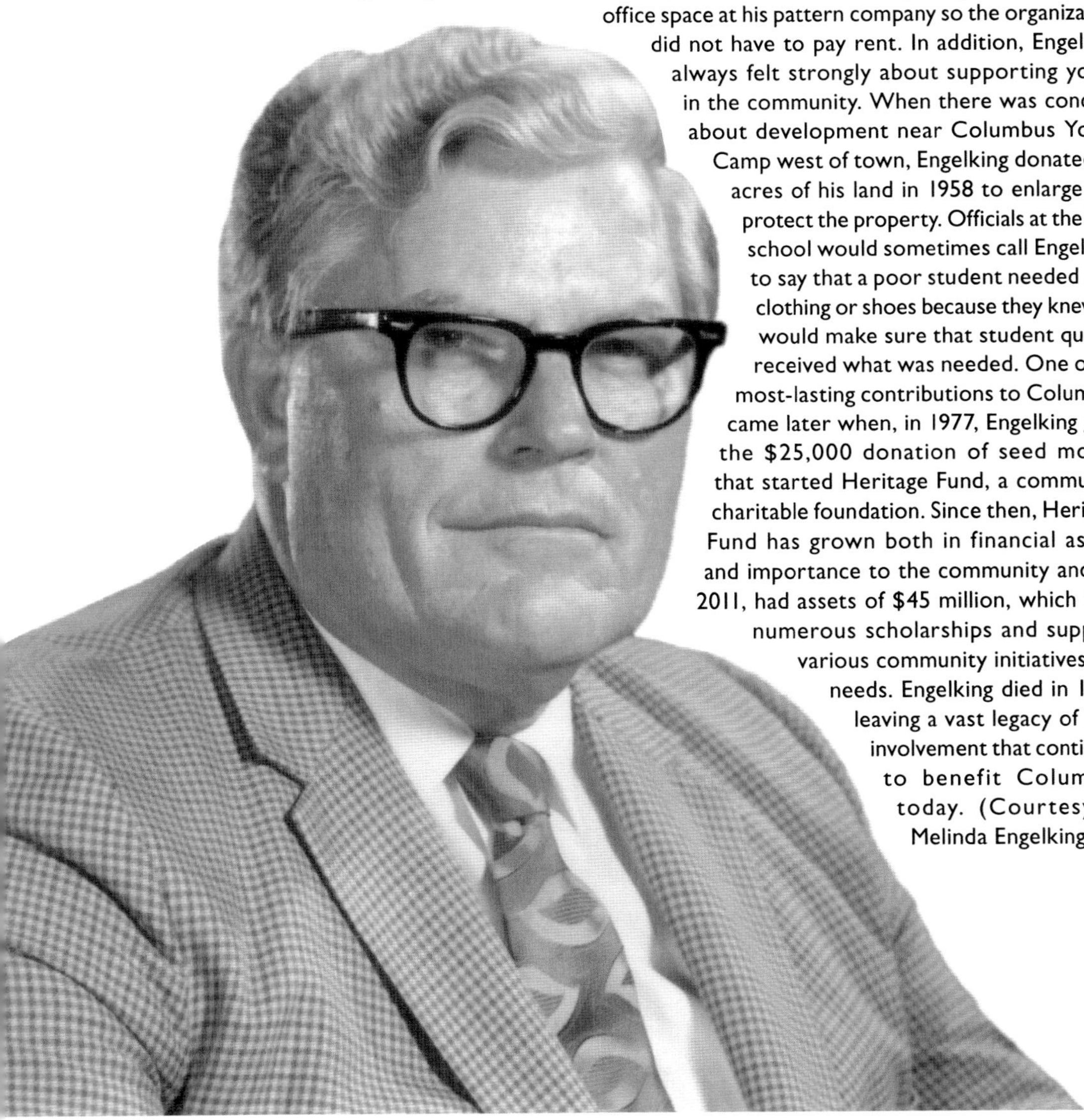

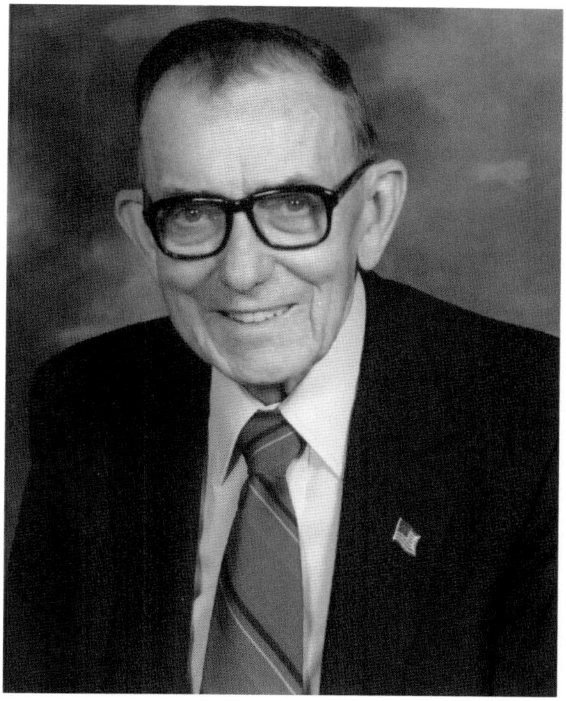

W. Calvert "Cal" Brand
From a very young age, hard work and responsibility were necessary parts of life for Cal Brand. Born into poverty in Brown County, his mother died when he was very young, and his father proved unable to care for him and his five siblings. Brand began to work at age 11, first at odd jobs for his boardinghouse owner and later for Dunlap's, a local lumber company. He worked to support himself and also helped his siblings find good foster homes, something of which he was always proud. In 1935, he graduated from Columbus High School and later served in the US Army during World War II. Over many years, he rose through the ranks at Dunlap's and became a vice president before leaving the company. He eventually bought his own lumberyard in 1967 to start Brands, Inc. He was a perfectionist and a harsh critic of those who were not performing up to his standards and worked hard trying to stay in front of new innovations in building techniques. He built two homes for his family in Columbus, including the first home in town to use geothermal heating. Active in several building trades organizations, he served as president of the Indiana Building Congress and the National Lumber and Building Materials Dealers Association. Brand was also active in multiple community organizations in Columbus, including the Columbus Chamber of Commerce, Junior Chamber of Commerce, and the Columbus Area Arts Council. He was president of both the Evening Kiwanis Club and Columbus Foundation for Youth and was chair of Heritage Fund. He was a longtime member of First Presbyterian Church and served as a deacon, elder, trustee, and Sunday school teacher. In addition to his civic involvement and his family-owned business, Brand had a prolific political career, beginning with election to the Columbus City Council in 1955 and moving on to the Indiana House of Representatives from 1966 to 1970. He was proud to serve as Gov. Edgar Whitcomb's legislative council administrative assistant—a position that required him to work with both parties to pass bipartisan legislation—and as state budget director. During the Ronald Reagan Administration, Brand was named assistant secretary of the US Department of Housing and Urban Development. He served on national election committees for two Republican senators and was a Republican presidential elector. In honor of Brand's extensive service to the state, five governors awarded him the state's highest honor, Sagamore of the Wabash. The Cal Brand Meeting Room in the Columbus City Hall also serves to honor his contributions to the city of Columbus. (Courtesy of Rev. D. Calvert Brand and Jesse Brand.)

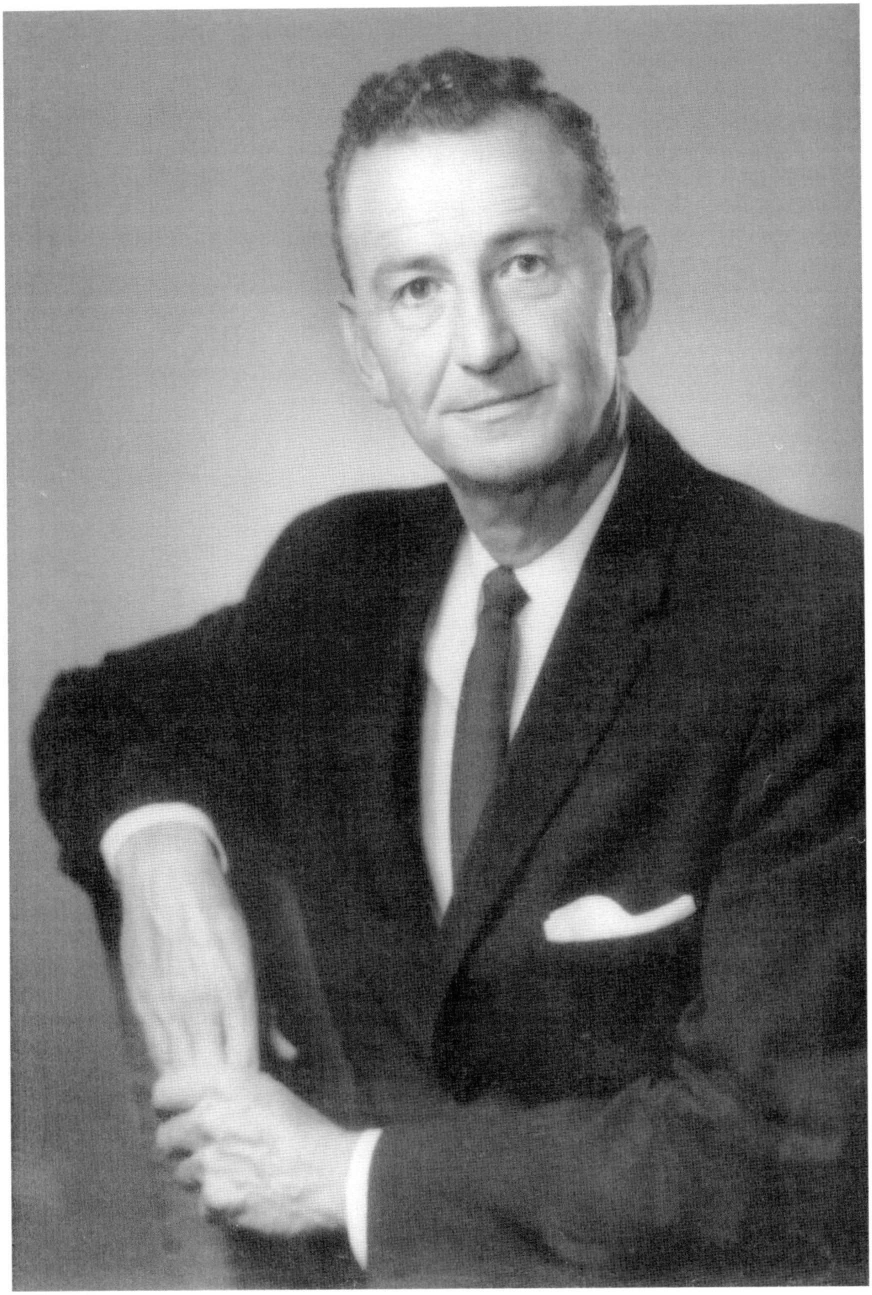

Bob Marshall

When reporter Bob Marshall married Betty Brown, daughter of *Evening Republic* editor Raymond Brown, it did not take him long to prove his value to the paper and to the community. Marshall moved through the ranks of the paper during his 36-year career, serving as city editor, news editor, associate editor, and, eventually, editor prior to retiring in 1972. He was extensively involved in the community as well, working as an original River Rat to clean up the future Mill Race Park, helping found Heritage Fund, and editing and annotating the 1976 reprinting of the 1888 county history. Marshall loved playing golf and planted and cared for many of the trees at the golf course at Harrison Lake. (Courtesy of Ann Knobloch.)

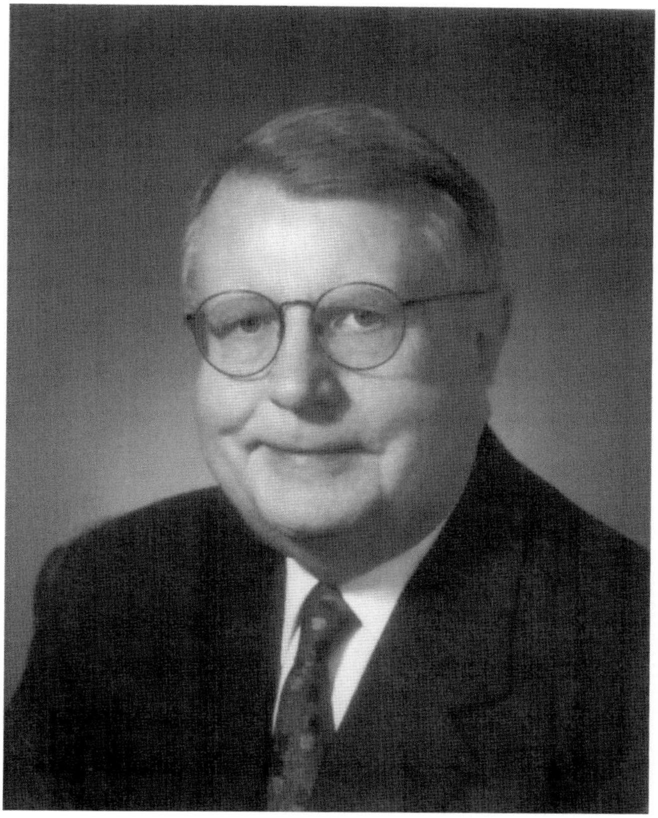

Dick Johnson

Dick Johnson epitomized the tradition of Columbus business people who are community-minded and willing to step up if called on to help fill a community need. Johnson's career began in 1957 when he bought a small Shell Oil distributor with a loan cosigned by his father. He began with two trucks and a small warehouse and drove a truck himself at the start. Johnson was hardworking and focused, and gradually, the business grew as opportunities arose to supply more gasoline stations farther away from town. Johnson Oil was a true family business with the whole family often pitching in around the dinner table to send invoices and generate ideas. In the 1970s, Johnson Oil expanded when it bought a Sunoco distributor, but the biggest expansion of the company began in the early 1980s with the opening of a Shell Food Mart near Nashville, Indiana. This was a new idea at a time when convenience stores were not commonplace, and as more stores were added, the name Bigfoot Food Stores evolved. From its humble beginnings, Johnson Oil eventually became one of the nation's largest independent gasoline distributors, and in 2000, Johnson was named the Ernst & Young Retail Entrepreneur of the Year. The following year, the family sold the business and formed Johnson Ventures. Over the years, as Johnson became more successful, he had more time to support local Columbus endeavors with both his time and money. Johnson and his wife, Ruth, supported a variety of causes and were great patrons of education, with Johnson serving as chair of the Community Education Coalition. He was perhaps most proud of the Johnson Center for Entrepreneurship & Innovation at the Kelley School of Business at Indiana University, which was established in 1998 with a financial gift from the Johnsons. Also supporters of the arts, Dick and Ruth bought over 100 paintings by Brown County wildlife artist Bill Zimmerman to support the book *Birds of Indiana* by Zimmerman and Charles Keller and then loaned them to Indiana University. Prior to his death in 2009, Johnson never retired but, gradually, shifted more of his time to community activities, continuing to promote his belief in the importance of public-private partnerships to solve problems. (Courtesy of Rick Johnson.)

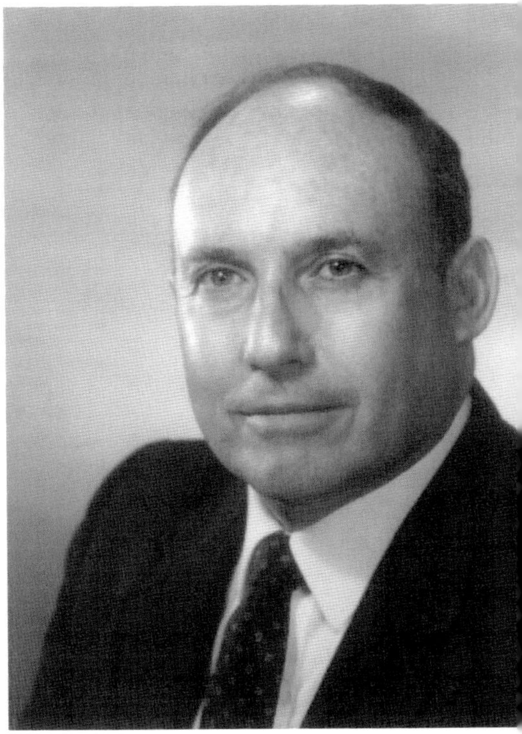

Bob Haddad

When the Harrison Lake Country Club was in danger of closing in 2005, Columbus businessman Bob Haddad stepped forward with a significant financial investment to purchase the club, an institution in Columbus since 1946. Haddad felt the club was a community asset essential to the social and family culture of Columbus that would aid in economic development. To preserve the investment, he created a new business strategy for the club's operation, drawing on years of experience running his own business. In 1975, the box company for which Haddad had worked wanted to relocate, and Haddad decided to start his own company rather than leave Columbus. Columbus Container was founded that year in a building with 13,000 square feet and six employees and has since grown into one million square feet and 300 employees. Haddad and his wife, Helen, are also longtime benefactors of the Columbus Indiana Philharmonic, and they own the building in which the philharmonic currently operates. (Both, courtesy of Columbus Container, Inc.)

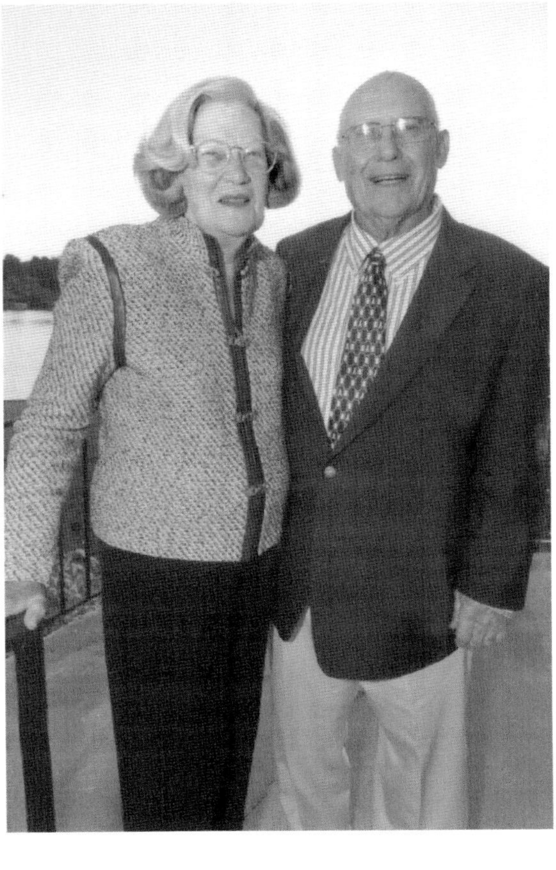

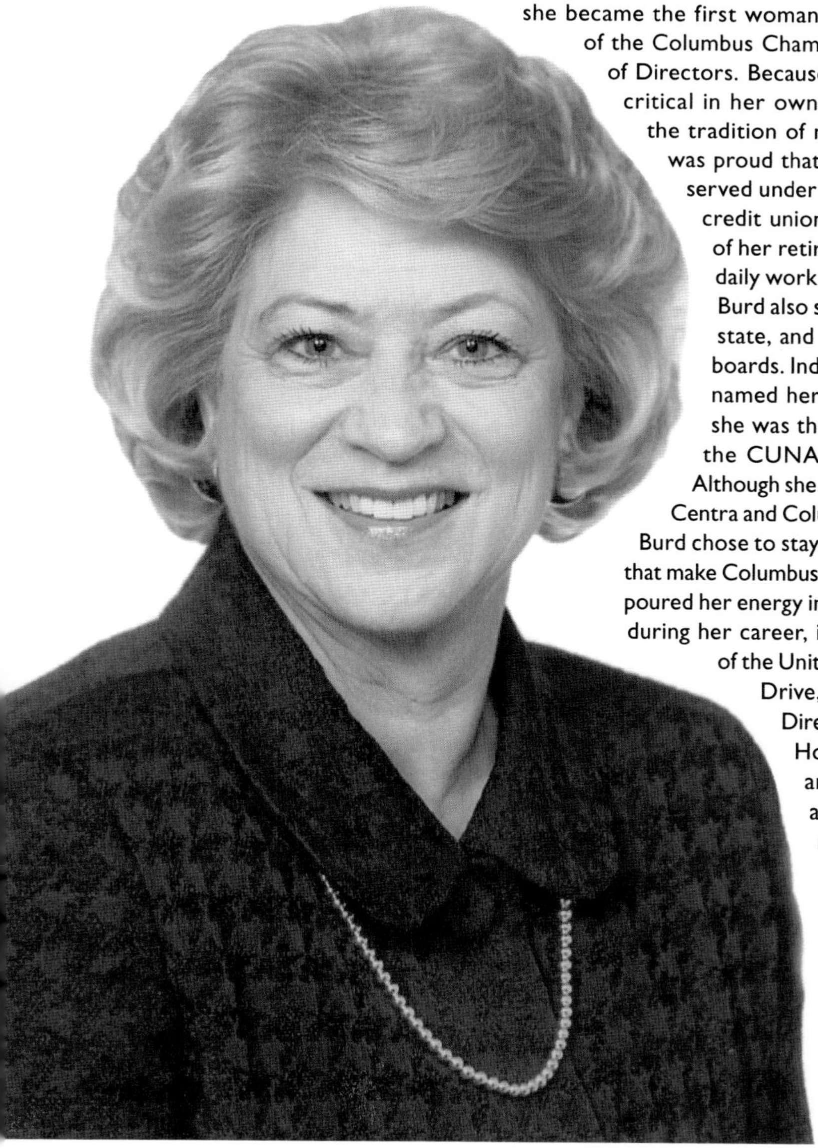

Loretta Burd

When Loretta Burd started at Centra Credit Union in 1965, a strong glass ceiling for women existed that made it impossible to imagine she would retire in 2012 as chief executive officer of the organization 47 years later. Starting at a time when the organization had fewer than 10 employees and only $4 million in assets was an advantage, as Burd had the chance to work in multiple areas and do a little of everything, including working as a teller, in clerical and bookkeeping roles, and in the loan department. Throughout her career, Burd had wonderful mentors who allowed her to take on new challenges and assume new positions, all of which was crucial to allowing her to break through the glass ceiling. In 1987, after serving as a branch manager and vice president of administration, Burd took over the position of chief executive officer. Then, in 1993, she became the first woman to become chairperson of the Columbus Chamber of Commerce Board of Directors. Because mentoring had been so critical in her own career, Burd continued the tradition of mentoring at Centra and was proud that five vice presidents who served under her had moved on to run credit unions elsewhere by the time of her retirement. In addition to her daily work as chief executive officer, Burd also served on numerous local, state, and national committees and boards. Indiana Credit Union League named her "CEO of the Year," and she was the longest-serving chair in the CUNA Mutual Group history. Although she had opportunities to leave Centra and Columbus for other positions, Burd chose to stay because of the attributes that make Columbus feel like a family town. She poured her energy into numerous local causes during her career, including serving as chair of the United Way Community Fund Drive, Heritage Fund Board of Directors, Columbus Regional Hospital Foundation Board, and kidscommons Board, among others. A few months before her retirement, Loretta Burd was proud to watch the company she had led for 25 years pass the symbolic $1 billion in assets mark in early 2012. (Courtesy of Centra Credit Union.)

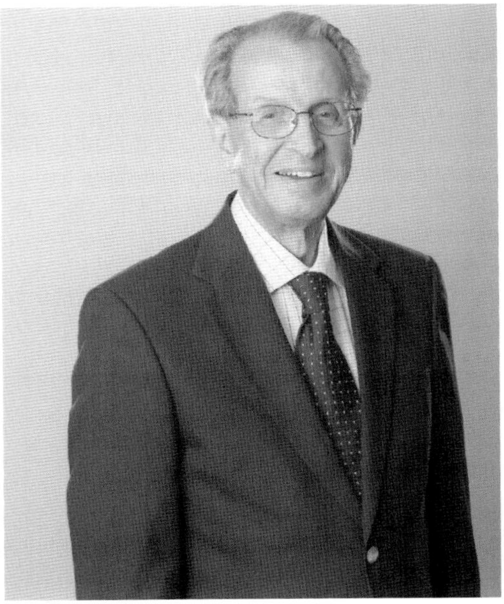

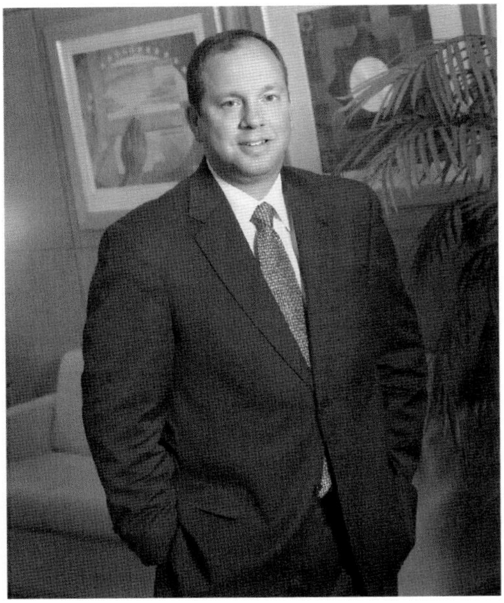

Elwood Family

In 1980, David Elwood started a preemployment testing company in Columbus that would become Elwood Staffing. Elwood's three sons gradually joined the business, with Mark (top right) in 1987, John (bottom left) in 1996, and Mike (bottom right) in 2004. In 2008, the Indiana Chamber of Commerce named Elwood Staffing one of the "Best Places to Work in Indiana" and *Inc. 5000* recognized the company as one of America's fastest-growing private companies. The Elwoods believe that their emphasis on strong relationships has helped fuel the company's success. In 2013, Elwood Staffing bought a competitor out of Salt Lake City, allowing the firm to expand into a total of 33 states and become one of the 20 largest staffing companies in the country. The company has partnered its business growth with community involvement, supporting the People Trails, Heritage Fund's Grant a Wish program, and the Columbus Indiana Philharmonic, among other charitable causes. (Courtesy of Elwood Staffing.)

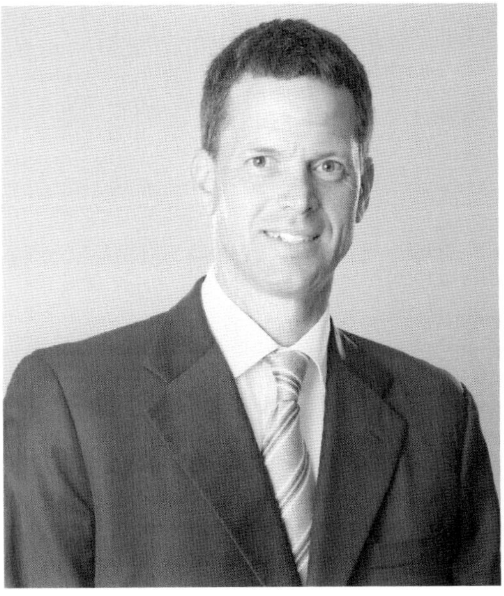

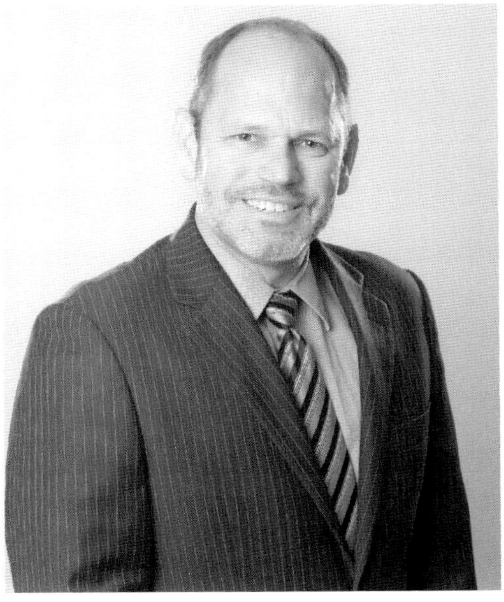

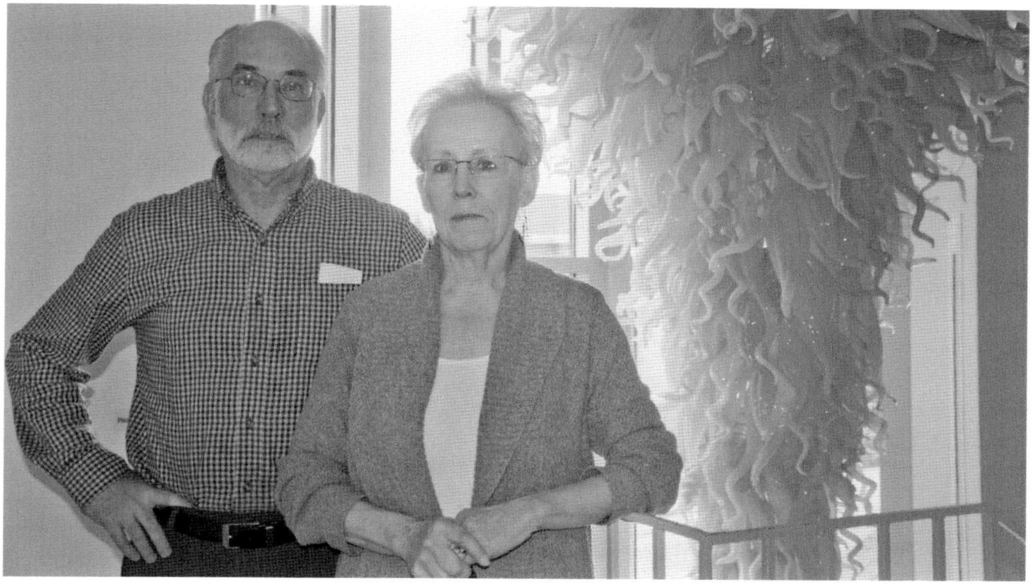

Terry and Susan Whitaker

Owners of one of Indiana's oldest independent bookstores, Terry and Susan Whitaker have owned Viewpoint Books since they purchased it from Susan's parents in 1979. Avid readers themselves, the Whitakers have made Viewpoint an important part of downtown Columbus, even as the world of online bookselling and electronic books effected the demise of many other bookstores. After residing in the original Commons until 2007, Viewpoint Bookstore now occupies the old post office building at Washington and Sixth Streets. (Photograph by author.)

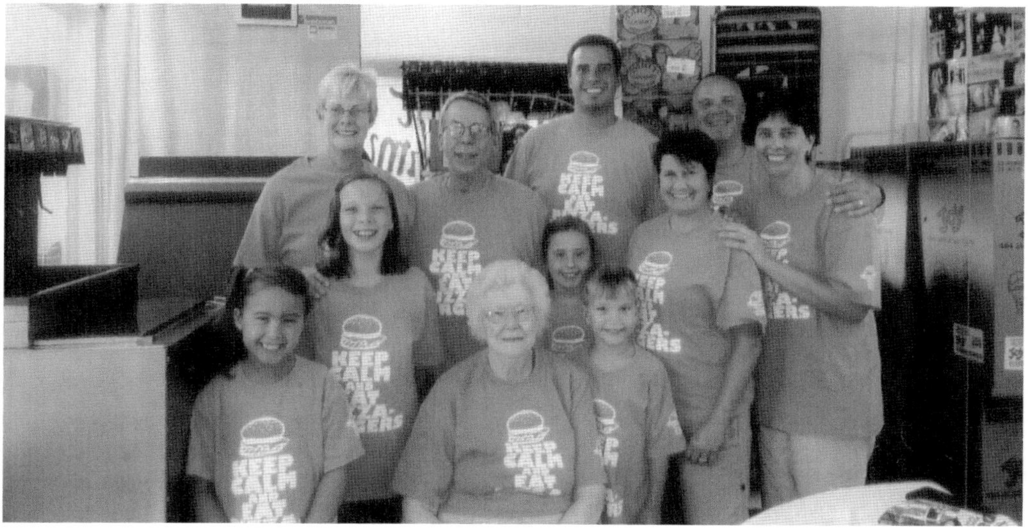

Musillami Family

For more than 50 years, generations of Columbus residents have enjoyed Pizzaburgers, the most popular menu item at Musillami's Drive-In on Jonesville Road. Mike Musillami (second from left in back row) took over the business when his mother, Helen (front row center), retired in 1986. Helen and her husband, Jasper, started the business in 1957, and now the fourth generation of the Musillami family is learning about providing good food and good service to their customers. (Courtesy of Mike Musillami.)

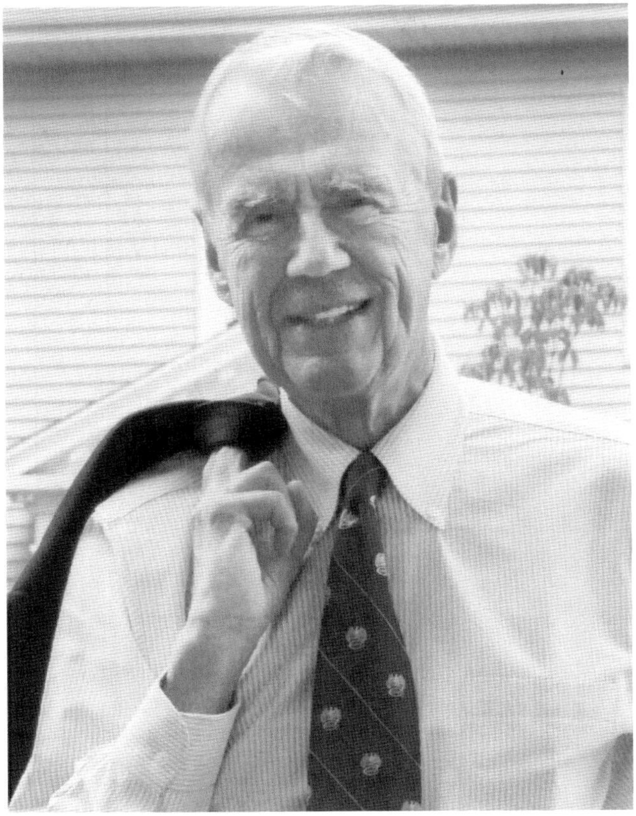

Jim Henderson

According to Jim Henderson, some of the credit for his remarkable career is attributable to the luck of being in the right place at the right time. A native of Culver, Indiana, and a graduate of Culver Military Academy, Henderson was at Harvard Business School after serving five years as an officer with the US Navy—including teaching at the US Naval Academy—when J. Irwin Miller, who was chairman of Cummins at the time, invited him to Columbus for an interview. Henderson was duly impressed with Miller, Cummins, and Columbus and, in 1964, accepted a position as Miller's personal assistant for a year. Because of Miller's involvement in numerous corporate boards, national and international philanthropies, and political causes, Henderson gained much experience both in and outside of the business world during this time. He also heeded Miller's call to "get involved" and started his decades of civic involvement in Columbus. After a year working for Miller, Henderson was transferred to Cummins and initially charged with attracting management talent for the growing company. Other managerial assignments followed quickly. In 1977, Henderson became president and chief operating officer, a role he held until assuming the top jobs of chief executive officer in 1994 and chairman in 1995. Unlike many Cummins executives, Henderson and his wife, Toots, were never asked to move with their four children to another Cummins location. They remained in Columbus, and Henderson remained engaged in various community organizations, including Heritage Fund, United Way, the Columbus Area Chamber of Commerce, and Junior Achievement. He also spent time on many corporate boards including AT&T, International Paper, Inland Steel, and Hillenbrand, Inc. He led the board of trustees at Culver as either president or chairman for more than 20 years. Henderson inevitably found himself involved in many fundraising projects, including chairing a major campaign at Princeton University, his undergraduate alma mater, where he also served as chairman of the board. When the Commons was rebuilt in Columbus in the early 2000s, Henderson successfully led the campaign for the funding from private sources, and the James A. Henderson indoor playground was named in honor of his efforts. (Courtesy of Culver Academies.)

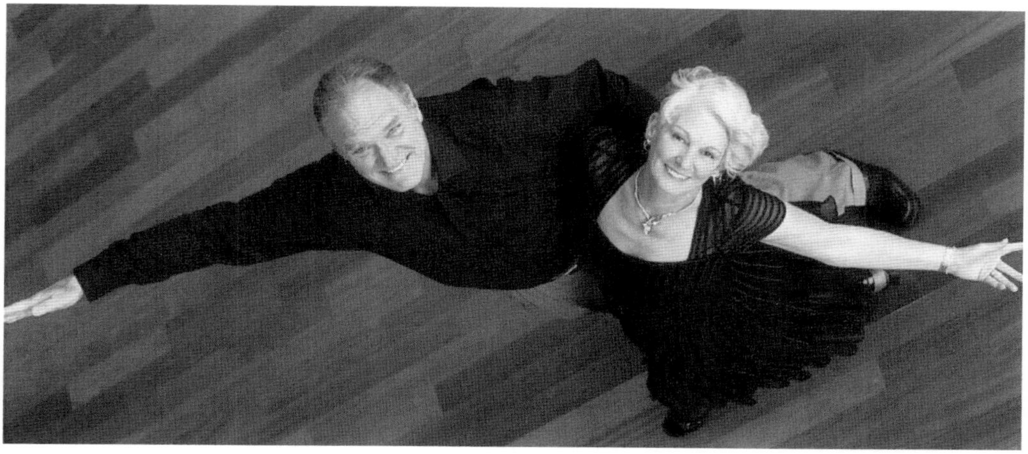

Bob and Barbara Stevens

One of the greatest business success stories of Columbus in the past 30 years started from what seemed like horrible luck. Bob and Barbara Stevens moved with their family to Columbus in 1985 so Bob could be closer to his job at a forge in North Vernon. Two weeks later, that company was sold, and Bob was not rehired. In a remarkable story of vision, hard work, and luck, the Stevens and four friends decided to start their own forge in an empty building in Woodside Industrial Park. They secured their first customer by promising to be in production within three months, an amazingly short period in which to secure capital, improve the building, buy equipment, and hire employees. The business and banking communities in Columbus were incredibly supportive of the venture, and Impact Forge did open in March 1986. Beginning with 10 employees, the company later expanded into a total of four related factories (Impact Forge, Net Forge, Omni Forge, and Impact Precision Forge). In 1989, Bob was named "Entrepreneur of the Year" for Indiana (pictured below), and the Small Business Administration named him "SBA Person of the Year" in 1990. The Stevens continued to run the company until selling Impact Forge Group in 2007. Over the years, the Stevens developed a love of Columbus and a strong desire to give back to the community. The family enjoys biking and being outdoors, and they supported the expansion of the People Trail system in Columbus and the installation of colorful bike racks downtown. An attorney, Barbara also spent many years on the Human Rights Commission. After years of attending performances and nonprofit fundraisers at the Commons, the Stevens felt passionate about the reimagining and rebuilding of the Commons in the early 2000s, and Bob chaired the committee involved in the rebuilding, offering his expertise about reusing the steel structure and supporting the installation of a Brazilian cherry hardwood floor in the performance space. When the Commons reopened in 2011, Bob and Barbara were asked to have the first dance (pictured above) in a space now available for all of Columbus to enjoy. (Above, courtesy of the *Republic*/Alton Strupp; below, courtesy of Bob and Barbara Stevens.)

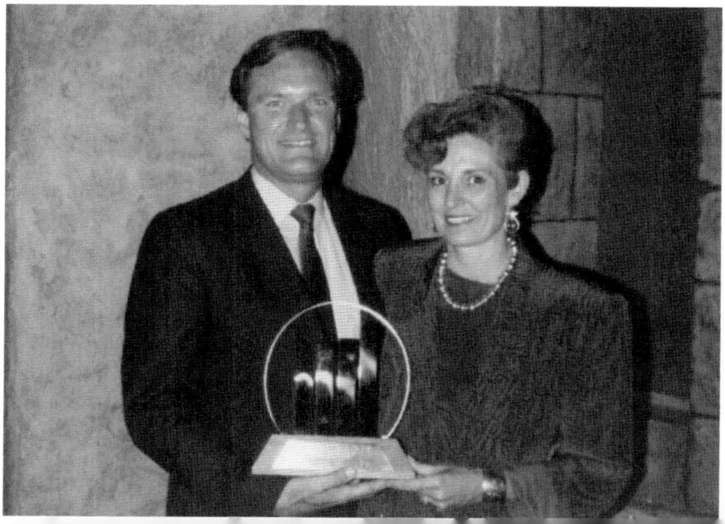

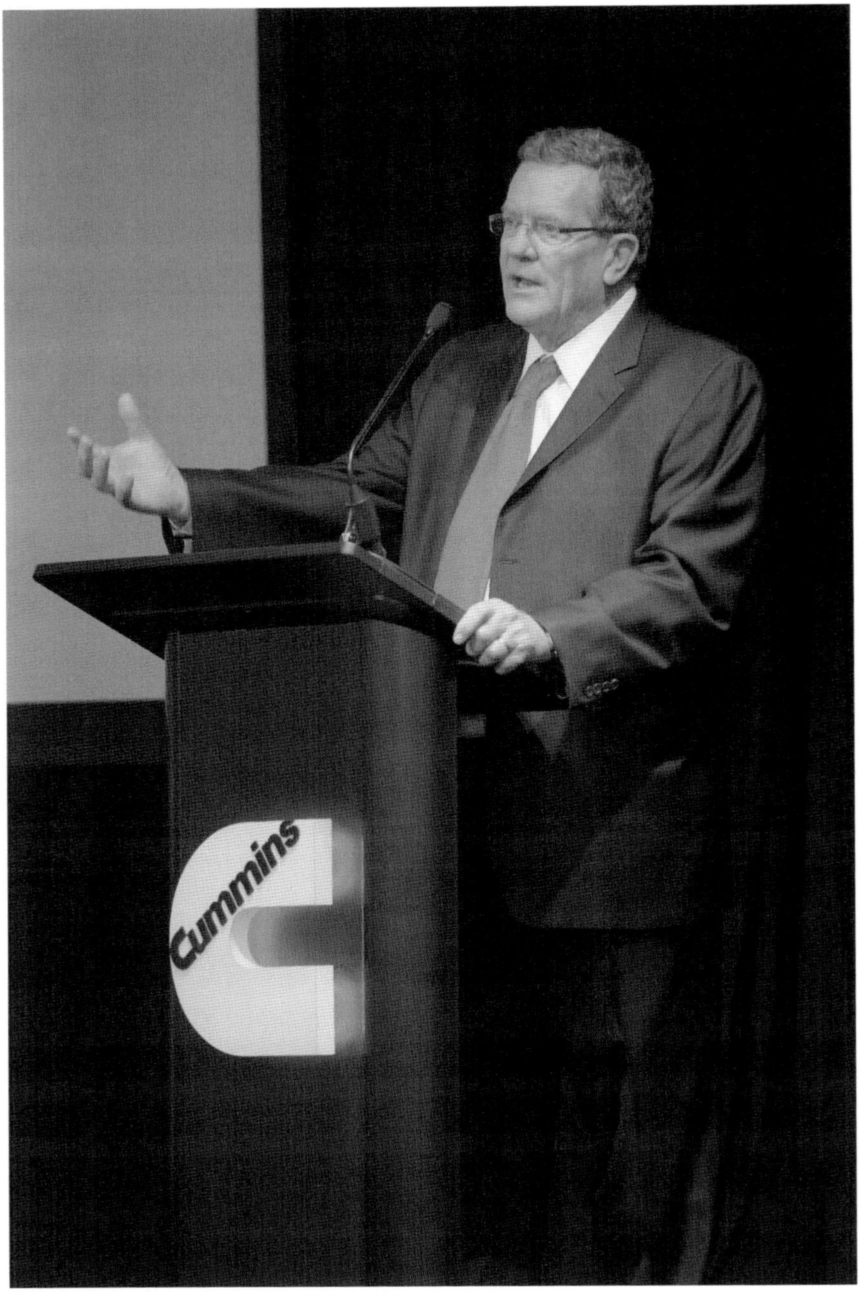

Tim Solso

As chief executive officer of Cummins from 2000 through 2011, Tim Solso led the company through a remarkable period of growth. During this time, Cummins doubled its sales, its stock price multiplied, and international business assumed a more prominent role. Solso spent 40 years at Cummins and earned many accolades for his leadership, including being named by *Marketwatch* as one of the five finalists for "CEO of the Decade" in 2010. In 2011, President Obama appointed Solso to the President's Management Advisory Board, and in 2013, *Harvard Business Review* designated him No. 51 on the list of best-performing chief executive officers in the world. (Courtesy of Cummins, Inc.)

CHAPTER THREE

Serving and Giving Back

The history of Columbus is full of individuals who have served others and their community in a variety of ways. Some of these individuals include local soldiers who gave their lives in service to their country and are honored by the Bartholomew County Memorial for Veterans. The 25 forty-foot-tall limestone pillars are engraved with names and excerpts of letters from soldiers to their families.

Since 1942, Columbus has been home to an airport. Originally built as an air support base during World War II, today it is called Columbus Municipal Airport. In the 1980s, many of the original 1942 barracks and buildings were slated for demolition when the idea was hatched to turn one of the old buildings into a museum. Instead, a new building was constructed, and since 1992, the Atterbury-Bakalar Air Museum has been sharing the stories of the base's history and the men and women who passed through. Volunteers continue to maintain the museum, which includes displays about local veterans and information about and models of World War II aircraft.

Other public servants from Columbus include politicians at all levels of government who have guided the city or represented its citizens at the state and national levels. Columbus's first mayor, Smith Jones, was elected in 1864, when Columbus was incorporated more than 40 years after the county's founding. Beyond the local level, Bob Garton was Indiana's longest-serving Senate president pro tem, spending more than three decades in the Indiana Senate. Several other Columbus citizens have served in the Indiana legislature as well. On the national level, Lee Hamilton left a Columbus law practice in 1965 after election to the US House of Representatives. He went on to a distinguished career in Congress that spanned more than 40 years. In 2012, native son Mike Pence was elected Indiana's 50th governor after also serving in the US House of Representatives.

In other fields, Columbus citizens have served the community as well. When Bartholomew County Hospital opened in 1917, five physicians were on staff. Dr. Bertha Clouse was one of the first female physicians in Columbus and served as the school physician at Columbus High School. After Dr. Clouse's death, Dr. Dorothy Teal and Dr. Eleanor Clay were the only female physicians in town for many years. Today, more than 240 physicians—67 of whom are female—staff Columbus Regional Hospital.

Other individuals served as leaders of community organizations or nonprofit groups, some for extended periods of time and many with extraordinary accomplishments during their tenures. Hospice, the philharmonic, and the senior center are examples of organizations that have benefited from remarkable leaders.

Among the many narratives of Columbus's growth and success, the stories of a few of the many citizens who have served their community, state, or country are worthy of sharing.

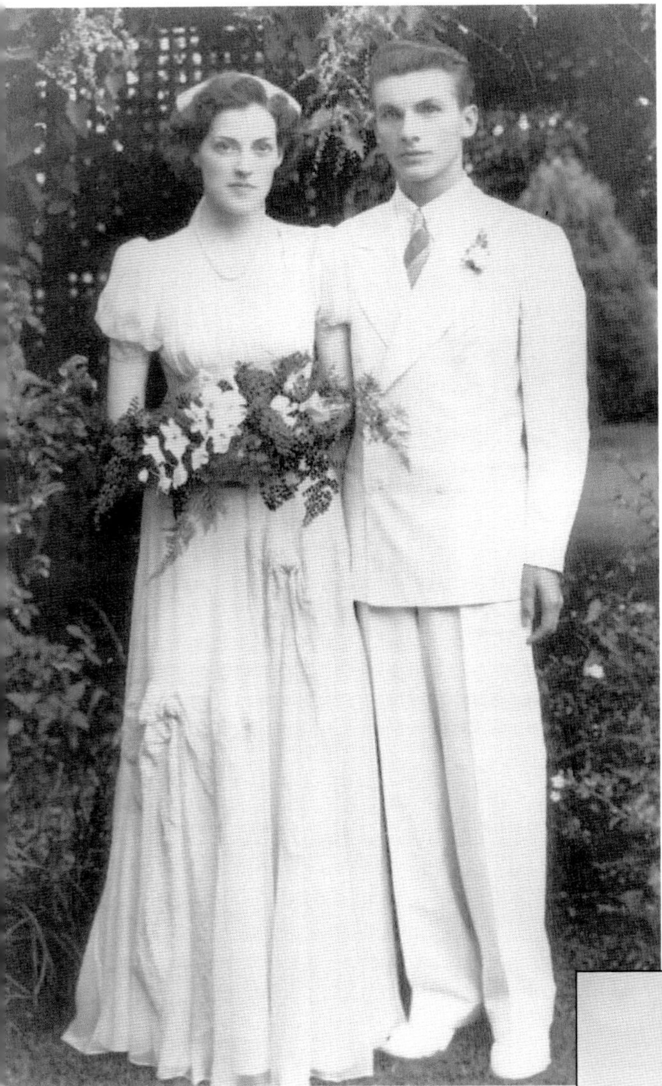

Jeanne Norbeck

Jeanne Lewellen Norbeck was born in Columbus and graduated from Columbus High School in 1929. She and her husband, Edward Norbeck, are pictured at their 1940 wedding in Hawaii, where they were living when Pearl Harbor was bombed in 1941. Her husband joined the Army, and Jeanne became one of the first women to serve as pilots in the US military when she joined the Women Airforce Service Pilots (WASP). More than 25,000 women volunteered to join the WASP, and Norbeck was one of only 1,074 successfully to complete the training. Except for combat training, the WASPs received the same training as male pilots and flew 78 different kinds of aircraft. In 1944, Norbeck was killed during a test-flight crash in South Carolina. Because the WASPs were civilians, the military did not pay for her funeral or those of the more than 30 other female pilots who were killed. In 2009, President Obama awarded the WASPs the Congressional Gold Medal, the nation's highest civilian honor, for their service. Norbeck is buried in Garland Brook Cemetery in Columbus, and the original Bakalar Air Force Base Chapel in Columbus has been named after her. (Both, courtesy of Lewellen family and Atterbury-Bakalar Air Museum.)

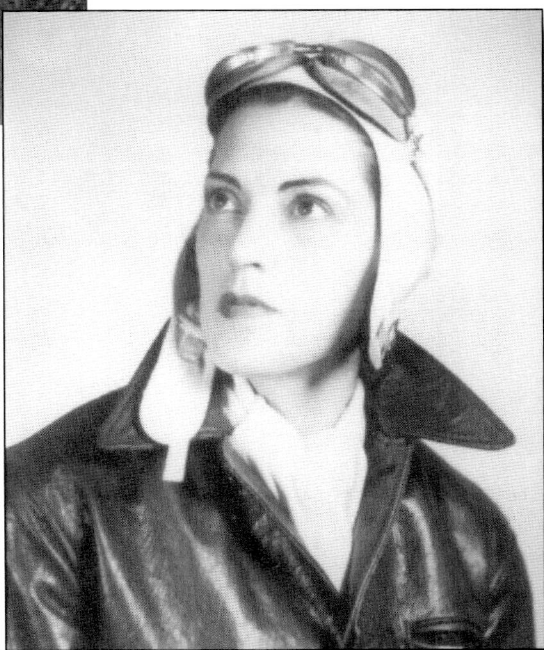

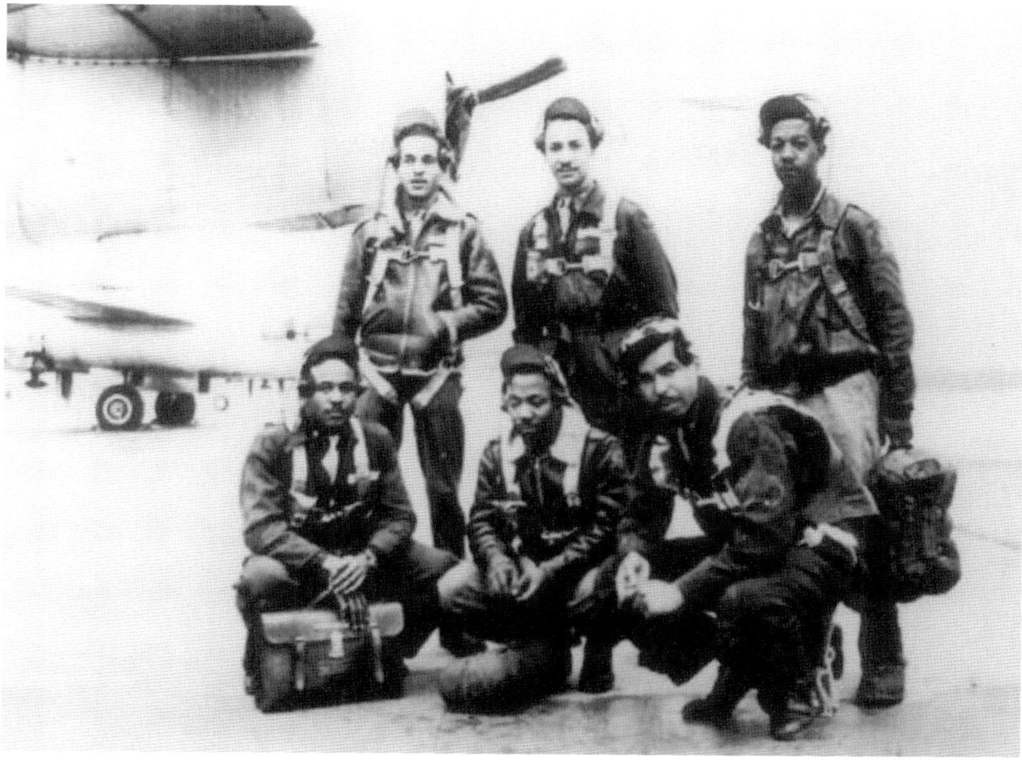

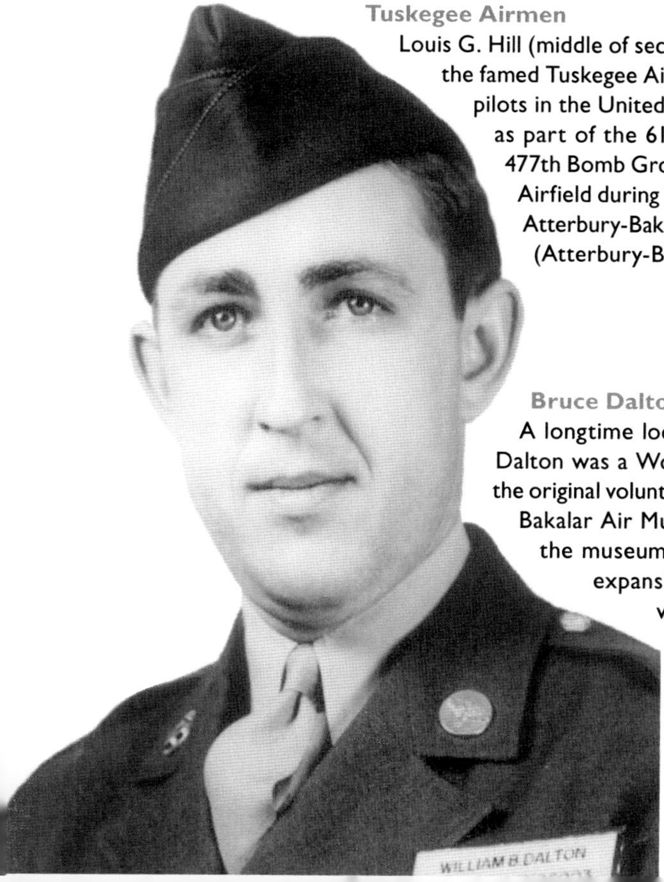

Tuskegee Airmen
Louis G. Hill (middle of second row) and his crew were members of the famed Tuskegee Airmen, the first African American military pilots in the United States. They flew the B-25 Bomber and, as part of the 618th and 619th Bomb Squadrons of the 477th Bomb Group, they served and trained at Atterbury Airfield during World War II. Hill was a supporter of the Atterbury-Bakalar Air Museum prior to his death in 2007. (Atterbury-Bakalar Air Museum Collection.)

Bruce Dalton
A longtime local businessman and civic leader, Bruce Dalton was a World War II glider pilot as well as one of the original volunteers who worked to make the Atterbury-Bakalar Air Museum a reality. After his death in 2007, the museum was able to realize Dalton's dream of expansion. Today, visitors to the museum can visit the Bruce Dalton Media Center, which was designed to look like the inside of a World War II glider, complete with portholes and flashing lights designed to resemble tracer fire. (Atterbury-Bakalar Air Museum Collection.)

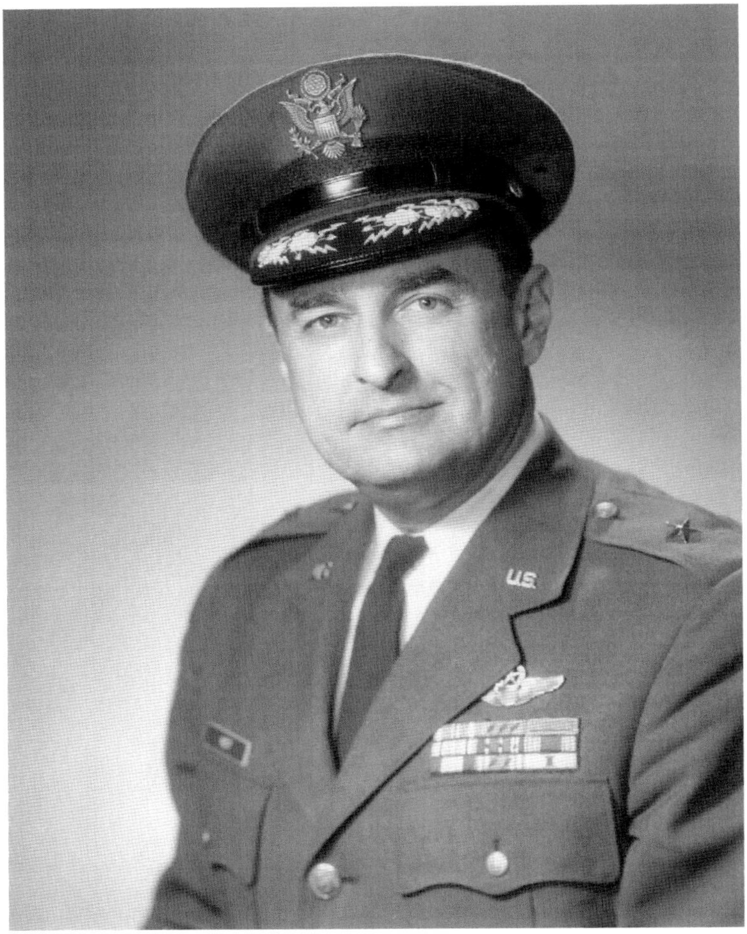

Maj. Gen. John Hoff

Maj. Gen. John Hoff served a long and distinguished career as a military aviator and leader. Beginning in the US Army Air Force (USAAF) in 1943, Hoff became a B-17 Bomber pilot during World War II. For his first combat mission, he flew with more than 2,000 other heavy bombers in December 1944 to stop advancing German troops in the Battle of the Bulge. After the war, Hoff elected to continue his career with the US Air Force, the successor to the USAAF. Several years after the war, he assumed the role of chief controller of the Caribbean Air Command, which served to protect the Panama Canal. In 1960, Colonel Hoff became commander of Bakalar Air Force Base. He served in this role until 1967 and was the longest-serving Bakalar base commander. Hoff was also 434th Troop Carrier Wing Commander from 1962 to 1967, during which time the 434th Troop Carrier Wing was called to active duty during the Cuban Missile Crisis and temporarily transferred to Florida as a deterrent to Russian missiles from Cuba. For their role in preventing escalation of the crisis, Pres. John F. Kennedy personally commended Colonel Hoff and his troops and shook hands with Hoff. Over his long career, he received numerous awards, including the Distinguished Flying Cross, World War II Victory Medal, National Defense Service Medal, and Command Pilot Wings. After retirement, Hoff became active in preserving military history and was instrumental in the planning and creation of the Atterbury-Bakalar Air Museum in Columbus. He helped restore the World War II–era chapel on airport property and volunteered for the museum until his death in 2011. Hoff also served as cochairman of the Celebration 95 project, which organized a community commemoration of the end of World War II in 1995, and helped raise funds for the Bartholomew County Memorial for Veterans. (Atterbury-Bakalar Air Museum Collection.)

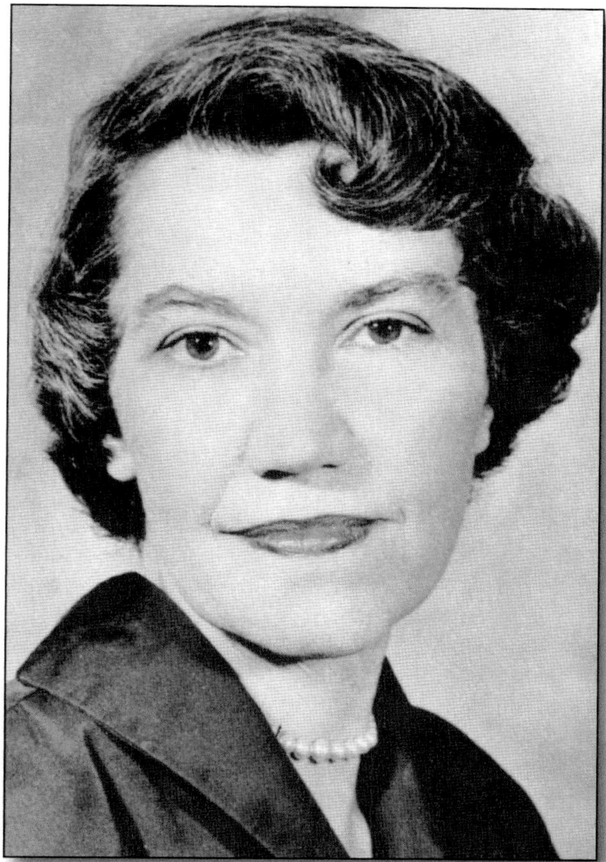

Olive Murphy
Olive Murphy was the longest-serving Bartholomew County Hospital administrator, serving from 1939 to 1967. In addition to overseeing a great period of hospital growth, Murphy helped start both the Blue Cross Blue Shield insurance company in Indiana and the Hospital Foundation in Columbus. She served on the state licensing council and was instrumental in passing rules to allow licensure of licensed practical nurses (LPNs). (Courtesy of Columbus Regional Hospital.)

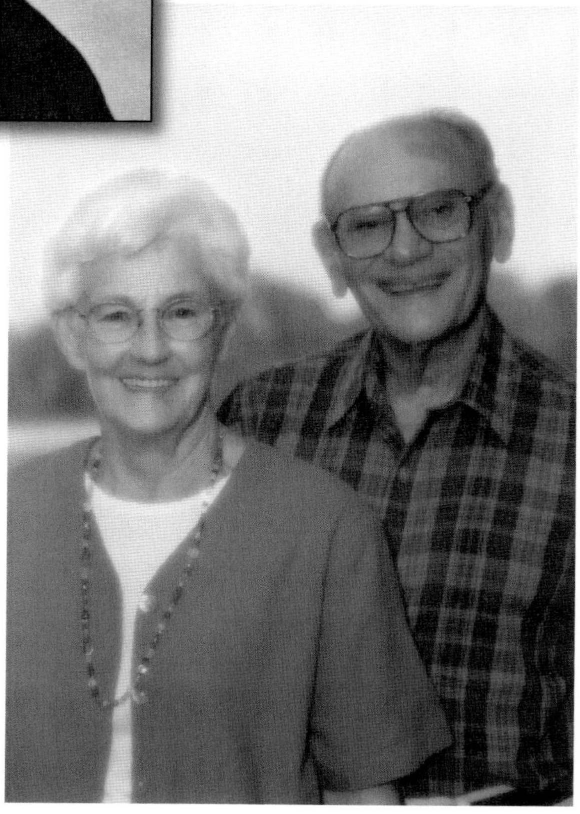

Dr. George and Mary Weinland
Dr. George Weinland came to Columbus in 1960 as the town's first psychiatrist and director of its new mental health center. Born in Hope, Weinland served the mental health needs of area patients until his retirement in 1990, and Weinland Clubhouse peer support center is named in his honor. His wife, Mary Weinland, was a native of Hartsville and a longtime teacher whose passion was volunteer work. For her efforts, she earned the *Republic's* "Woman of the Year" award in 2010. (Courtesy of Laura Weinland Young.)

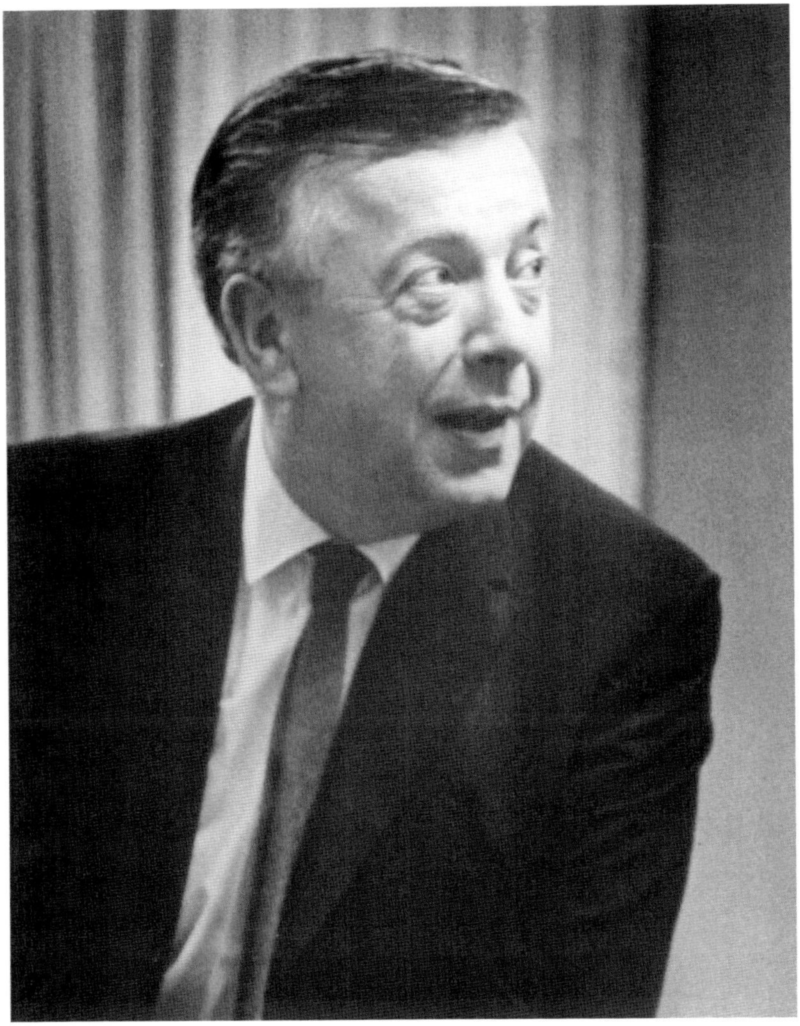

Rev. William R. Laws

During the 26 years in which Rev. Bill Laws served as pastor of First Presbyterian Church, Columbus changed greatly. When he assumed the pastorship in 1950, Columbus was a much smaller, less diverse town with issues of racial inequality, and Reverend Laws became a vocal supporter of equal opportunity for minorities in housing and education. He believed that a pastor should speak about social issues of the time, even if it made people uncomfortable. Reverend Laws worked with microbiologist Mickey King (page 100), attorney Lee Hamilton, and others to encourage realtors to sell homes to black residents at a time when most neighborhoods were segregated. The fact that a black man could not get a haircut in Columbus at that time upset him, and he convinced a Columbus barber to cut the hair of black men who would otherwise have to drive as far as an hour away for a haircut. In addition, he established a scholarship fund to help minority youth from Columbus attend college, and he started the first preschool and day care programs in Columbus. In 1970, Reverend Laws assumed a one-year appointment as moderator of the General Assembly of the Presbyterian Church, a national leadership role. In 1976, he and his wife, Ellen, left Columbus to spend four years at a church in Iowa; they returned to town after his retirement in 1980. Today, there are many reminders of Reverend Laws's efforts, including the annual Laws Peacemaking Lecture and the Columbus Human Rights Commission's annual William R. Laws Human Rights Award. (Courtesy of Marty Ahlemeyer.)

Lee Hamilton

Few people have had as distinguished a career in public service as Lee Hamilton, who represented Indiana's 9th District in the US House of Representatives from 1965 to 1999. Hamilton practiced law for several years in Columbus before his election to Congress, and while Columbus was a welcoming place for Hamilton and his family in the early 1960s, the town was struggling with its own civil rights issues at the time. Hamilton got involved with other community leaders—including Mickey King and Rev. Bill Laws—and helped develop the Columbus Human Rights Commission. Hamilton later recalled "a sense of progress and moving forward" in Columbus as leaders worked together to tackle problems of the time. Although he initially represented Columbus, redistricting later altered the district to include other parts of southern Indiana. When Hamilton first arrived in Washington in 1965, the political environment was friendlier, and a sense of cooperation between political parties existed, with the overriding sentiment felt by most legislators that they had a responsibility to make the country work. Over more than three decades in Congress, Hamilton experienced that atmosphere changing, with an increase in partisan politics as the media presence and money in politics increased. His accomplishments during his long tenure in Congress include considerable time working in the areas of intelligence, foreign affairs, and national security, including chairing several Congressional committees. After his retirement from Congress, Hamilton was chosen by Pres. George W. Bush to be vice chairman of the bipartisan 9/11 Commission, which was charged with investigating the events surrounding the attacks of September 11, 2001. Since then, he has continued to travel back and forth between Indiana and Washington as a trusted member of many boards and commissions, including the Iraq Study Group and the Homeland Security Advisory Council. Currently, Hamilton serves as director of the Center on Congress at Indiana University, an organization whose mission is to help all Americans understand how their representative democracy functions and what their role in their own government should be. (Courtesy of Center on Congress at Indiana University.)

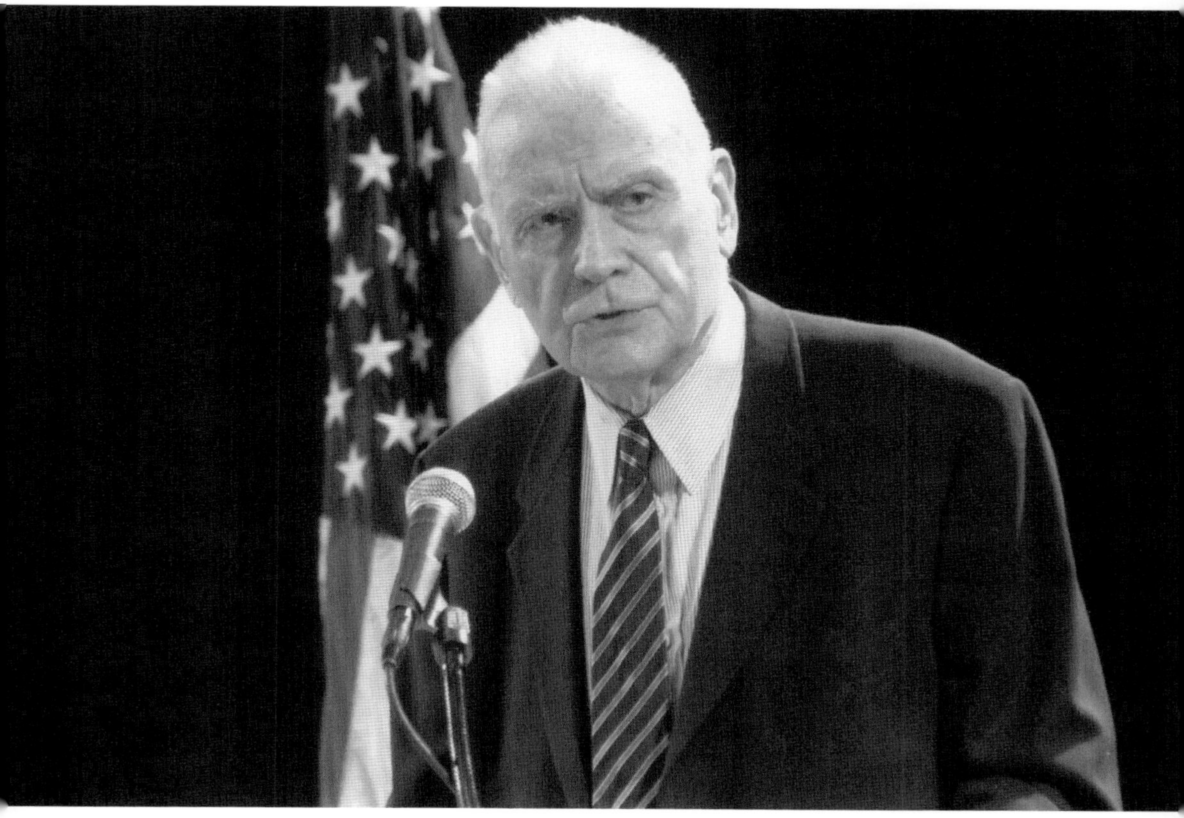

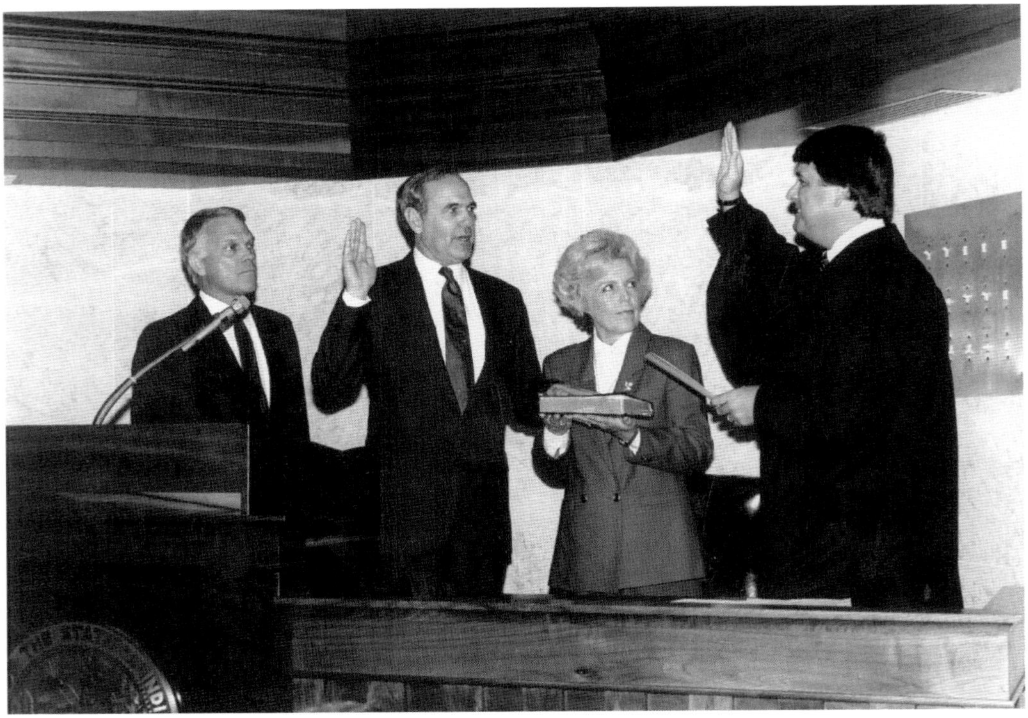

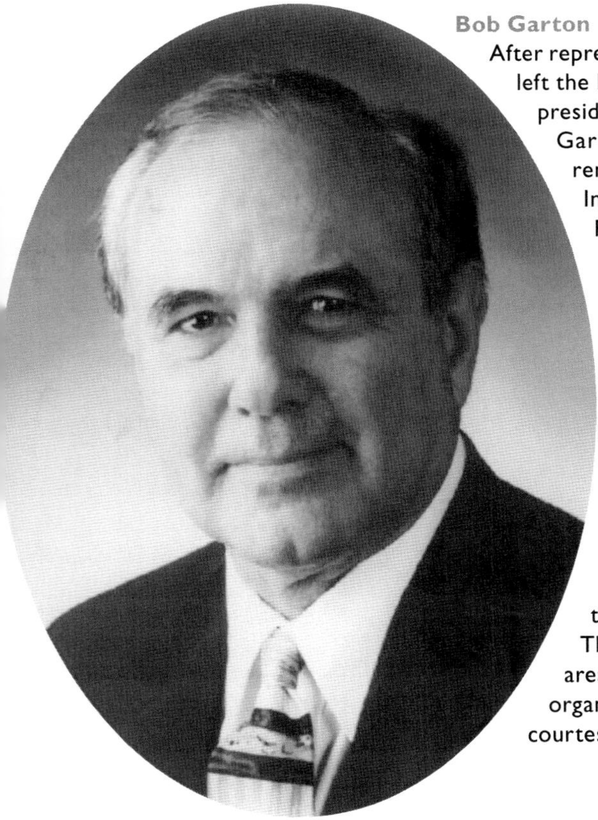

Bob Garton

After representing the Columbus area for 36 years, Bob Garton left the Indiana Senate in 2006 as the longest-serving Senate president pro tem, having held that position for 26 years. Garton's accomplishments during his tenure include removing the sales tax from grocery purchases, leading Indiana to become the last state to ratify the Equal Rights Amendment, and guiding the legislature into the digital age by becoming wireless and installing electronic voting. In addition, Garton served as chair of the select committee responsible for overseeing the writing of a historical volume commemorating the first 100 years of the Indiana General Assembly and of two volumes of biographical sketches of legislators. In 1999, Garton received the William Bulger Excellence in State Legislative Leadership Award, and the Robert D. Garton Veterans Plaza on Second Street honors his service. Both Garton and his wife also spent many years in leadership positions at Ivy Tech in Columbus, where Barbara was chair of the Columbus Region Board of Trustees for 24 years. The Gartons have also been supporters of numerous area causes, including Mill Race Center and various arts organizations. (Above, courtesy of BCHS Collection; left, courtesy of Bob and Barbara Garton.)

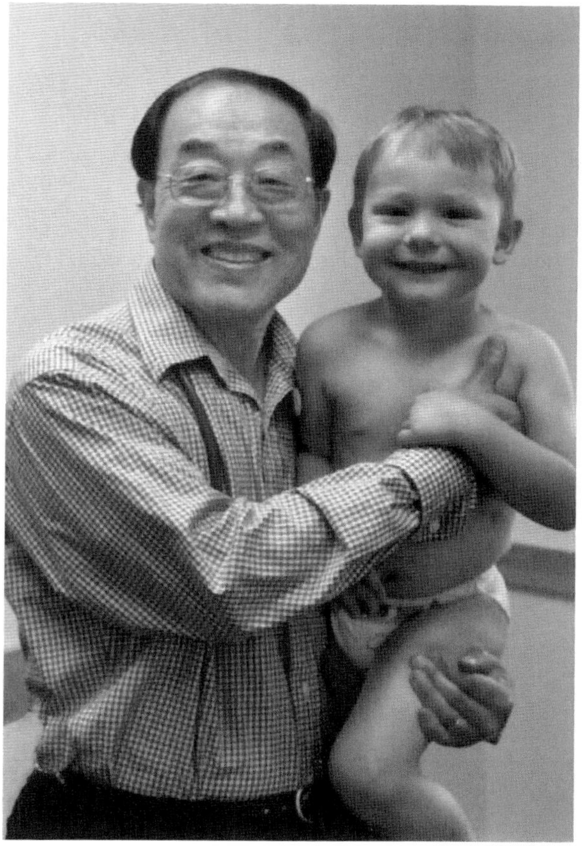

Dr. C.B. Kim
When Dr. C.B. Kim opened his solo pediatric practice in 1972, his dedication to his patients was evident when he gave parents his home phone number for emergencies. Dr. Kim developed the Level II Nursery at Columbus Regional Hospital and was the first doctor in Columbus to do lifesaving procedures on newborns, including neonatal intubation and umbilical artery catheterization. Prior to his retirement in 2006, thousands of Columbus children received their medical care from Dr. Kim, pictured here with Grant Emerick after surgery to correct a heart problem diagnosed by Dr. Kim. (Courtesy of C.B. Kim.)

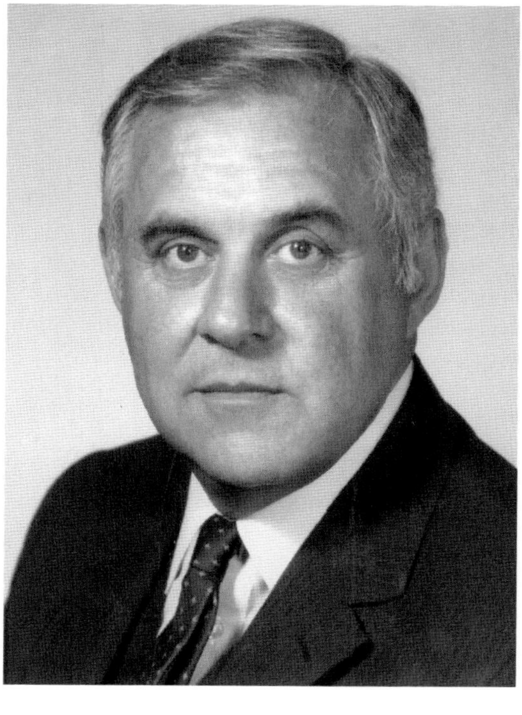

Mayor Bob Stewart
Bob Stewart's accomplishments as mayor from 1984 to 1996 included diversity training in response to minority complaints about police treatment and starting a study of a possible trail system in Columbus, the result of which is Columbus's extensive People Trail system. Stewart also created 6,500 jobs, many from the Japanese companies he recruited to Columbus. Every October, thousands still enjoy Ethnic Expo, founded in 1984 by his wife, Barbara Stewart, who was also very active in the community. In honor of Bob Stewart's work with the Front Door project of the 1990s, the Second Street Bridge was renamed in his honor in 2013. (BCHS Collection.)

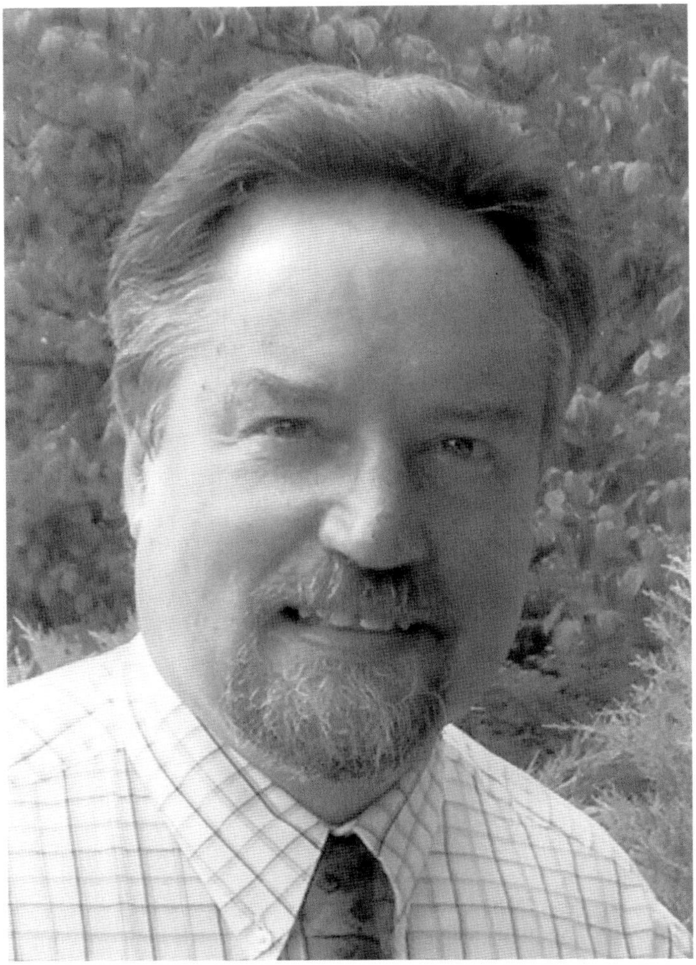

Bob Pitman

Today's Mill Race Center in Columbus is the epitome of what a senior center should be—a place where seniors can gather for social, educational, recreational, and health-related activities. When Bob Pitman became the director of the senior center in Columbus in 1985, it was housed in the old waterworks building, a facility that lacked space for many of the services now available, including a fitness center, computer lab, and rehabilitation center. As early as 1990, Pitman and others began to imagine the type of facility that would allow them to grow and provide more services to Columbus's senior population. Many obstacles made the realization of this dream difficult—including issues with funding, space, and conflicting ideas from members—but Pitman was determined and worked through the challenges. After almost 20 years of consideration and planning, including a challenging six-year capital campaign, construction on the Mill Race Center took place from 2009 to 2011. In the first year and a half after the facility's opening in 2011, membership increased by more than 1,000 members. During his time as director, Pitman also became involved in advocacy for seniors on a state and national level, including serving as chair of the National Institute of Senior Centers and receiving the organization's Founder's Award in 2009. The local community also recognized his tireless work advocating for the rights of seniors by awarding him the William Laws Human Rights Award in 2012. Pitman is proud that Columbus—far from the traditional warm weather of the Southeast or Southwest—has become a retirement community to many people not from the area who are looking for a place with a good quality of life for seniors, as he believes that Mill Race Center is a big part of this. (Courtesy of Bob Pitman.)

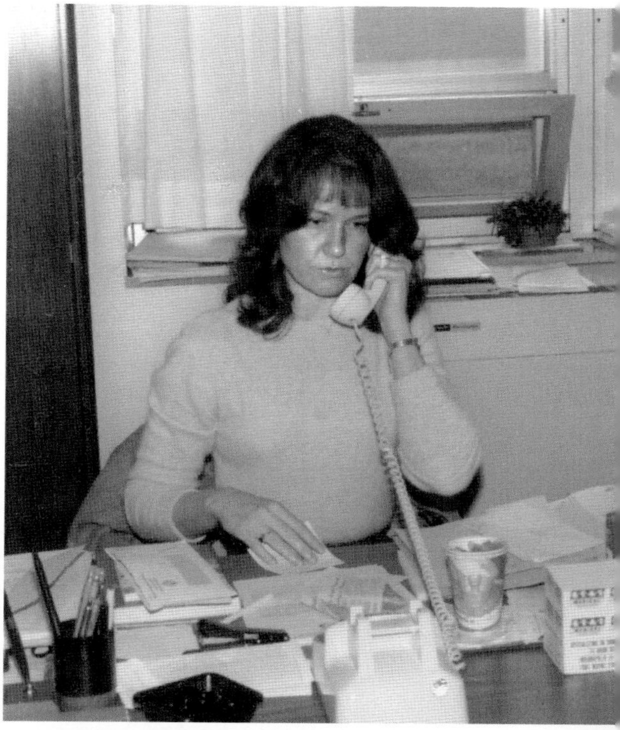

Sandy Carmichael

When Sandy Carmichael started working with terminally ill patients, she was not allowed to wear a name tag with the word "hospice" when she visited patients because it made people uncomfortable. In 1980, when hospice was incorporated and Carmichael was named its first director, many physicians did not even tell patients when they had cancer. Carmichael had been the head nurse on a medical-surgical floor at Bartholomew County Hospital and she knew that patients in the end stages of illness had needs that were not being met in a hospital setting. As a group of physicians and community members worked together in the early years of hospice, more patients wanted to have comfort care at home near the end of their lives and not spend this time in a sterile hospital setting, and more caregivers agreed that terminally ill patients should have a choice in what kind of care they received. Carmichael was not only instrumental in the development of the local hospice system, but she also founded the Indiana Association for Hospice in 1979 after learning that other hospitals were interested in this new idea too. As a referral system developed, the local program cared for 60 patients in its first year. Initially, growth was slow, as insurance companies did not reimburse for hospice services. Carmichael worked hard to make the program profitable, and under her guidance, the local hospice remained in the forefront of end-of-life care, becoming the first licensed hospice in Indiana in 1989. For her work as a leader in the national hospice movement, Carmichael was invited to a White House reception in 1991 given by First Lady Barbara Bush. A few years later, she began to consider the idea of a freestanding in-patient hospice building. In order to convince the board of directors and the community about the value of such a center, she traveled to many national and international meetings and studied other in-patient hospice centers. After years of research, a feasibility study, and a large capital campaign, the in-patient hospice center opened in 2004 and is now a valuable community asset, providing care to patients and their families near the end of life. After more than 30 years of Carmichael's leadership and the hard work of many, Our Hospice of South Central Indiana today cares for around 1,000 patients per year. (Both, courtesy of Sandy Carmichael.)

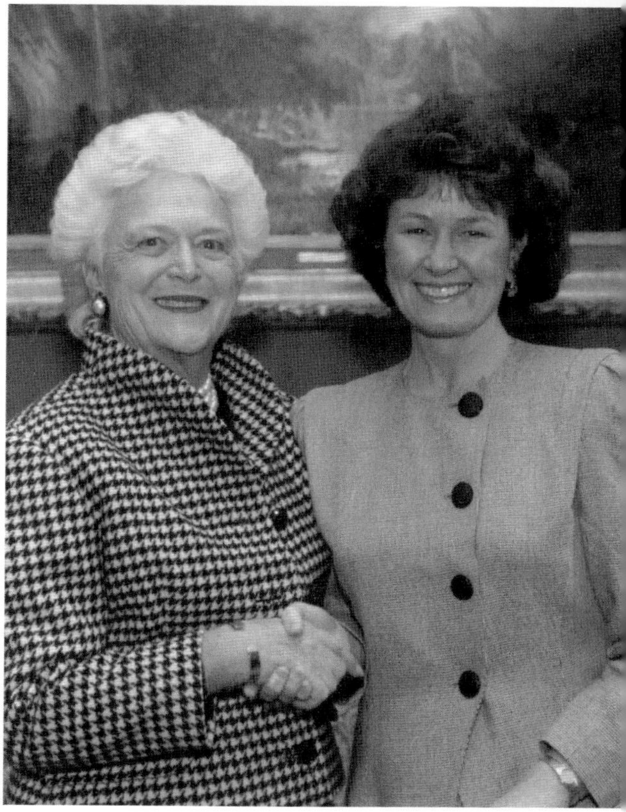

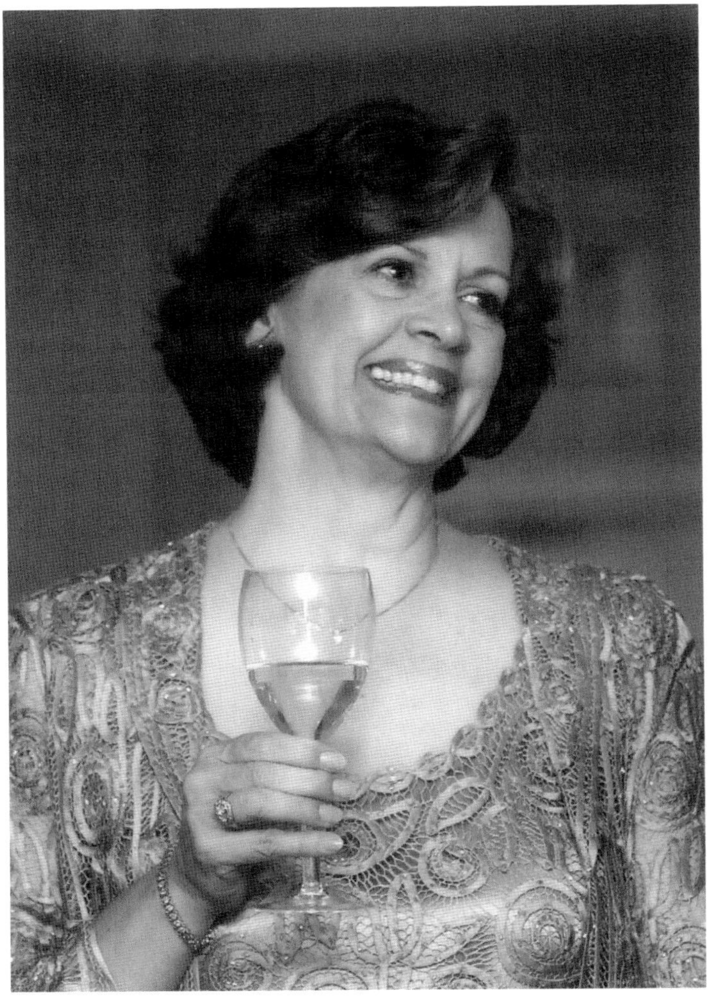

Alice Curry

Alice Curry served as the executive director of the Columbus Indiana Philharmonic from 1987 to 2010, except for a two-year period away from Indiana. Under her leadership, the orchestra was transformed from a small volunteer group to a well-respected professional orchestra, and with the help of music director David Bowden, the Columbus Indiana Philharmonic has won numerous awards and received national acclaim. Alice studied music education during college, and during her time at the helm, the philharmonic also expanded its educational opportunities for children in the community with a youth strings program in local schools, a summertime strings camp, and the formation of the Columbus Indiana Children's Choir in collaboration with the Indianapolis Children's Choir. Alice was known for her enthusiasm for the arts in Columbus, and she continued to work for the philharmonic, even after being diagnosed with Stage IV lung cancer in 2009. Not one to let this hurdle stop her, she continued with the organization for another year, before stepping down in 2010. Instead of retiring quietly, she then took on two new causes, the first being the reopening of Columbus's major arts venue downtown, the Commons. Although she had never smoked, Alice knew the dangers of secondhand smoking, to which she had been exposed much of her life, and she devoted a great deal of time in her last year of life championing antismoking bans at both the city and state levels, even testifying at the Indiana Legislature supporting a statewide smoking ban. Her very personal knowledge of the effects of lung cancer gave strength to her fight until the day she died in 2011. (Courtesy of Jerry Curry.)

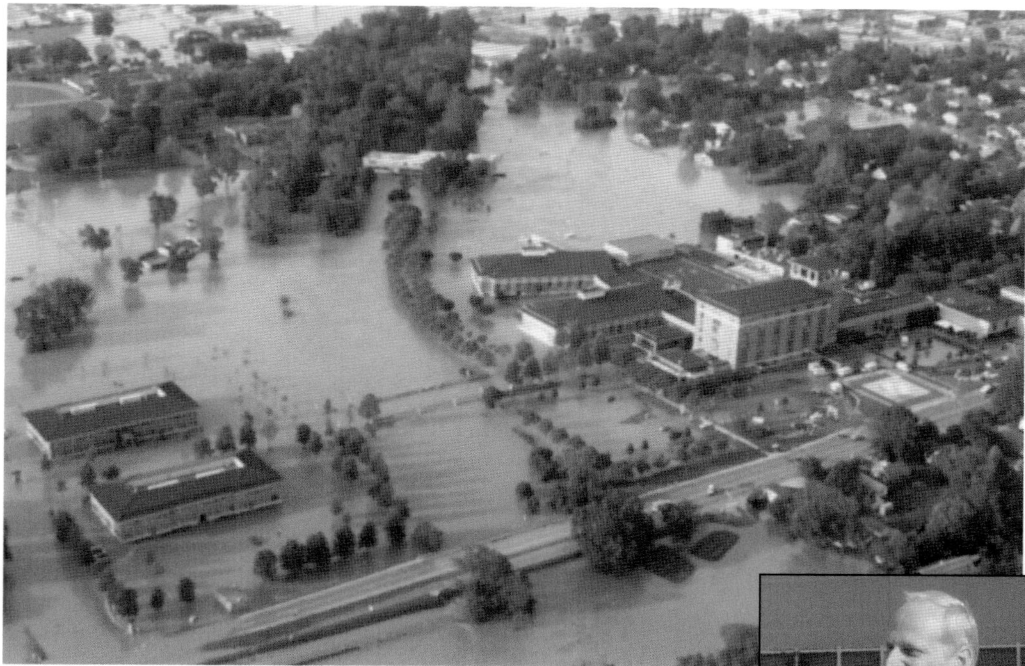

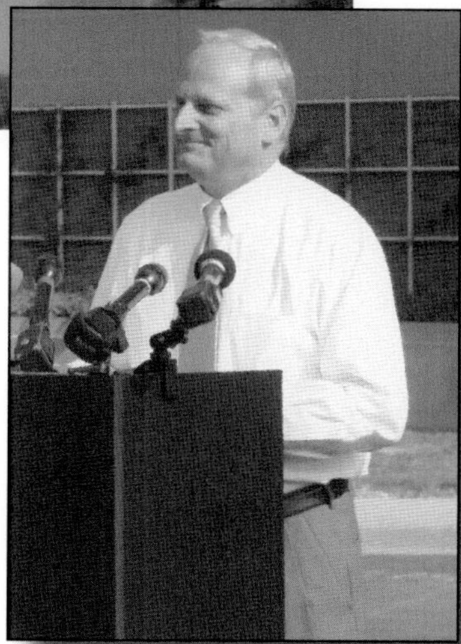

Jim Bickel

In June 2008, a historic flood devastated much of Columbus. Columbus Regional Hospital chief executive officer Jim Bickel was on site at the hospital that day after attending an emergency meeting about rising water levels around the county with the mayor and other city officials. He watched the usually quiet Haw Creek steadily rise and move closer to the hospital, and by 3:00 p.m., he knew the situation was dire as floodwater rushed onto the hospital loading dock and into the basement. Because numerous vital structures and operations were located in the basement, including dietary services, elevator controls, boilers, pharmacy, laboratory, sterilization services, and medical gases such as oxygen, the loss of the basement was disastrous. Within an hour, Bickel was forced to order the evacuation of the hospital. Although it was a weekend, administrators, staff, and physicians worked together, and the hospital was evacuated in less than three hours. The teamwork of everyone involved, along with trust and good training—including from a mock disaster drill one year prior—helped the process go smoothly. The evacuation itself was just the beginning of a stressful four-month period, during which the hospital worked to reopen. Less than 24 hours after the flood, Bickel met with hospital leaders at city hall to discuss the next steps. All involved were aware that livelihoods of many employees were at stake, as was health care for the entire community with the hospital closed. At that first meeting, the seeds of an amazing commitment to the hospital staff were sown when Bickel and hospital leaders decided to continue paying staff while the hospital was closed. The hospital had a significant amount of cash on hand to begin a planned building project, but the decision was made that using that money to pay staff was critical to retaining that staff during recovery. For four months, staff members continued to receive their paychecks, as they aided in cleanup and volunteered around Columbus. Bickel and the leadership team saw an opportunity for excellence in recovery from the flood, just as they had always strived for excellence in day-to-day operations. Within two weeks, a temporary emergency department (ED) was operational, and after two months, the ED was back in the hospital building. On October 27, 2008, Columbus Regional Hospital reopened and was ready to provide Columbus with the quality care it was known for. (Both, courtesy of Columbus Regional Hospital.)

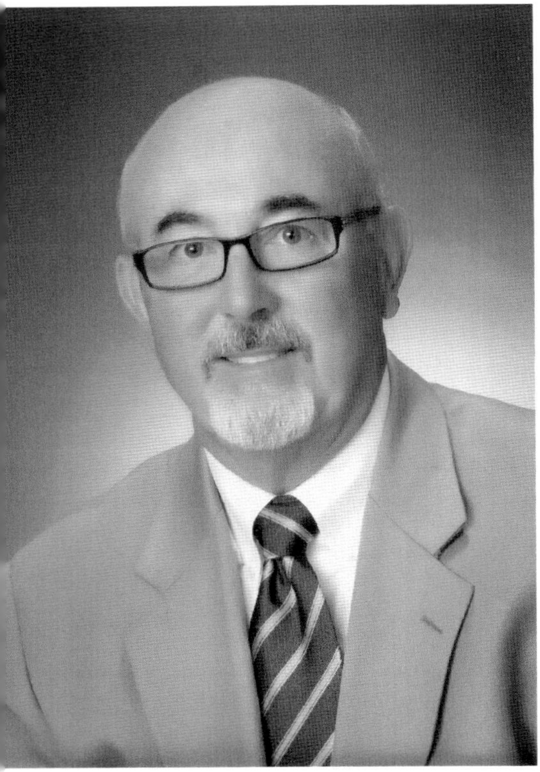

Mayor Fred Armstrong

Having the opportunity to work with many dedicated and talented people was the best part of being mayor of Columbus for Fred Armstrong. Mayor Armstrong lists his proudest achievements as the downtown revitalization that occurred and the no-smoking ordinance that was passed during his tenure. A former police officer, Armstrong worked in the private sector before returning to public service and eventually becoming Columbus's longest-serving mayor from 1996 to 2011. (Courtesy of Fred Armstrong.)

Ethan Crough

Ethan Crough has never let achondroplasia (commonly known as dwarfism) stand in the way of his goals. He has lived all over the country and worked as an actor, comedian, tour guide, and teacher. Crough is currently serving on the national Board of Directors of Little People of America, an advocacy and support group, as vice president for membership. He has always tried to connect with the community in which he is living and, in 2012, he became executive director of the Bartholomew Consolidated School Foundation, although he continues with public speaking and diversity education. (Courtesy of Ethan Crough.)

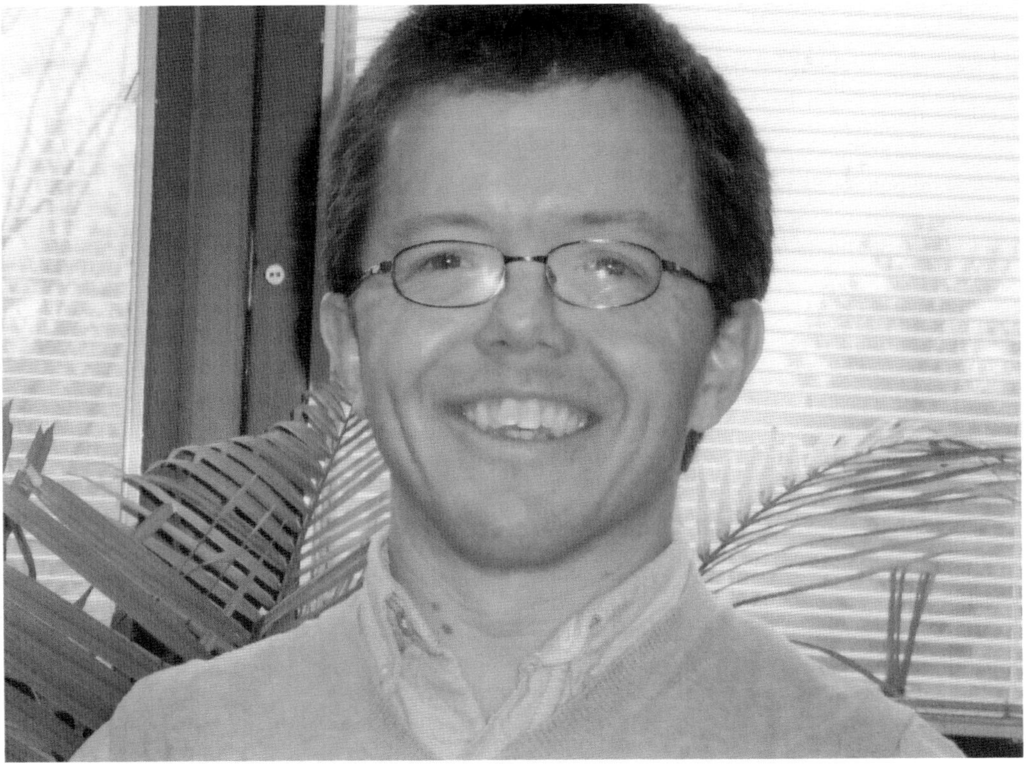

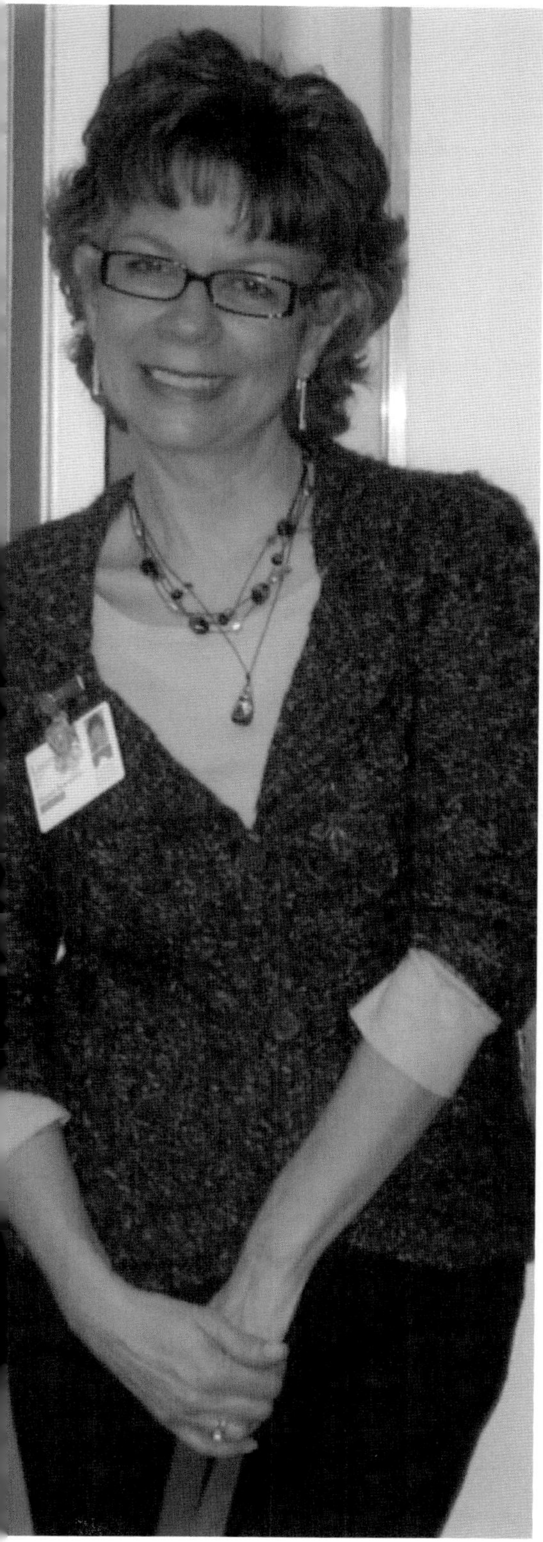

Laura Hurt

In the late 1990s, Laura Hurt began to see more and more Spanish-speaking people around Columbus who seemed disconnected with the rest of the community. A native of Mexico, Hurt had enrolled in medical school there, but after moving to the United States and starting a family, she chose a career in nursing. She was hired in 1998 by Columbus Regional Hospital and quickly began to receive phone calls from all over the hospital to interpret and translate for Spanish-speaking patients. The Healthy Communities Initiative in Columbus had also noticed the growing Latino community and asked Hurt for ideas about how to address their health needs, and a new team called Proyecto Salud was formed under her leadership in 1999. Proyecto Salud partnered with the Volunteers in Medicine Clinic, which had opened in 1996 to serve uninsured residents of Bartholomew County; assembled lists of volunteer interpreters who could aid expectant mothers and patients at doctors' offices; and opened an unstaffed phone line for health-related inquiries. In 2000, Hurt took a new trial position at the hospital to increase the staff's cultural awareness and to teach the basics of medical Spanish, eventually being named director of diversity strategies, but maintained her volunteer role as chair of Proyecto Salud. Other challenges to integrating this population into the community arose, including unaddressed mental health issues, family fragmentation, the need for school programs to aid nonnative speakers, and the opposition from many landlords and landowners, who felt that many individuals were not deserving of assistance due to their undocumented status. With the goal of teaching self-reliance within the health care system, Proyecto Salud developed a Promotora Program, which identifies people from within the target community to become trusted messengers of health education and disease prevention practices. The Promotoras have functioned in workplaces, churches, neighborhoods, and health centers with a large percentage of Spanish-speaking individuals. Hurt is very proud of the Promotora Program, which has been identified as a model for other communities. Although her original career goal changed, Hurt's journey through the health care field has improved the health of many who might otherwise have been without care. (Courtesy of Laura Hurt.)

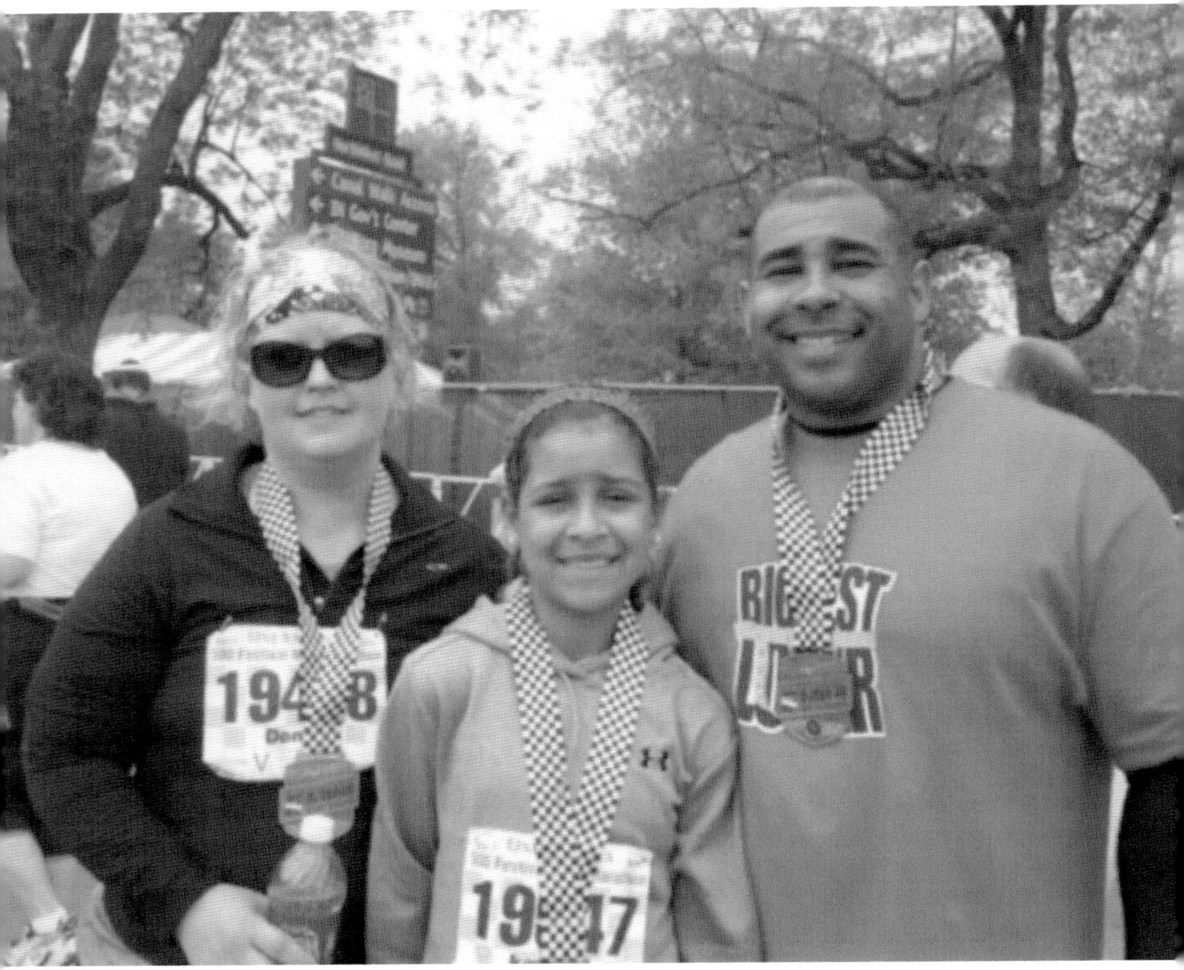

Allen Smith
Many people across the country were introduced to Allen Smith as a contestant on the NBC television show *Biggest Loser* in 2009–2010. Smith, however, had achieved local fame prior to this when he won election for county coroner in 2008, becoming the first African American ever elected to county office in Bartholomew County. A firefighter for 15 years, Smith had always had an interest in politics and had served as deputy coroner before running for coroner. As a member of one of the city's oldest black families, Smith was born and raised in Columbus and graduated from Columbus East High School. His grandmother was Prentess Smith (page 98). He has traveled extensively around the United States and around the world, but he and his wife, Frankie, chose Columbus to raise their daughter, Taylor. (Courtesy of Allen Smith.)

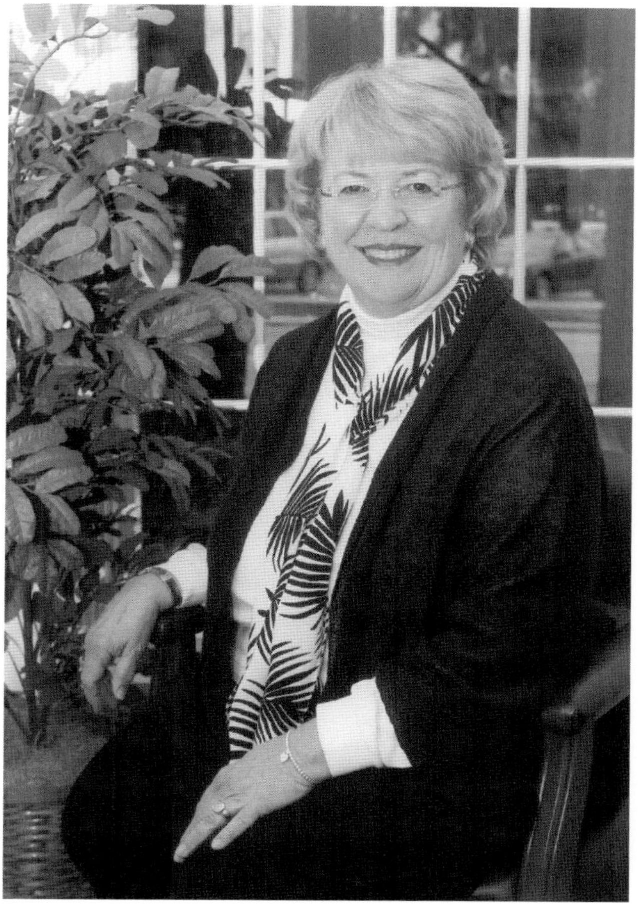

Sherry Stark

Although not originally from Columbus, Sherry Stark has a long history of community involvement in her adopted hometown. She served as one of the Columbus Area Visitors Center's early tour guides and tour guide trainers in the 1970s, and she spent 10 years in Columbus Service League, which gave her essential knowledge about Columbus and taught her how to get things done. She was hired by Mayor Bob Stewart to be senior deputy mayor and executive director of the community development department during his time in office and helped spearhead the many Focus 2000 Projects. In this role, she played a large part in the downtown streetscape project, the Front Door project, the renovation of Mill Race Park, and the development of what later became Lincoln-Central Neighborhood Family Center. Before leaving this position when Mayor Stewart left office, Stark ran unsuccessfully for mayor. She then moved to the nonprofit world and led the Columbus Area Arts Council for two years before, in 1999, becoming president and chief executive officer of Heritage Fund–the Community Foundation of Bartholomew County. During her tenure, the fund's assets grew from $17 million to a high of $70 million, and the organization strived to become a catalyst for important change in the community. The Welcoming Community Initiative was started at Heritage Fund and gave rise to both Columbus Young Professionals and CAMEO (Columbus Area Multi-Ethnic Organization), and Heritage Fund led the way in supporting fundraising for the construction of the new Commons. Stark is especially proud of the EcO15 initiative (Economic Opportunities through Education by 2015), which received a $38-million grant from Lilly Endowment to develop job training programs in southeast Indiana. Since retiring from Heritage Fund in 2011, Stark has undertaken new challenges, including establishing Centra Foundation in 2012 and serving as its first executive director. (Courtesy of the *Republic*/Joel Philippsen.)

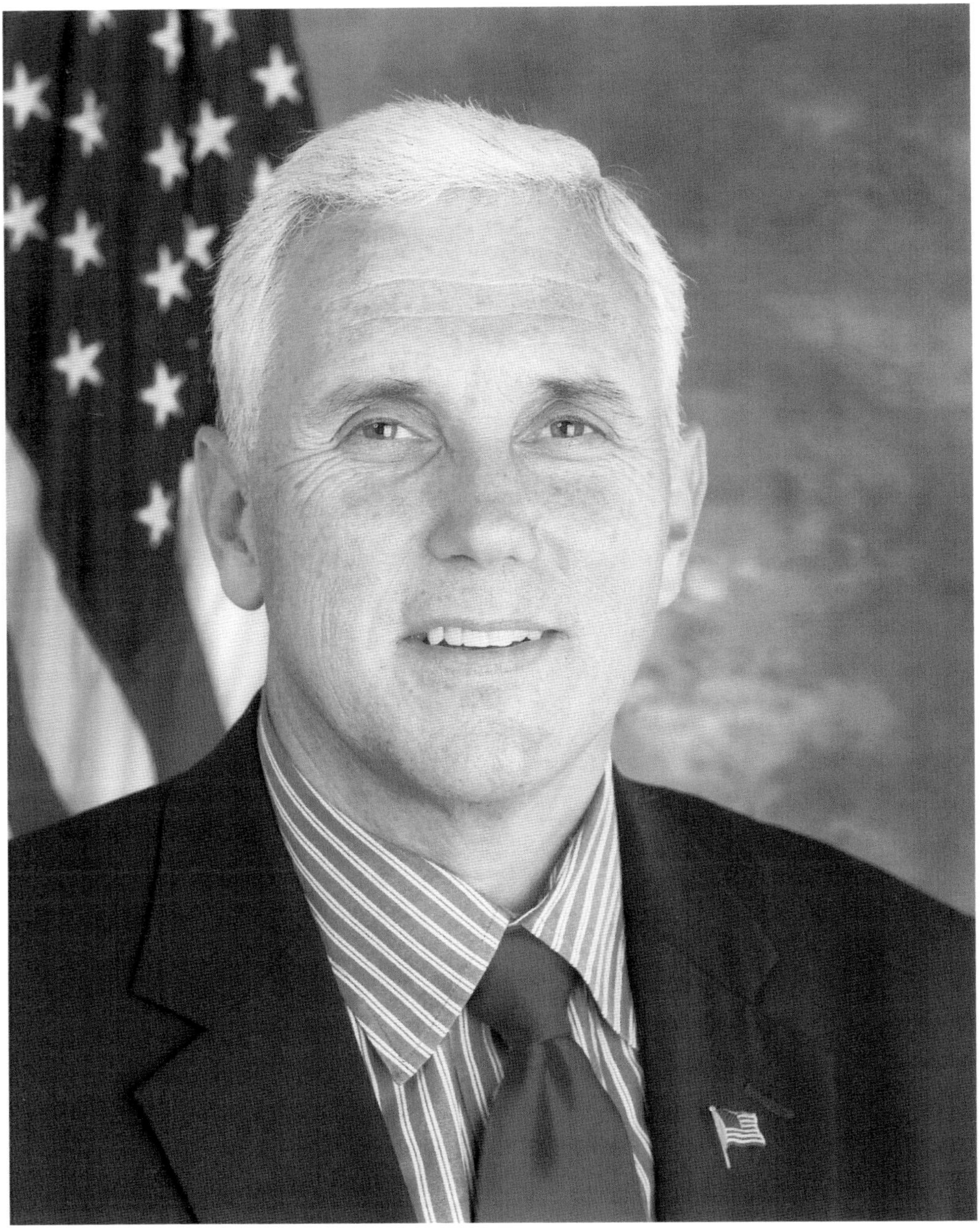

Mike Pence

Columbus native Mike Pence was elected Indiana's 50th governor in 2012 and inaugurated in January 2013. A graduate of Columbus North High School, Pence went on to earn degrees from Hanover College and Indiana University School of Law. First elected in 2000, Pence served in the US House of Representatives from 2001 to 2013, representing the 6th District of Indiana, an area that includes most of Bartholomew County. During his six terms in Congress, Pence served in a variety of Republican leadership roles, including House Republican conference chairman, and he was known as a champion of fiscal conservatism. (Courtesy of US House of Representatives.)

CHAPTER FOUR

Educating the Community

A long line of exceptional educators in Columbus includes the teachers after whom schools were named. Mabel McDowell, Lillian Schmitt, Frances Smith, and W.D. Richards were honored with elementary schools named after them, as were the Fodrea sisters, Hazel, Bess, and Mabel.

In addition, certain teachers have had careers noteworthy for innovative teaching methods and long-lasting effects on generations of students. Longtime teacher Edna Folger started her career in a one-room schoolhouse and finished at Columbus High School. The annual award for most outstanding Columbus teacher is named in Folger's honor. Evelyn Seward graduated from Columbus High School at age 15 and taught journalism, French, and Latin for many years. Seward also served in the Navy during World War II and was involved in local politics. The longest-serving teacher in school corporation history, Shirley Lyster chaired an English department that won national awards for its innovative methods of teaching writing, and Lyster won the first Edna Folger Award. She is one of many individuals from Columbus who have earned trips to the White House to meet presidents or first ladies after winning national awards.

After Columbus East High School opened in 1972, two of its original teachers—art teacher Phil Miller and science teacher Jack Young—created a love of learning in their fields for numerous students year after year. The art center and science laboratory at Columbus East are named for Miller and Young respectively.

An example of innovative teaching that captures the interest of students is American Pie, the annual concert of music from the 1950s, 1960s, and 1970s, which teaches history through music. It was started by Ed Niespodziani in 1985. Niespodziani also took students on numerous educational trips, including to the American West to study the effects of Westward migration on Native American populations and to Washington, DC, to study representative democracy up close.

Other teachers, such as Candy Carr, have also taken special interests in specific areas. Carr, a longtime elementary teacher, has created a curriculum for other elementary teachers to teach local history to their students. Carr collaborated with historian Susanna Jones on *It Began With Bartholomew*, a book for fourth graders about early Bartholomew County history. She also created materials for teachers to lead field trips for students through City Cemetery, downtown Columbus, and throughout the county.

As the demographics of the school corporation have shifted with an increase in Spanish-speaking students, Mary Ellen Nelson has led a group called Family-School Partners to reach out to families of these children to improve their chances of being successful in school. Nelson's bilingual skills allowed her to go into the homes of Spanish-speaking preschool children to help prepare them for school, and once families learned of the available services, the referrals to the program exploded.

From preschool through postgraduate education, students in Columbus have benefited from the many outstanding educators who have taught them.

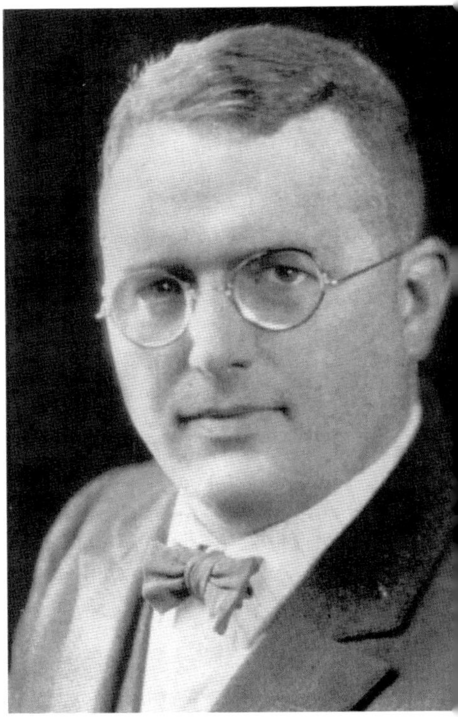

Donald DuShane

Donald DuShane was an advocate for teachers, not just in the Columbus schools, for which he served as superintendent from 1918 to 1941, but for teachers everywhere. DuShane was an active member of the National Education Association (NEA) and was elected president of the nationwide organization in 1940. He fought against political interference in schools, and the NEA created a fund in his name to aid in the defense of teachers unjustly accused of wrongdoing. (1934 *Log*/BCHS Collection.)

Judson S. Erne

Judson Erne was principal at Columbus High School from 1949 to1972, during which time more than 12,000 students graduated and two new high schools (Columbus North and Columbus East) were built. When an Indianapolis radio station ran a contest in the 1960s for the area's favorite principal, Erne received 210,000 votes—at a time when the student body of his school was 2,400, and all votes had to be written on paper! Today, the Columbus North auditorium is named for Erne. (1958 *Log*/BCHS Collection.)

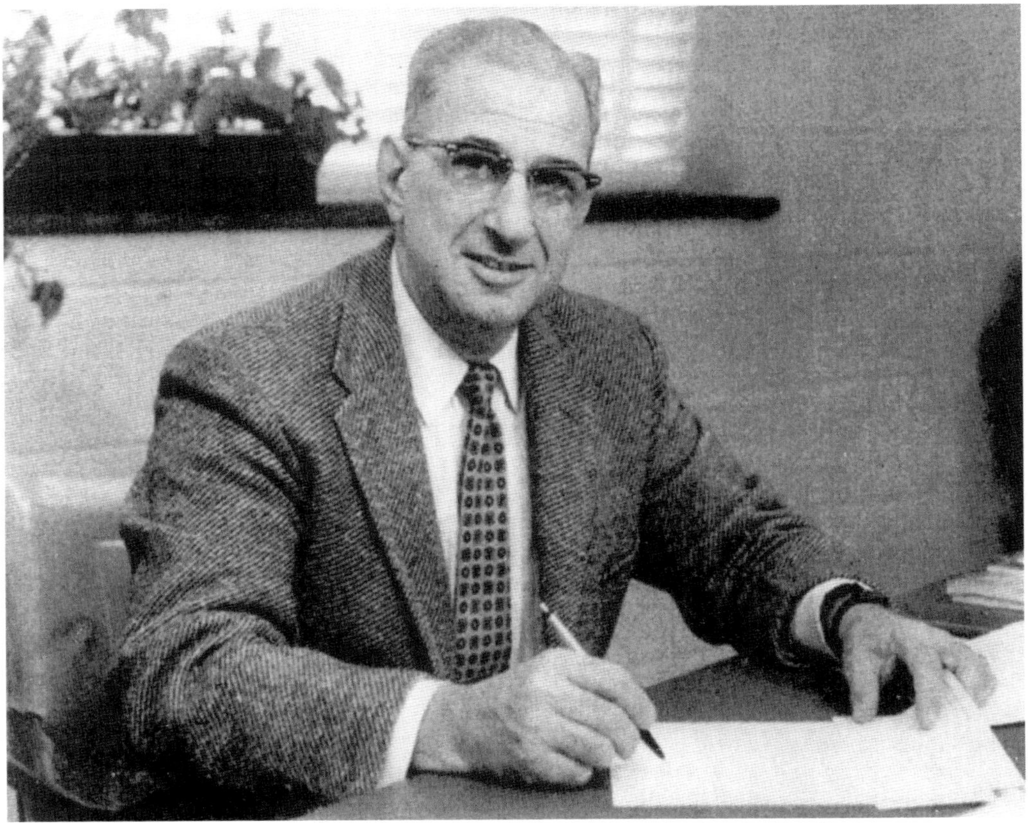

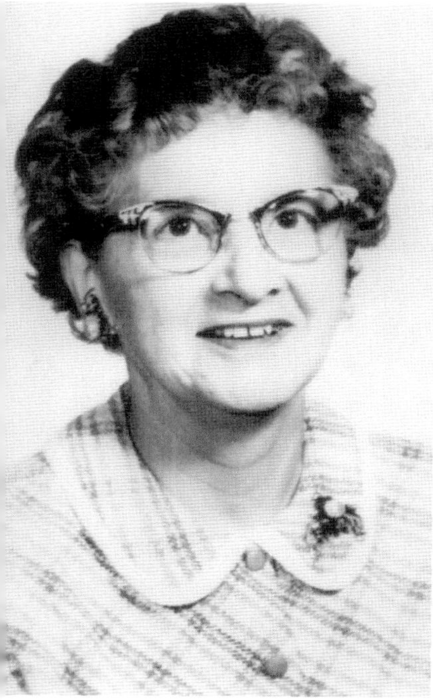

Edna Folger
When people hear Edna Folger's name today, they are likely to think of the distinguished teaching award named for her and given to a Columbus teacher each year. Folger herself taught math for 46 years, beginning in a one-room schoolhouse then spending most of her career at Columbus High School. (BCHS Collection.)

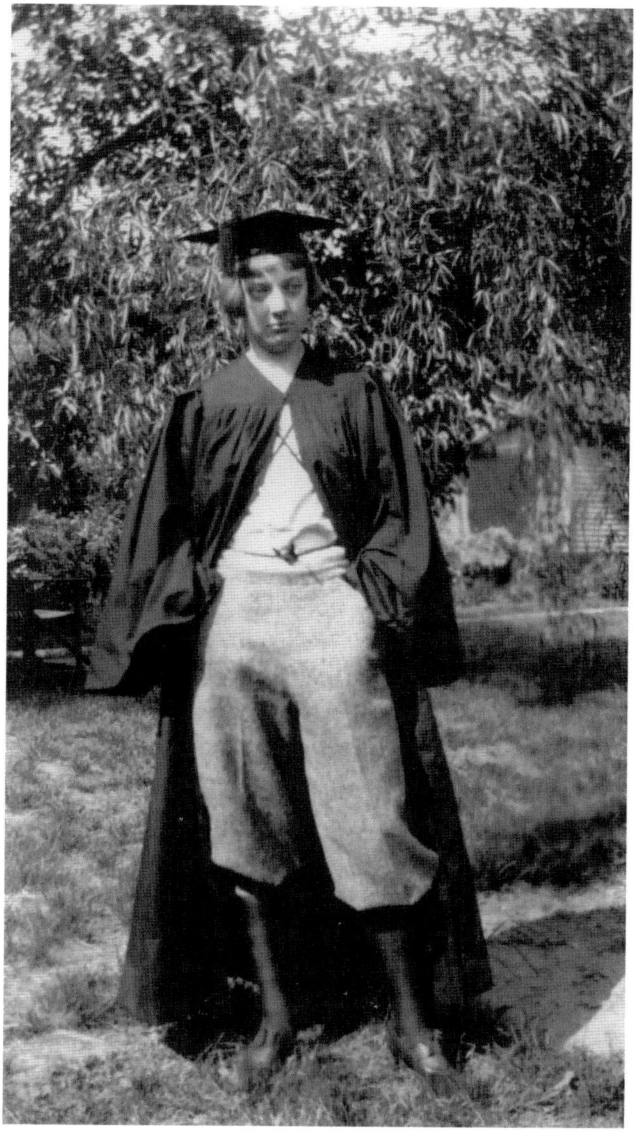

Evelyn Seward
The granddaughter of a cofounder of the *Republic*, Evelyn Seward taught high school from 1930 to 1972. In 1944, she enlisted in the WAVES (Women Accepted for Volunteer Emergency Service), an all-female division of the Navy, in which she served two years before returning to teaching. After her retirement, she was active in local politics and other community causes. Seward never married, and upon her death in 1993, she willed her two homes and property, including a large amount of historic documents related to her family history, to the Bartholomew County Historical Society. (BCHS Collection.)

Fodrea Sisters

Fodrea Community School (now Columbus Signature Academy [CSA] Fodrea) opened in 1973 and was named after three sisters, Hazel and Bess Fodrea and Mabel Fodrea Jordan, who were teachers in Columbus schools. Mabel (standing second from right) taught in a one-room schoolhouse before marrying and moving to Seymour. Bess (sitting at center) taught seventh- and eighth-grade students at McKinley School for many years. Hazel (standing at center) was a beloved first-grade teacher at Garfield Elementary who had two rooms—one regular classroom and a room for bunnies, baby chicks, and other exciting and unconventional learning opportunities. There were eight Fodrea sisters in all, and they sang in a double quartet in perfect harmony all over Indiana. (Courtesy of Ivadel Simpson Hannah.)

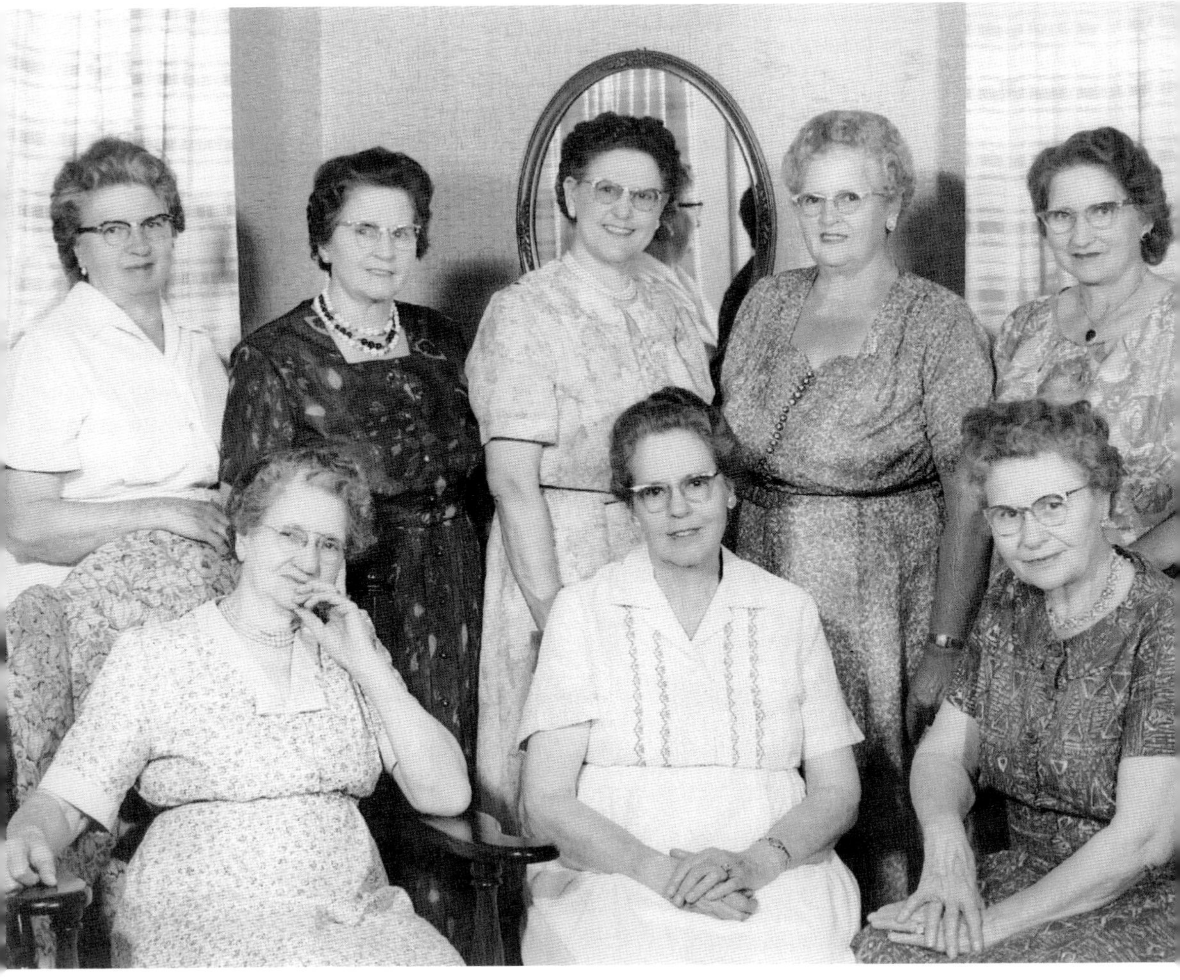

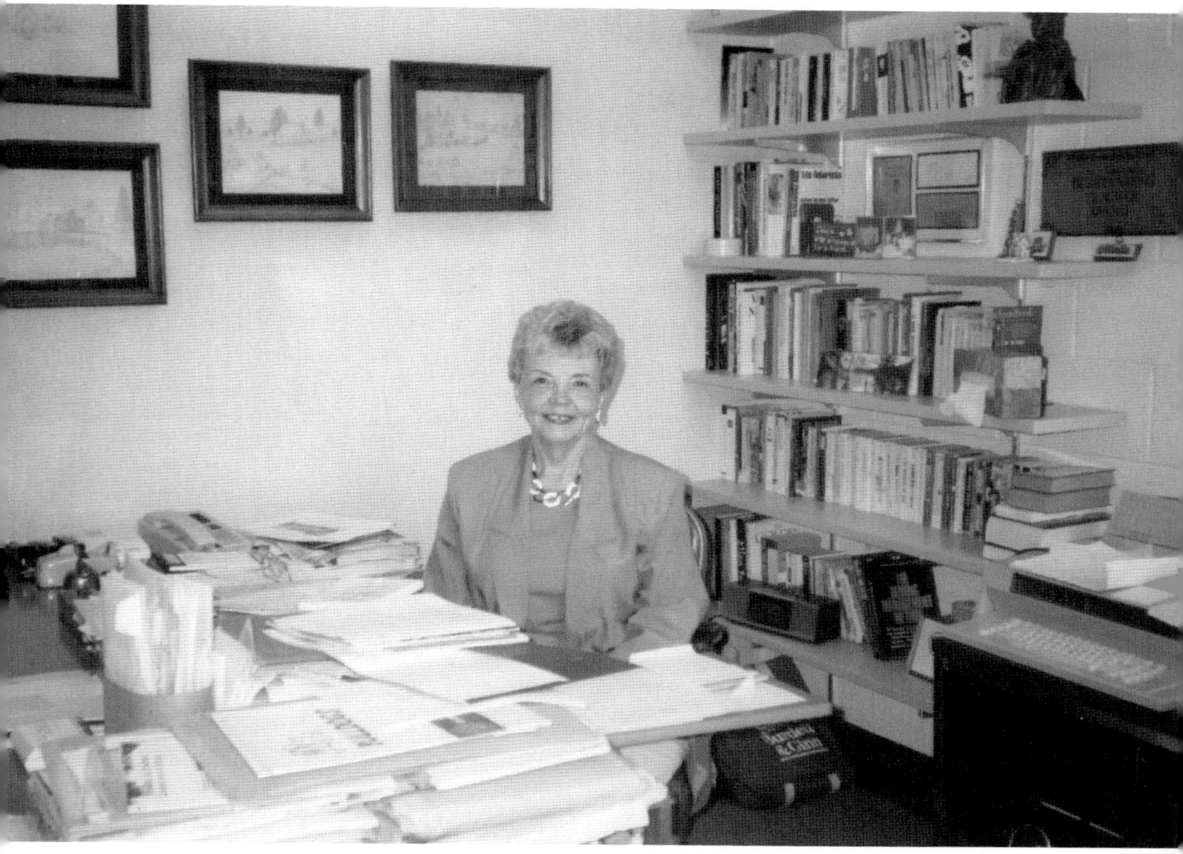

Shirley Lyster

To say that no one has as much history with Bartholomew County schools as Shirley Lyster would not be exaggerating. When she retired in 2004 after more than 52 years as a teacher, she was the longest-serving teacher in the history of Columbus schools. Lyster was born in Columbus and graduated from Columbus High School in 1947, returning to do her student teaching there in 1951 after graduating from Franklin College. During that time, a teaching position opened up, and she began her long career. Lyster taught English for 52 years at Columbus High School and Columbus North High School and was English department chair for 33 of those years. During that time, she built a department of excellent English teachers and developed a writing program that received local and national accolades for its strong preparation of students for college writing. Numerous English departments adopted her innovative ideas years after she implemented them in Columbus, including a computerized writing center, cumulative writing portfolios for students, and a phase elective program combining core courses and electives. For many years, at least one Columbus North student won the prestigious National Council of Teachers of English (NCTE) Achievement in Writing Award, recognizing the best student writers in the nation. During Lyster's tenure as department chair, the English department also received the prestigious NCTE Center of Excellence Award, given to only 32 schools in the nation, a source of great pride for her department. Lyster was the first recipient of the Edna Folger Outstanding Teacher Award in 1983 and several Indianapolis Star Academic All-Star students named her as their most influential teacher. Twice she traveled to Washington, DC, with students who earned the elite title of Presidential Scholar and honored her as the teacher who impacted them the greatest. This allowed her to meet former president Bill Clinton and former first lady Laura Bush. After her retirement, Lyster remained incredibly active in the community, reading and teaching literature to book clubs, civic groups, and through the Partners in Education adult education classes in Columbus. (Courtesy of Kim Stover.)

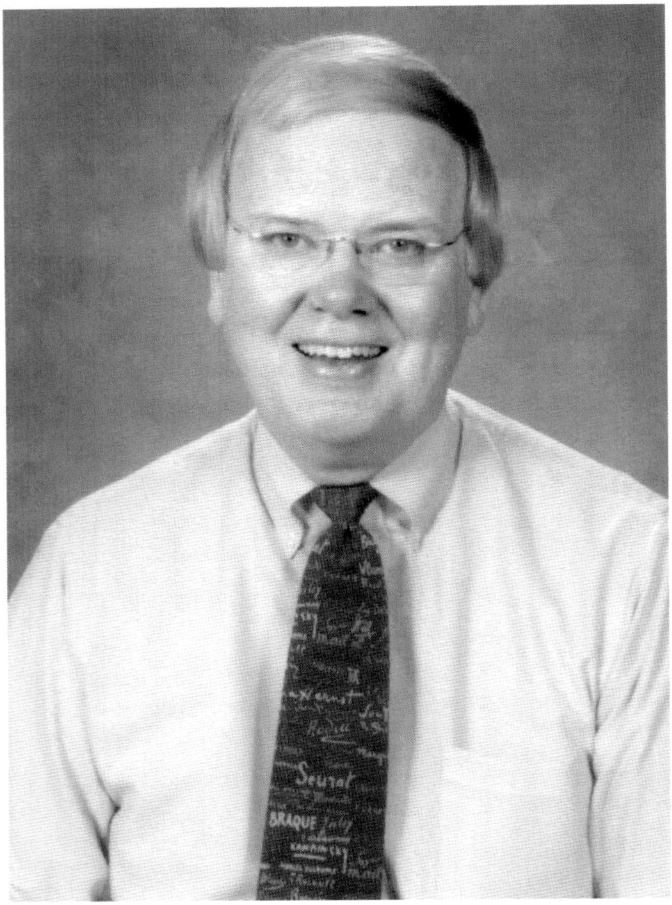

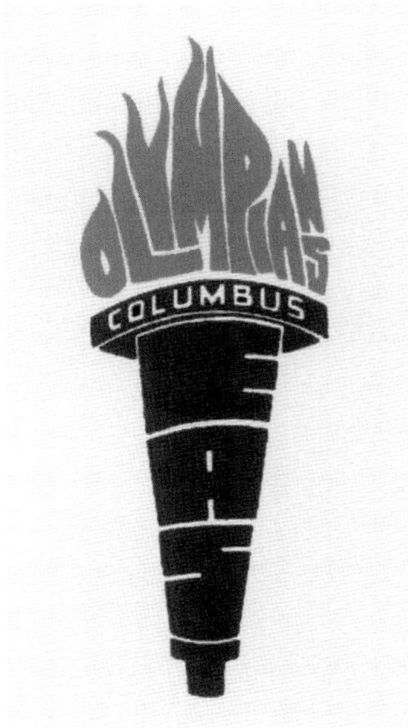

Philip Miller

Phil Miller's love of art and the mutual respect between art teacher and art student is still evident all over the house he lovingly restored with his wife, Irida, before his death in 2009. Miller was the first art teacher at both Columbus East High School and Indiana University-Purdue University Columbus (IUPUC) and nurtured thousands of student artists over more than four decades of teaching. The Millers' historic home is not only full of custom woodworking, glasswork, and art pieces Miller himself created but also many of his students' works of art. To support promising students, Miller purchased many pieces from them and proudly displayed them in his home. After his death, the collection grew as former students sent other artworks to Irida in memory of Miller's influence on their education and careers. Born in Columbus, Miller graduated from Columbus High School in 1962 and, eventually, earned a master's in fine art from Ball State in 1968. He was interested in and skilled at multiple genres, including woodworking, drawing, painting, graphic art, and logotype design. In addition, Miller had a passion for history. He taught US history on occasion and was an avid collector of World War II military memorabilia. Besides being a dedicated teacher, artist, and collector, Miller was a devoted husband and father to son, Alec, and daughter-in-law, Alisa. Over the years, students became accustomed to Miller's penchant for puns. His wit and sense of humor made him a favorite of many, and he was known for such truisms as "Never let your studies interfere with your education." One lasting contribution Miller made to Columbus East was the design of the school's iconic Olympian torch logo, intended to inspire excellence in Columbus East students. In honor and memory of Miller, the Philip R. Miller Scholarship for Visual Arts is now offered through Heritage Fund to Columbus East senior art students who intend to pursue art or art education studies at the university level. (Courtesy of Irida Miller.)

70

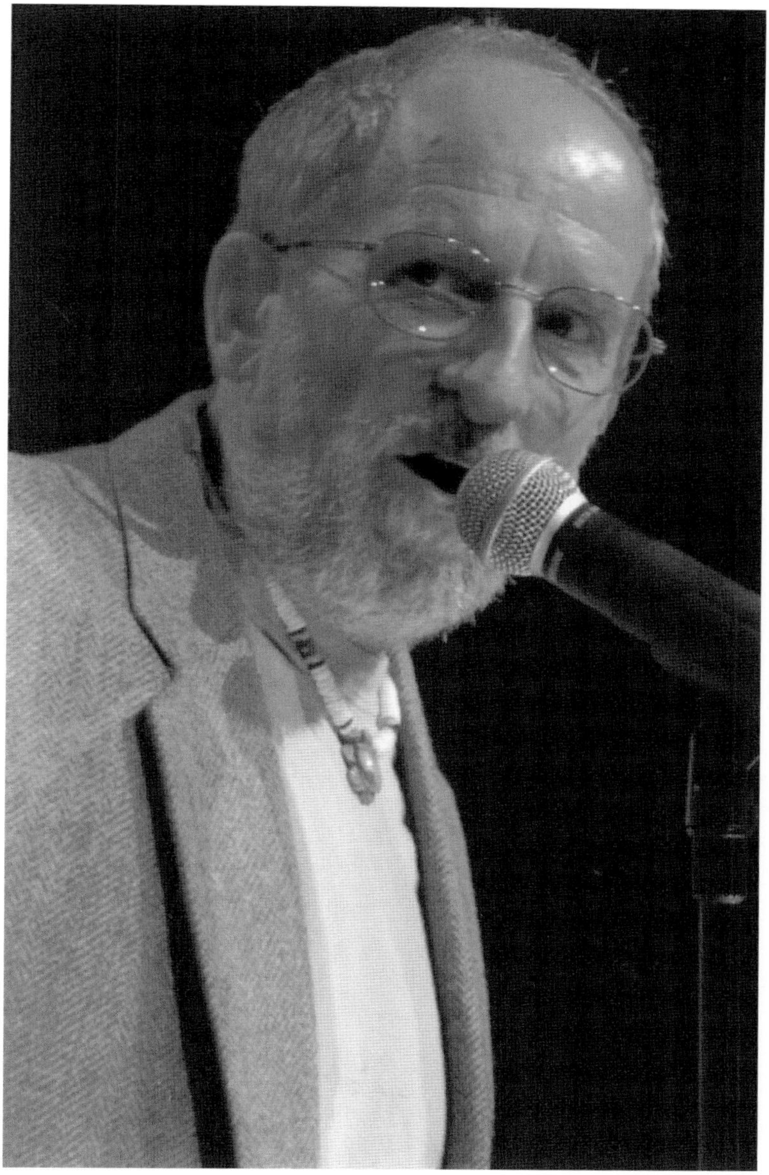

Ed Niespodziani

Retired teacher Ed Niespodziani believes music can transcend time and create a personal connection between people. In 1985, as part of an elective class he was teaching at Columbus North called "The '50s, '60s, & '70s," he started American Pie, a short concert by student musicians demonstrating how the music of that era both reflected and influenced the time. During the first few years, a growing audience of students eagerly crowded the auditorium to listen, learn, and enjoy the experience. American Pie was soon moved to the evening to prevent students from skipping class to attend, and professional musicians were added to improve the experience. English teacher Dennis Lindsey joined Niespodziani to add a literary context to the songs starting in 1989. Over almost three decades, the show has grown greatly in scope, now including more than 100 students who must audition for the chance to sing iconic songs of the 1950s, 1960s, and 1970s on stage for students, parents, and community members. (Courtesy of Ed Niespodziani.)

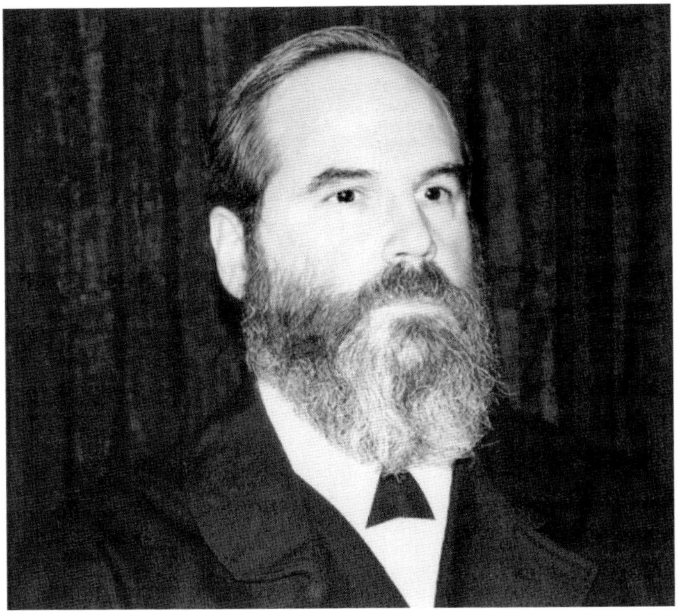

Greg Lewis

Making history interesting to kids is not always easy. Columbus East High School teacher Greg Lewis has become known for impersonating a variety of historical figures to make history come alive for his students. He becomes somewhat of a local celebrity around Presidents Day each year when, for more than 15 years, he transforms himself into a different US president. In 2011, Lewis (above) portrayed Pres. James Garfield (below). Initially conceived while he was teaching an interdisciplinary US history and literature course, Lewis worked to get students to question what makes a good leader. In 2010, he was recognized for his creative approaches and his dedication to his students when he was named the Preserve America History Teacher of the Year for the state of Indiana. (Courtesy of Greg Lewis.)

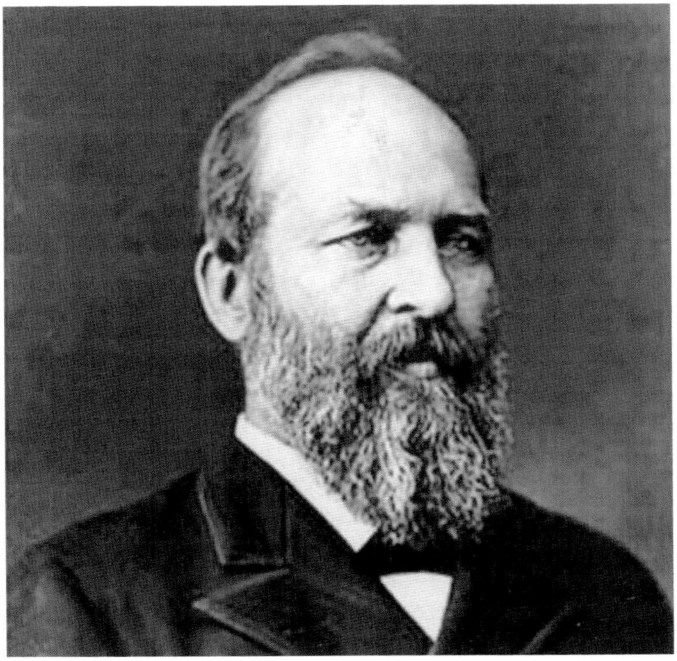

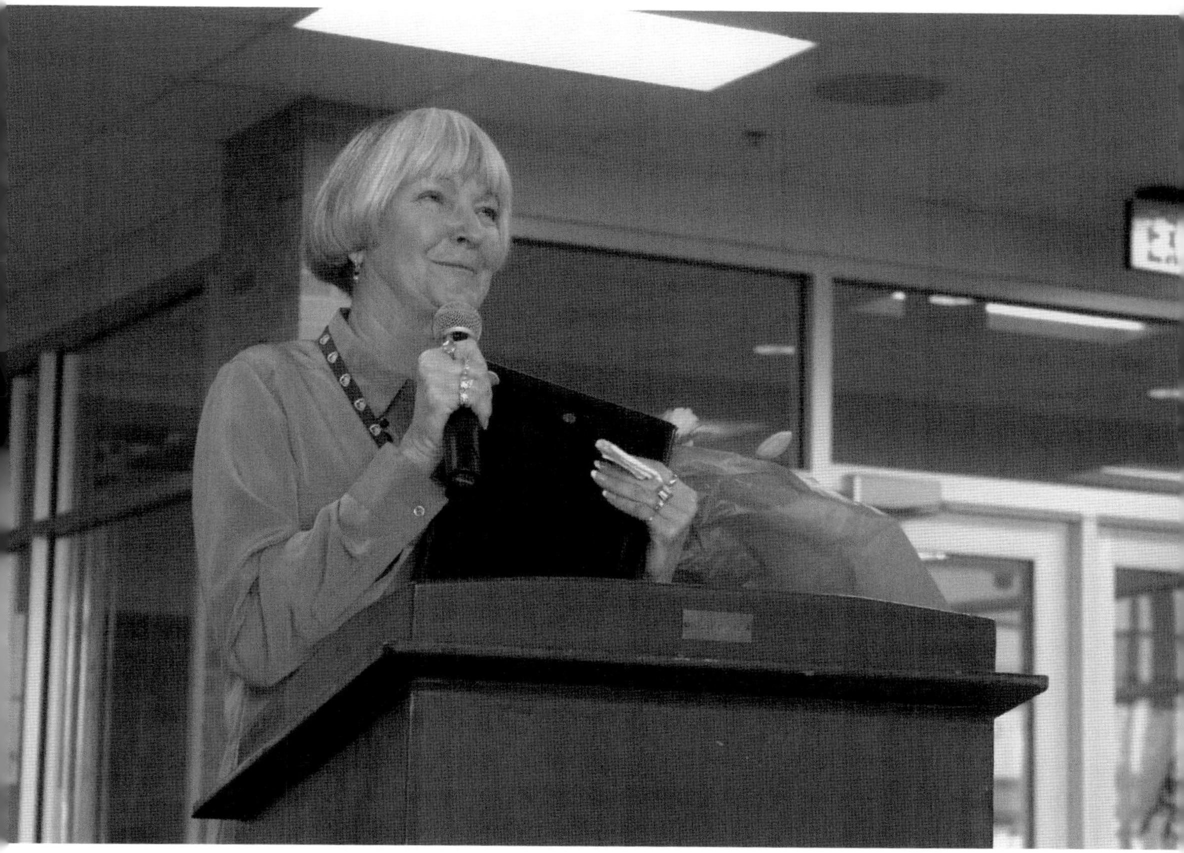

Kim Green
During Kim Green's time as a journalism teacher and advisor at Columbus North High School, both Green and her students have won numerous awards for the high quality of their work. The Journalism Education Association named Green 2011 Yearbook Advisor of the Year, its top national award. In addition, Green has shared her expertise with her peers by leading workshops for other journalism advisors all over the country. Green believes her role is to advise her students, who are given great responsibility and whose work is not reviewed or edited by staff. Many of her students have gone on to study journalism in college and then to careers at nationally known newspapers, a testament to the positive experience in journalism at Columbus North. (Photograph by Hannah Booth.)

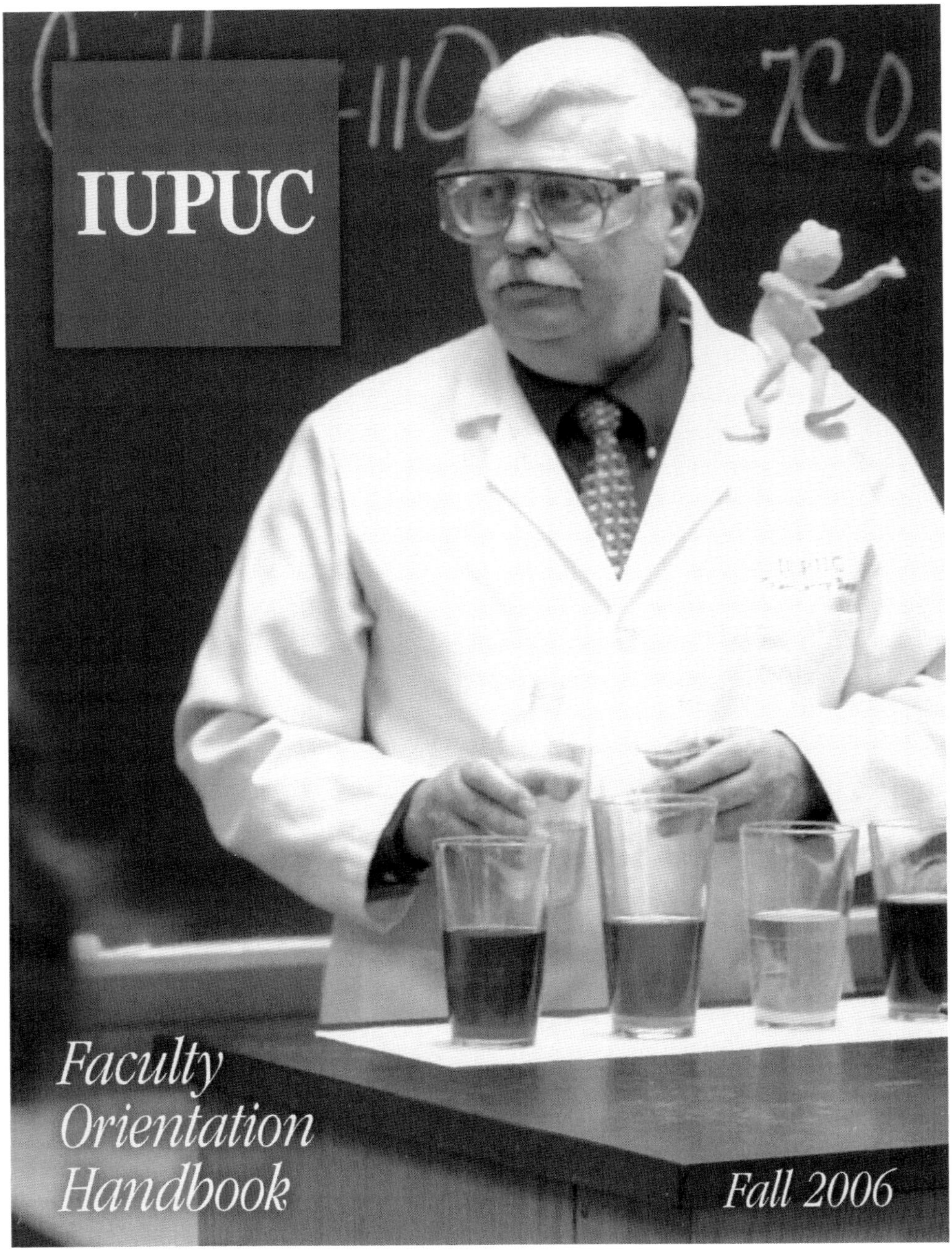

Jack Young

One of the original teachers at Columbus East High School when it opened 1972, science teacher Jack Young retired in 2005. His retirement was very short. One week later, he accepted a job teaching at IUPUC. He won awards at both the high school and college levels, including the *USA Today* All-USA Teacher Award in 1999 and the governor's Distinguished Hoosier Award. His positive attitude and sense of humor carried him through adversity in the final years of his life, first when his Columbus house was flooded in 2008 and later when he was diagnosed with advanced colon cancer. The science lab at Columbus East is named for Young. (Courtesy of Priscilla Young.)

CHAPTER FIVE

Celebrating the Arts

Today's vibrant arts scene in Columbus started slowly. Early in the city's history, concerts and recitals were held in old city hall. After the former railroad square was turned into a city park, the Columbus Band performed concerts in the bandstand. These concerts later moved to Donner Park after First Christian Church was built where City Park once stood. Similarly, the bandstand in the Hope Town Square was central to that town's social life as well.

In 1922, Chester Kitzinger started the Columbus Symphony, which today is the oldest symphony in Indiana. Columbus is also home to a professional orchestra, the Columbus Indiana Philharmonic (CIP), which was led for years by executive director Alice Curry. Music director David Bowden joined the CIP when it was founded in 1987 and has won numerous awards for his work. The philharmonic includes programming for children and youth to develop their love of music, and young people in Columbus have long had many opportunities for musical education through school music programs and talented private music teachers.

In 1948, brothers Ross and Don Barbour, members of the very musical Fodrea family, were two of the original members of the Four Freshmen, a Grammy-nominated vocal quartet. Their cousin Bob Flanigan, also a Columbus native, soon joined them, and the Freshmen were very popular during the 1950s, influencing later vocal groups, including the Beach Boys.

Many talented music teachers have taught countless Columbus youth over the years as well. Music store owner Tom Pickett has taught guitar students for more than 50 years. Piano teacher Charlotte Rowe taught hundreds of piano students in group lessons, along with giving workshops for other piano teachers, for 62 years until after her 80th birthday. Today, Dr. Stephen Reen continues the tradition of teaching piano to groups of children when he is not performing with his family, which includes nine children. Columbus native Janie Gordon has performed in community theater and sang with the band Forty Years of College. She serves as the choral director at Columbus North and has also taught private voice and piano lessons for many years. Several of her students have gone on to professional careers in music and theater.

Music is not the only active arts scene in Columbus. Former NATO chef Jim Gregory brought his European training and trademark red apron to Columbus in the 1960s to work for J. Irwin Miller. More recently Columbus native chef Daniel Orr, who has worked all over the world, has brought his signature blend of island and Midwest cooking to his Bloomington restaurant.

Artist and art teacher Marilyn Brackney has long reused found objects in her work and, lately, has made it the focus of a regular art show downtown. The late-contemporary artist Catherine Burris also left her mark on Columbus with multiple public art pieces, including murals in city hall and the downtown Dairy Queen. In 2013, more than 40 public art pieces ornament the city and complement its collection of modern architecture.

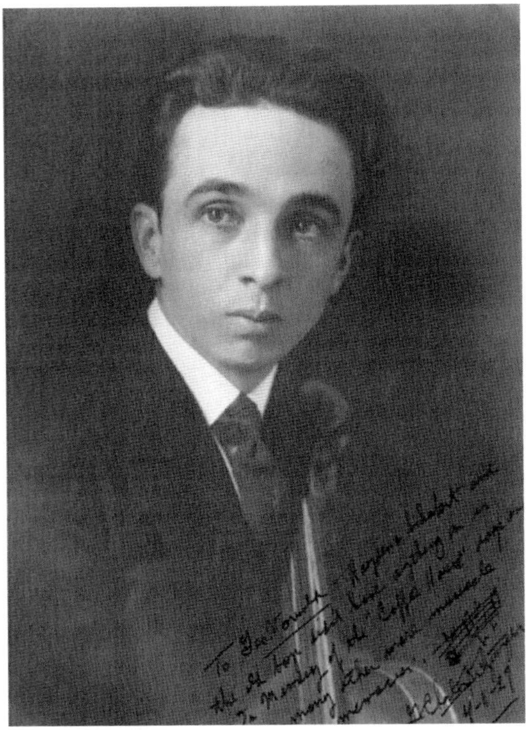

Chester Kitzinger

In 1922, violin teacher Chester Kitzinger started the Columbus Symphony with a group of his violin students and volunteer instrumentalists from the City Band. The first performance was in the Crump Theatre on Third Street. Even when many of the musicians were called to duty during World War II, the orchestra continued, and today, the volunteer orchestra is the oldest symphony orchestra in Indiana. Kitzinger remained the conductor until 1970. (BCHS Collection.)

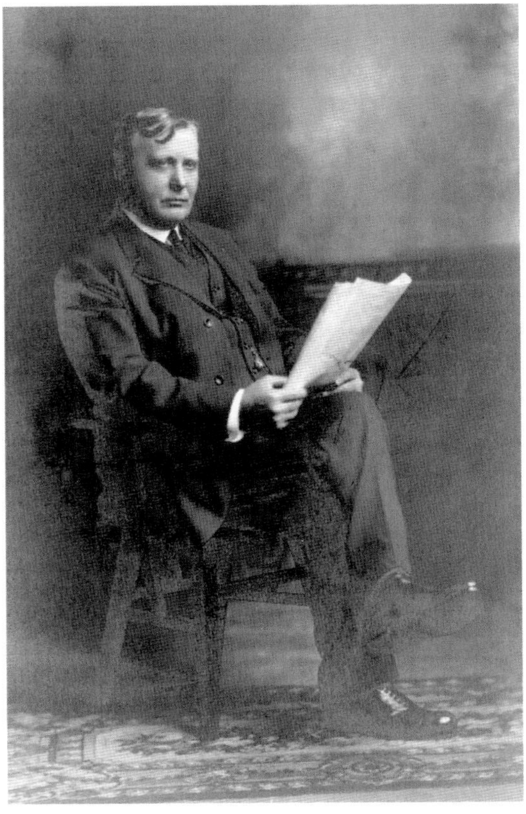

Ross Caldwell

The son of builder George Caldwell (page 28), Ross Caldwell was born in Columbus in 1895 and was also a builder and architect. In the mid-1940s he moved to Cherokee, North Carolina, where he was instrumental in the founding of the Mountainside Theatre, which would become home to "Unto These Hills," one of the longest-running outdoor dramas in the United States. Since 1950, more than six million people have seen the show. Caldwell died in 1981. (BCHS Collection.)

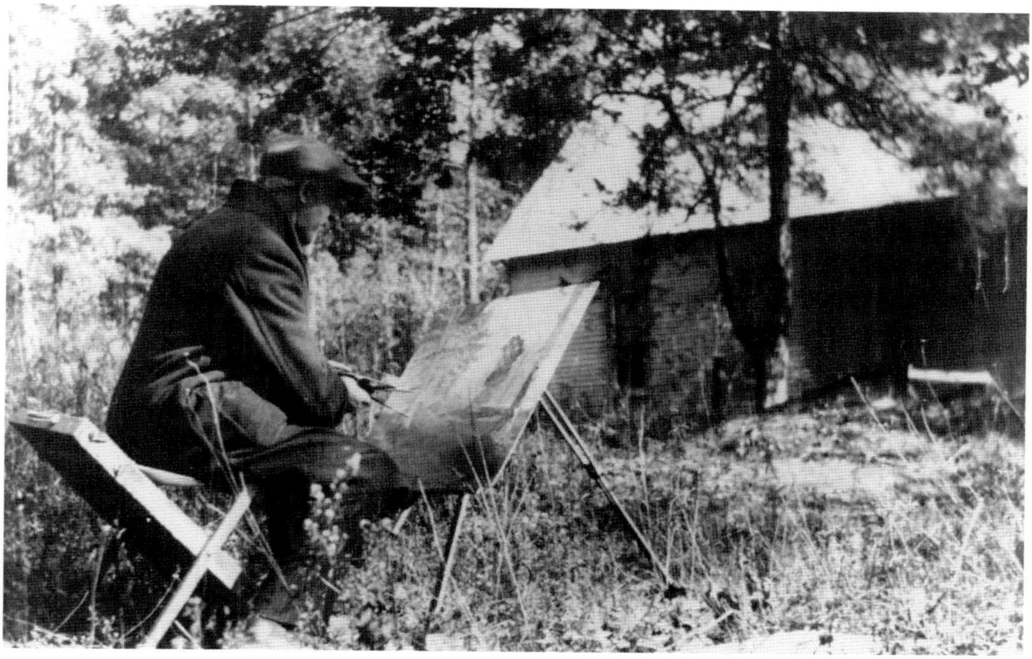

T.J. Koch
T.J. Koch was a teacher, painter, and composer. Born in Germany, Koch came to the United States at age four and later spent more than 40 years teaching art and music at St. Peter's Lutheran School. He created more than 800 paintings, most of which were landscapes from in and around Bartholomew County. Long after Koch's death in 1959, boxes of original music compositions were discovered at St. Peter's, and the extent of his musical legacy became apparent. (BCHS Collection.)

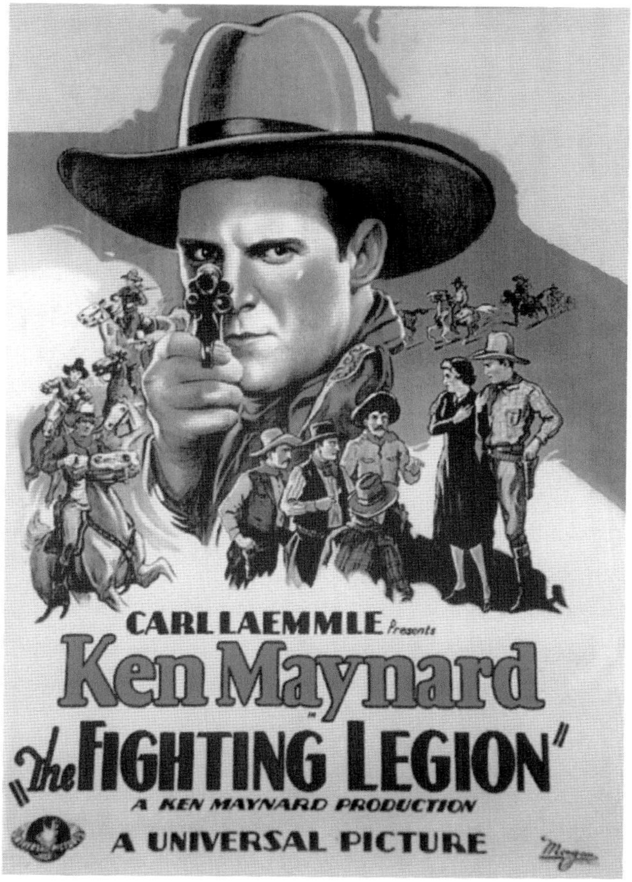

Ken Maynard
One of the first singing cowboys in the heyday of movie Westerns, Ken Maynard was born in 1895 in Vevay, Indiana, but grew up in Columbus. He began his career in the era of silent films in the 1920s and appeared in more than 90 films during his career, which earned him a star on the Hollywood Walk of Fame. His later life was marred by alcoholism, and he died penniless in California in 1973. (Author's collection.)

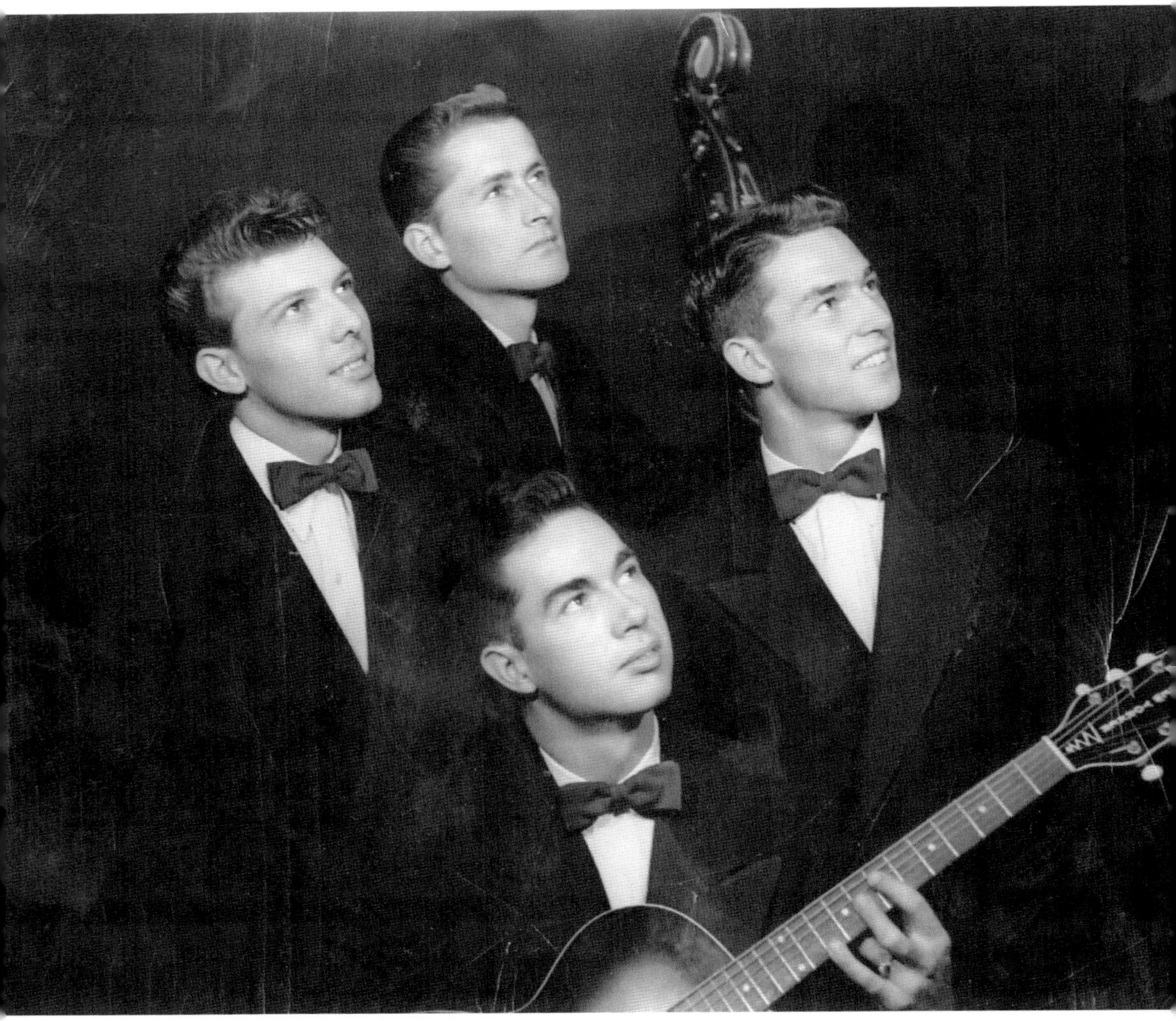

The Four Freshmen
Columbus natives Ross and Don Barbour were among the original four members of the Four Freshmen, a vocal quartet founded in the late 1940s. Ross and Don's cousin Bob Flanigan soon joined the group, and in 1950, they got their break when renowned bandleader Stan Kenton heard them perform and set up an audition with Capitol Records. Capitol offered the quartet a record deal later that year, setting off a successful decade during which the Four Freshmen was named best vocal group five times by *Down Beat* magazine. Over the years, new members have replaced old members, but the group has continued to perform as a vocal quartet. Original members Don and Ross Barbour died in 1961 and 2011, respectively. (BCHS Collection.)

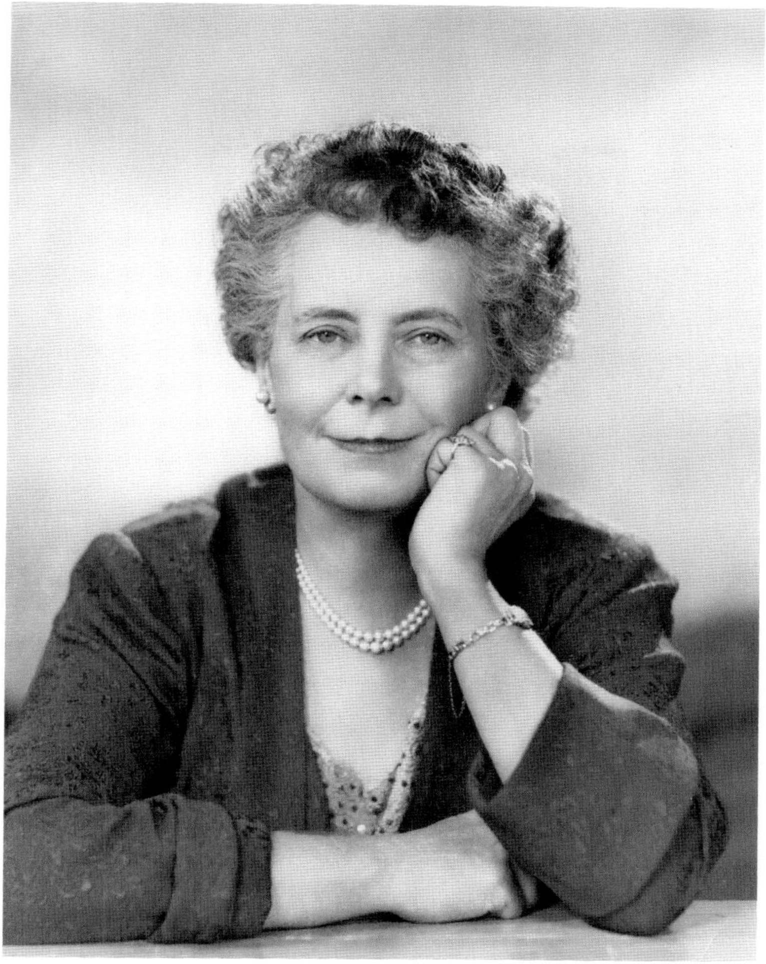

Elsie Sweeney

Elsie Sweeney was a great patroness of art and music and was the daughter of Zachary Sweeney (page 17) and the granddaughter of Joseph Irwin (page 16). She graduated from Columbus High School in 1905 and from Smith College in 1910. An avid pianist, she studied piano in Germany and New York City after college and played daily for most of her life. During World War II, Sweeney was active in relief work, starting a Bundles for Britain chapter to sew and collect clothing and raise funds for British victims of air raids. It was so successful that she later won a prestigious award from the British government. After the war, her love of music carried her to Bayreuth, Germany, for the famous Bayreuth Festival of opera music by German composer Richard Wagner. In 1955, Sweeney organized a benefit concert in Carnegie Hall, which drew opera singers from around the world to raise money to restore the Bayreuth Festival House. This earned her an Officer's Cross, Order of Merit from what was then West Germany. Sweeney also championed the arts closer to home, supporting the Indianapolis Symphony Orchestra and the Indiana University School of Music. An advocate for historic architecture, she photographed historic buildings in Columbus and gave slideshows about the city. She researched the appearance of the metal latticework that originally adorned the courthouse towers but had been removed due to deterioration and commissioned the installation of rust-proof replicas. Sweeney never married and closely supervised the construction and landscaping of her own home, Castalia, at Harrison Lake in 1962–1963. She often opened her gardens for benefit tours to share the beauty with others. Sweeney was proud of her Indiana heritage and was a great supporter of both the BCHS and the IHS. (Irwin-Sweeney-Miller Family Collection, IHS.)

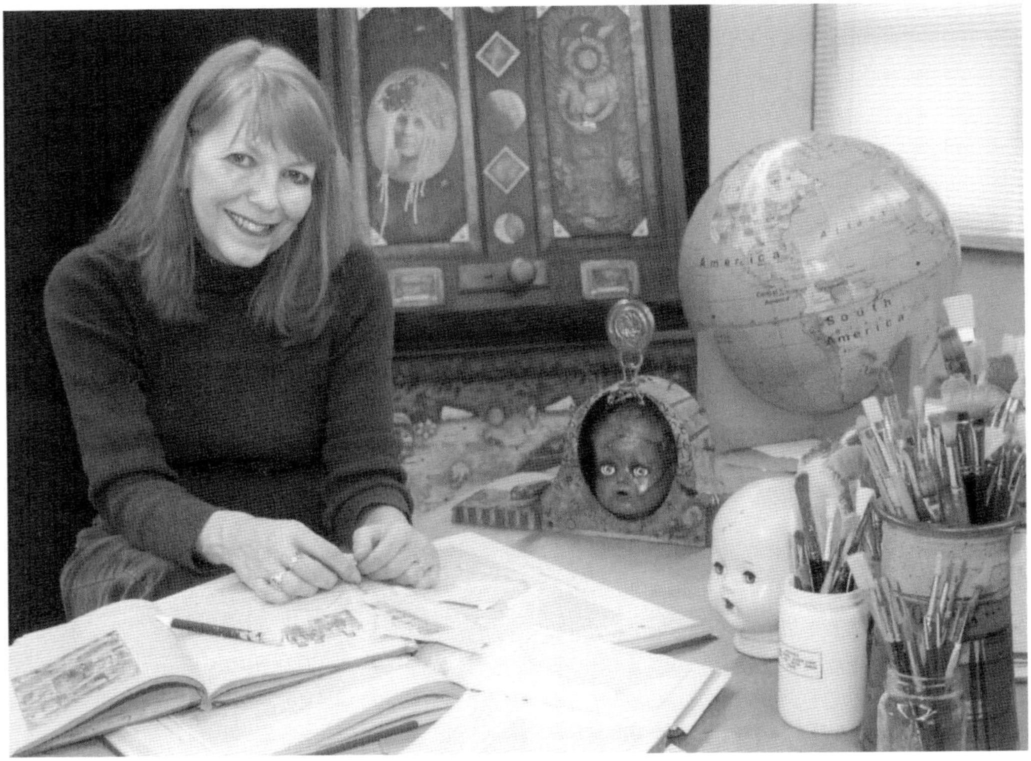

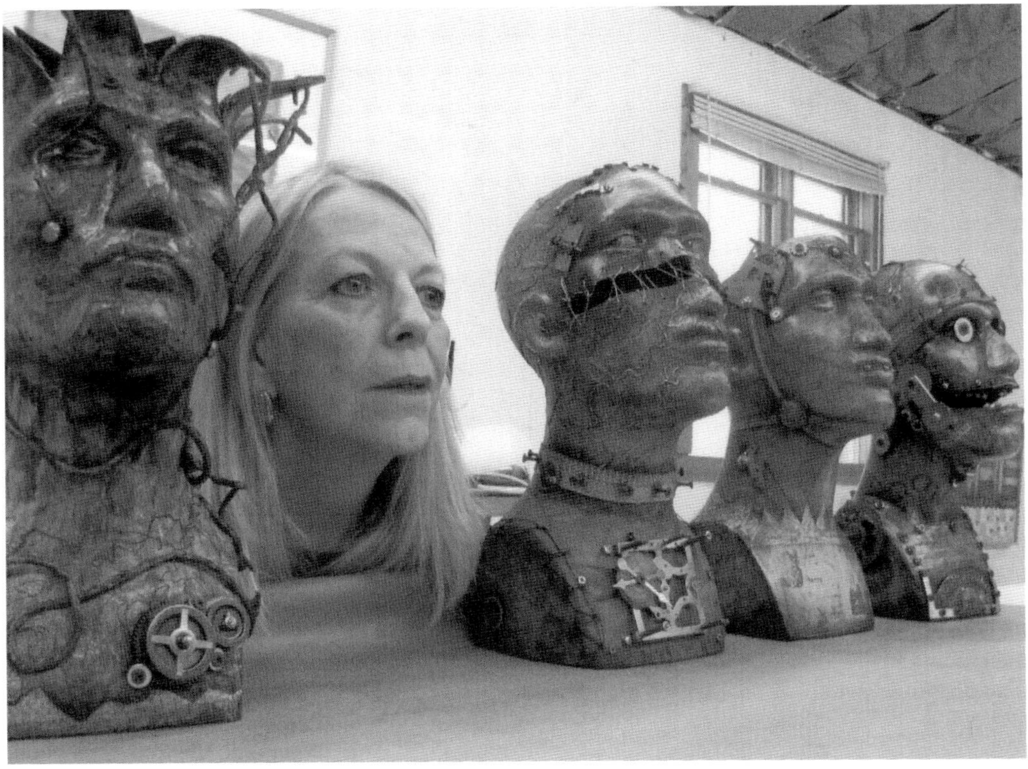

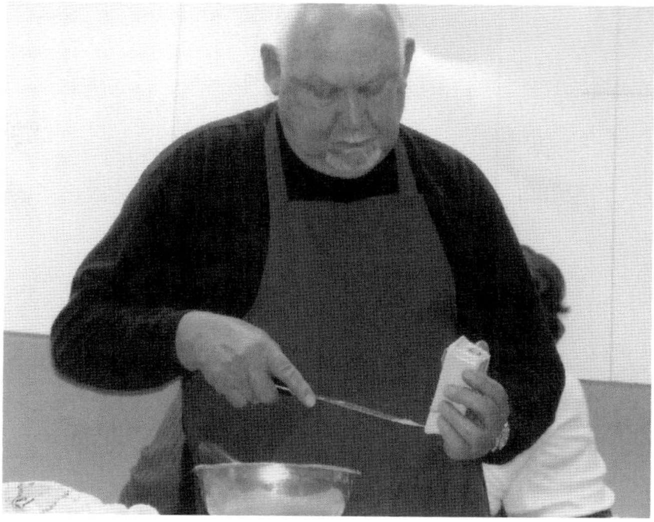

Chef Jim Gregory
Chef Jim Gregory has worn his trademark red apron all over the world. Trained at the prestigious Cordon Bleu in Paris (where he met Julia Child), Gregory was the executive chef at NATO before eventually coming to Columbus to work for J. Irwin Miller. Gregory worked as executive chef at Irwin Management for 17 years. Today, he continues to cook at his home in Columbus, advocating that quality ingredients are the most essential ingredients in good cooking. (Courtesy of Chef Gregory.)

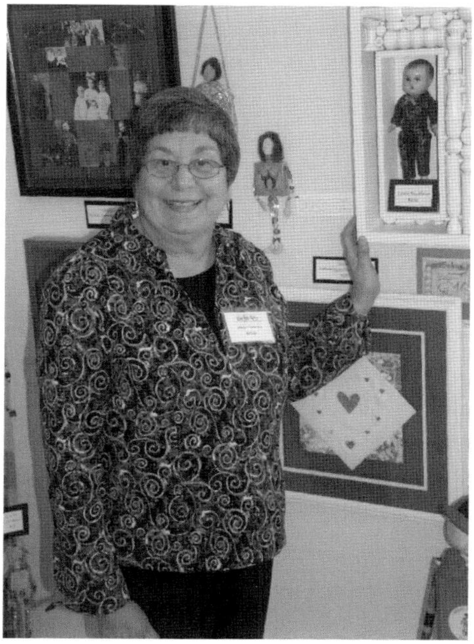

Marilyn Brackney
Long before reusing and recycling became widespread, Marilyn Brackney was reusing and recycling materials in her work as an artist and teacher. Originally starting out of necessity when she lacked funds to buy art materials for students, Brackney became adept at using found items in artwork. She received national recognition for her creative ideas in 1993 with an Environmental Woman of Action Award. In 2005, she started the Déjà Vu Art and Fine Craft Show in Columbus, showcasing artists from all over who "upcycle" items into their art. (Photograph by Dennis Stone.)

Catherine Burris (OPPOSITE PAGE)
Artist Catherine Burris's work was sometimes described as "Contemporary Narrative." Burris expected her art to tell a unique story to each viewer. She expressed her emotions in her art and enjoyed pushing the boundaries with unexpected images and details in many of her pieces. She primarily worked in acrylics but became drawn to mixed-media assemblages and collages near the end of her life. In addition, she had numerous public art pieces, including paintings and murals. Her lasting contributions to Columbus include the painting of" Jack the Bum" in city hall, the downtown Dairy Queen mural, and the Bartholomew County logo. She enjoyed teaching and working with young people and collaborated with troubled youth on mural paintings at the Columbus Animal Shelter. In 1992, Burris won the Mayor's Art Award, and her art is part of the permanent collection at the Indiana State Museum and the Kinsey Institute. (Courtesy of Bob Burris.)

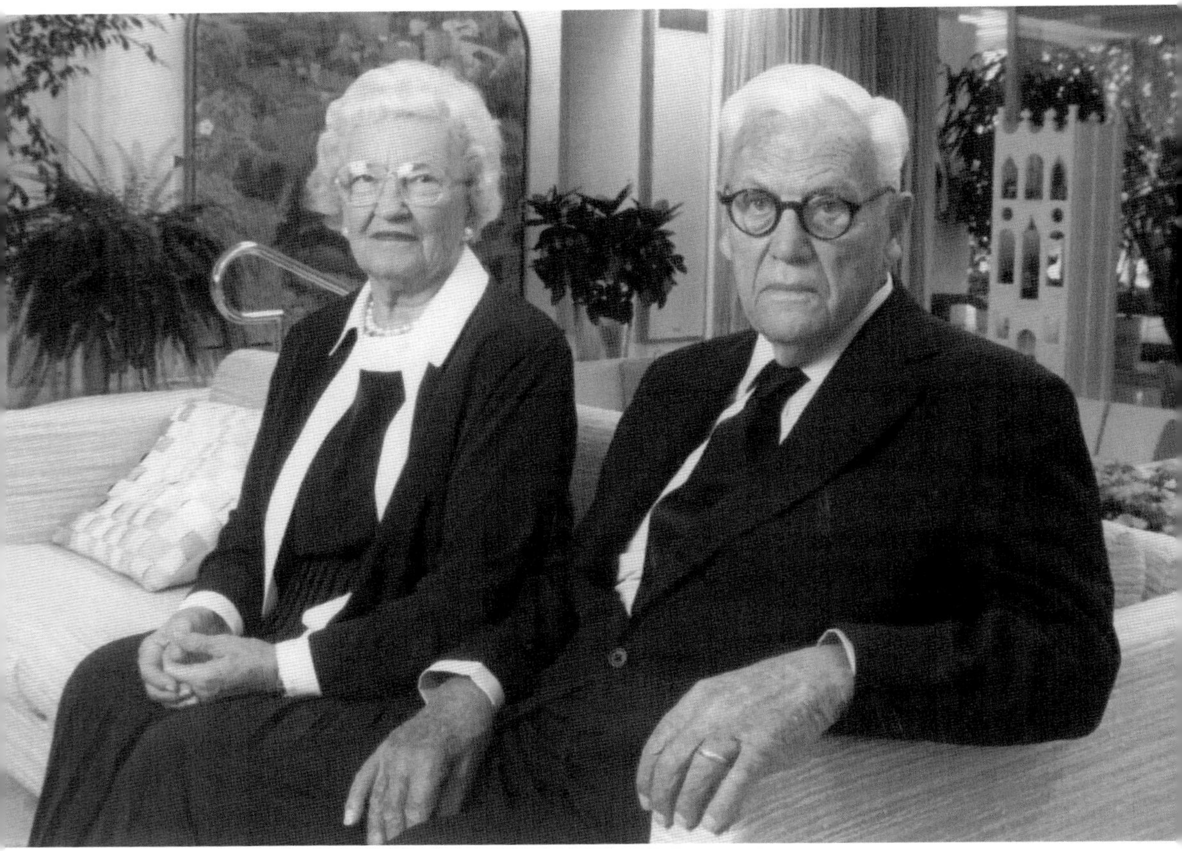

Xenia Miller

In 1943, Xenia Miller joined one of Columbus's most prominent families when she married J. Irwin Miller. A graduate of Columbus High School, she attended Indiana Business College and was the 14th woman hired at Cummins, where she met her future husband. Over the years, Xenia Miller became a great patroness of the arts in Columbus and beyond. While her husband was largely responsible for Columbus's great heritage of modern architecture, Xenia was instrumental in beginning a movement to preserve the community's historic architecture. She also played a leading role in making the city's architecture available to visitors with the development of the Columbus Area Visitors Center. Later, she was central to the expansion of the visitors center in 1997 that doubled its size when the Millers gave the gift to fund the renovation, which she personally supervised. The Millers also commissioned renowned glass artist Dale Chihuly to create the dramatic *Yellow Neon Chandelier*, which hangs in the visitors center. Two other prominent public art pieces in Columbus that were gifts of the Millers are sculptor Henry Moore's immense bronze piece titled *Large Arch* in library plaza and Jean Tinguely's kinetic sculpture *Chaos I* in the Commons. Xenia Miller was also very involved in the Indianapolis Museum of Art and helped establish the museum's first branch in Columbus. She worked closely with designer Alexander Girard on the family's modernist house, commissioned in 1953 and now a National Historic Landmark owned by the Indianapolis Museum of Art. She was also a founding member of North Christian Church. A great supporter of the Indianapolis Symphony Orchestra, she was a member of the Indiana Arts Commission and the first chair of the Indiana Endowment for the Arts. For her efforts, Xenia Miller received numerous awards over her lifetime, including being named by two Indianapolis publications as one of the state's most influential women and receiving the Indiana Arts Commission's Indiana Arts Award and the National Governors Association Award for Distinguished Service to the Arts. (Irwin-Sweeney-Miller Family Collection, IHS.)

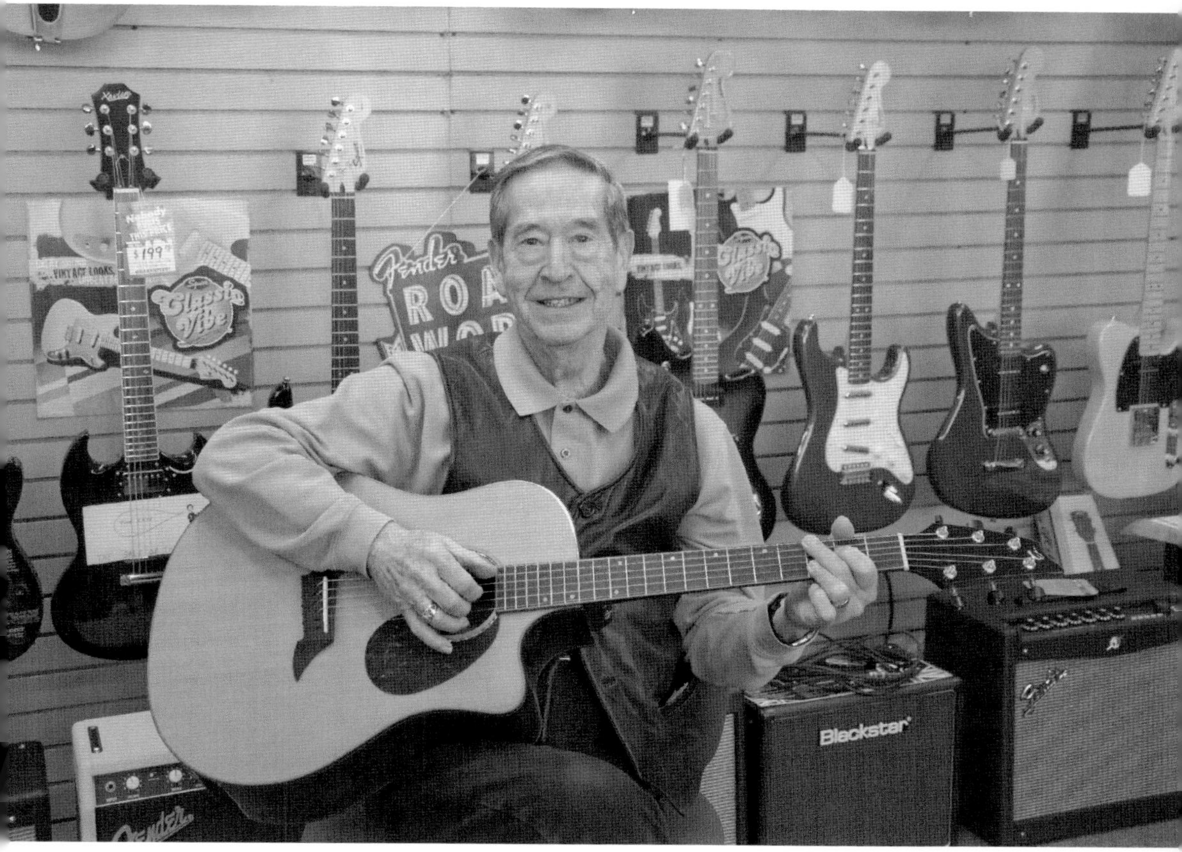

Tom Pickett

Tom Pickett came to Columbus in the 1950s while stationed as an air traffic controller at Bakalar Air Force Base. In that same decade, he opened his first music store on Washington Street, initially rationing himself to one meal a day to save money. Over the years, his store moved several times, including once after an early-morning gas line explosion destroyed his store across from the high school several hours before any students were in the area. Since 1983, Tom Pickett's has occupied a spot on National Road. Pickett has taught music students for over 50 years and has been involved for many of those years with summer musical variety shows at Donner Park. He still performs with the musical group he leads called Da Bums. In 2012, Pickett received the first annual Music Makes Your Life Award given by the Rotary Club in honor of longtime philharmonic director Alice Curry. He was honored in 2013 at a concert titled "Jammin' with the Stars," which included many of his former students, including Gov. Mike Pence. (Photograph by author.)

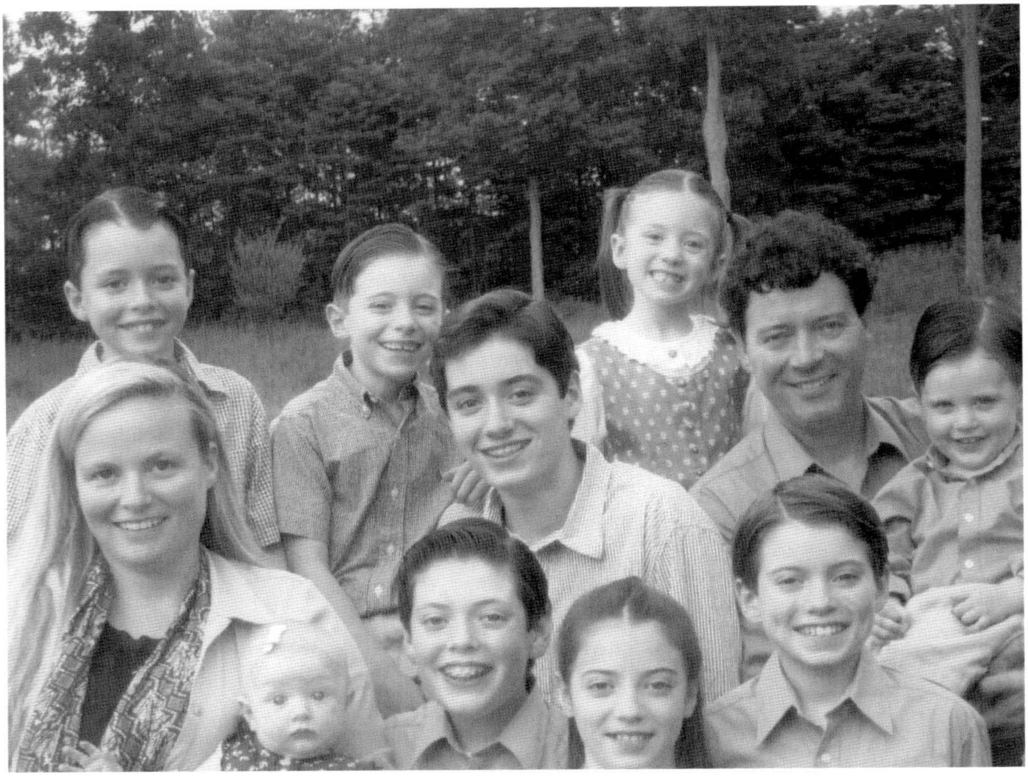

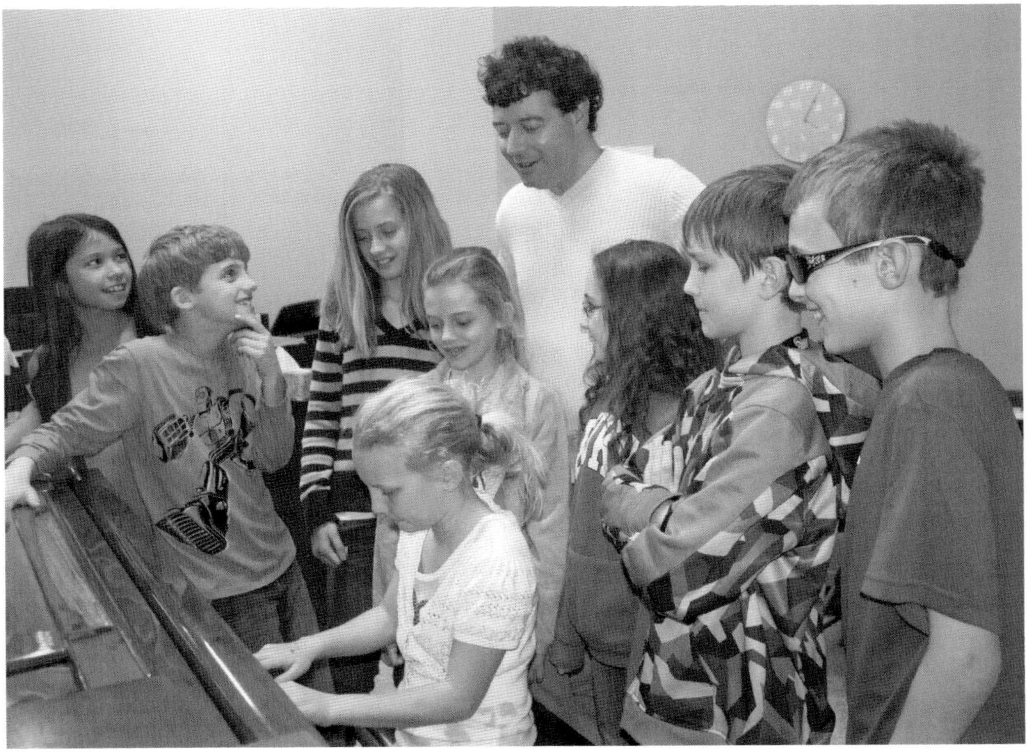

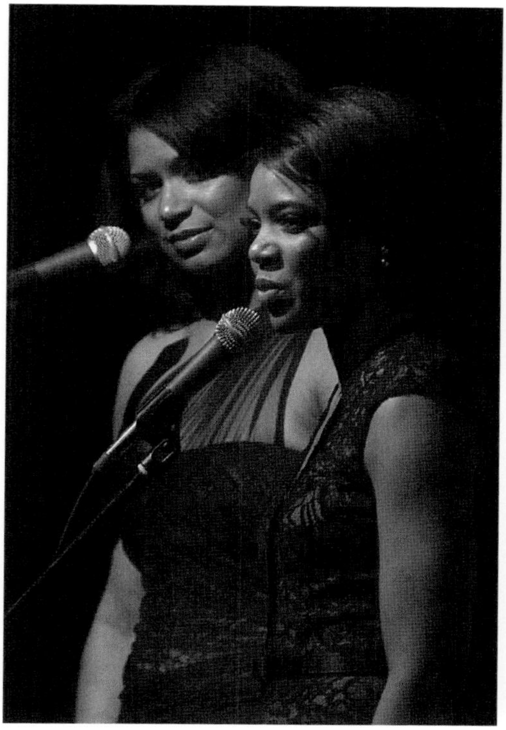

The Harmon Sisters
Marja and Chasten Harmon's talent, hard work, and passion for musical theater has brought them success on Broadway early in their careers. Among their notable roles, Marja (background) portrayed Maggie the Cat in *Cat on a Hot Tin Roof* on Broadway with a multicultural cast including greats such as James Earl Jones, and Chasten (foreground) played Eponine in the 25th anniversary touring production of *Les Misérables*. The sisters, both graduates of Columbus East, are pictured on stage together with the Columbus Indiana Philharmonic in February 2013. (Photograph by Chris Crawl.)

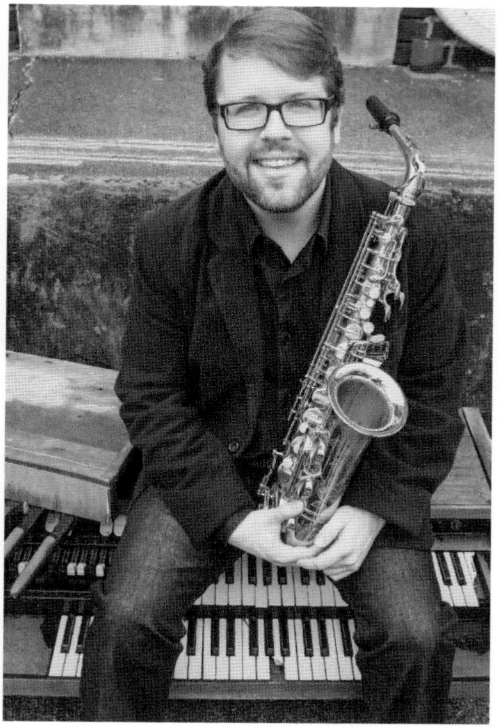

Cam Collins
At age 19, Columbus native and saxophonist Cam Collins won a prestigious position with the Naval Academy Band. Upon completion of his tenure with the Navy, Collins moved to New York City to be a freelance musician. He has appeared with many notable musicians, performed with touring Broadway musicals, and can be heard on numerous recordings. A graduate of Columbus North, Cam attended Indiana University and the Manhattan School of Music. (Photograph by DRGphotography.)

The Reen Family (OPPOSITE PAGE)
Music comes naturally to the nine children of Columbus piano teacher Dr. Stephen Reen and his wife, Sophie, a cellist. Steve has been teaching piano for more than 30 years, and his passion is teaching piano to young children in group lessons. The Music Teachers National Association honored Stephen as one of the top five group piano teachers in the nation in 2001. Sophie teaches piano and cello and has taught preschool music and movement classes. The Reens moved to the Columbus area in 1996 after studying at the Indiana University School of Music, and Steve has been teaching group piano lessons since then. Both Steve and Sophie Reen also perform on the piano and cello regularly, with and without their children. All of the Reen children sing, and the older children play piano and strings. The family performs all over the country as the Reen Family Singers, and the oldest three boys and Stephen are an award-winning a capella quartet. (Top, courtesy of the Reen family.; bottom, photograph by author.)

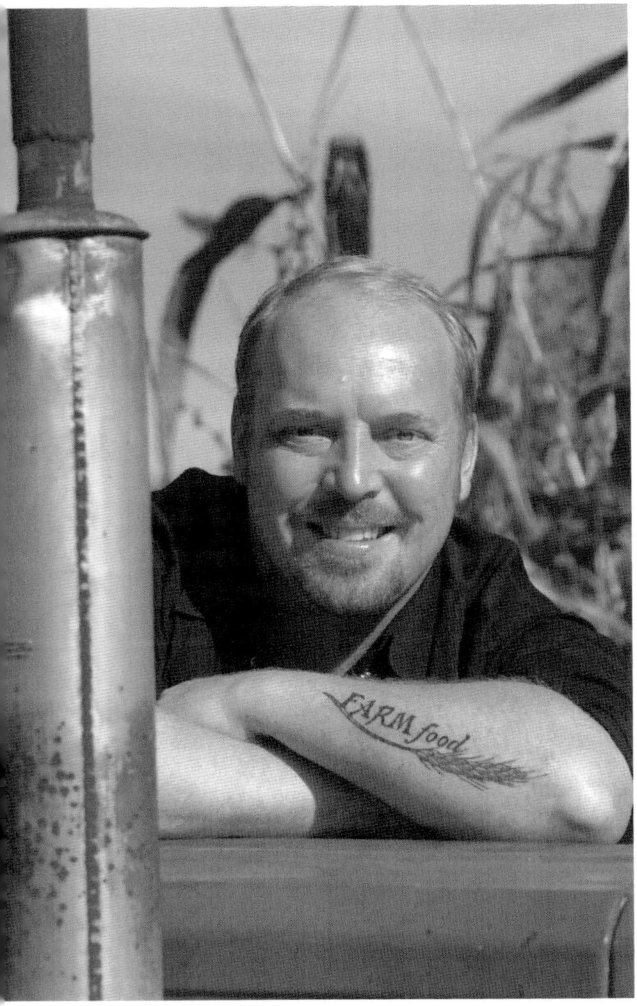

Chef Daniel Orr
Chef Daniel Orr owns FARM Bloomington, a restaurant that uses local ingredients to blend Midwest cooking and island cuisine. His restaurant is the product of a culinary career that began in his parents' Columbus kitchen as a child, stopped in some of the finest restaurants in France and New York City, and landed in Anguilla in the Caribbean. In addition, Chef Daniel has written three cookbooks and has a radio show and podcast on public radio. (Courtesy of MLKO Photography.)

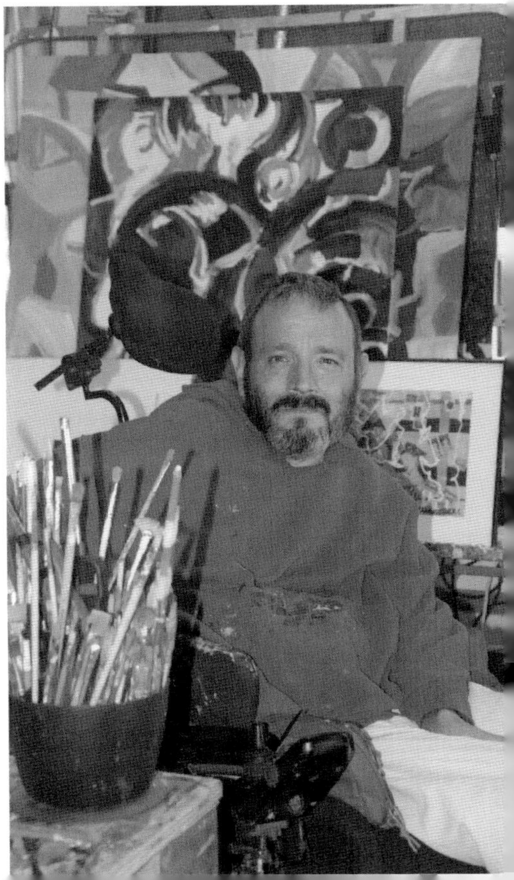

Paul Neufelder
After a diving accident at age 14 left him paralyzed, Paul Neufelder's dream to work in forestry was over. Luckily for him and the many students he has taught—especially the at-risk youth he so enjoys working with—Neufelder discovered his talent in art and began a career as an artist and art teacher. Now he paints and draws with his mouth. He credits his positive outlook to his parents, who always taught him to "leave the place better than you found it." (Photograph by author.)

CHAPTER SIX

Excelling in Sports

Columbus has a rich sports history starting with basketball—true to Hoosier tradition. Early high school basketball games were played in the second floor of old city hall before Columbus High School built a gym. In 1917, Chuck Taylor sported a bulldog jersey on the high school team. Although he went on to play professional basketball, he made a name for himself as a shoe salesman for Converse, and Chuck Taylor All-Stars still bear his signature today.

Certain Columbus basketball teams since then have made names for themselves as well. The 1963 and 1964 Bulldogs were undefeated and made it to the state finals in 1964. A trio of Bulldog players, Jerry Newsom, Butch Wade, and Steve Hollenbeck, went on to Indiana State where Newsom had a particularly successful collegiate career.

After class basketball began in Indiana in 1997, the Columbus North boys basketball teams struggled in their sectionals, but the girls team made it to the state finals in 2012 and spent much of the 2012–2013 season ranked number one in the state. As intended, class basketball improved the odds for smaller schools, and Hauser High School took advantage of this in 2006, winning a state championship that thrilled the town of Hope.

Football has also been important in local sports. Columbus East has had a storied football history, beginning in 1979 when quarterback Blair Kiel led the team to a state title. Kiel went on to a celebrated career at Notre Dame and several years playing professionally. More recently 2006 East graduate Stevie Brown had a successful collegiate career at the University of Michigan before moving on to the NFL.

Other sports with longtime success include gymnastics and volleyball at Columbus East High School. Columbus North has been known for its tennis, golf, swimming, and cross-country teams. In 2012, the Columbus North High School boys soccer team became the first Columbus team in a ball sport to win a state championship.

Helping athletes and teams find success, several local coaches have achieved their own fame. Hall-of-fame basketball coach Bill Stearman won more than 700 games in more than 40 years coaching at Columbus High School and Columbus North. Both Columbus East and Columbus North football fields are named after longtime coaches John Stafford and Max Andress. Swim coach Jim Sheridan is one of few coaches to have won a state championship at two different high schools, and cross-country coach Rick Weinheimer has taken his girls and boys teams to the state finals more than 40 times.

For years, radio was a primary source of local sports news, and many sports fans have followed local sports on the radio and have heard broadcaster Sam Simmermaker say, "Holy cow!" while covering sports during his more than five decades in broadcasting.

Finally, one of Columbus's most-famous native sons is race car driver Tony Stewart, who started racing locally as a youth and progressed to open wheel racing and, eventually, to NASCAR racing. Stewart's career includes many awards, including three NASCAR Sprint Cup Series championships—so far.

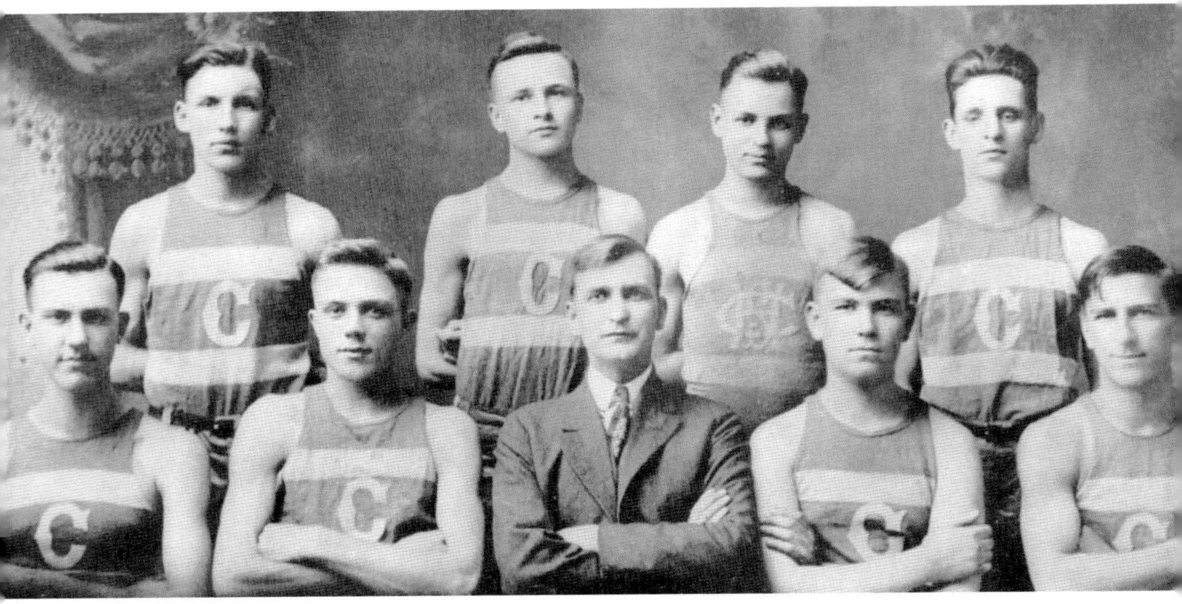

Chuck Taylor

One of the most famous names in American shoes was born in 1901 near Columbus. In 1917, Chuck Taylor (front row, far left) played basketball for Columbus High School wearing Converse shoes. He later played for several professional teams, including a team in Akron, Ohio, and a Converse All-Stars barnstorming team that played all over the country. After school, Taylor had gone to the Converse office in Chicago looking for a job. He became well known for traveling the country selling shoes and hosting basketball clinics, and he made suggestions to improve basketball shoes that prompted Converse to add his signature to the star patch on the ankle of Chuck Taylor All Stars. Taylor was inducted in to the Basketball Hall of Fame in 1969. (1917 *Log*/BCHS Collection.)

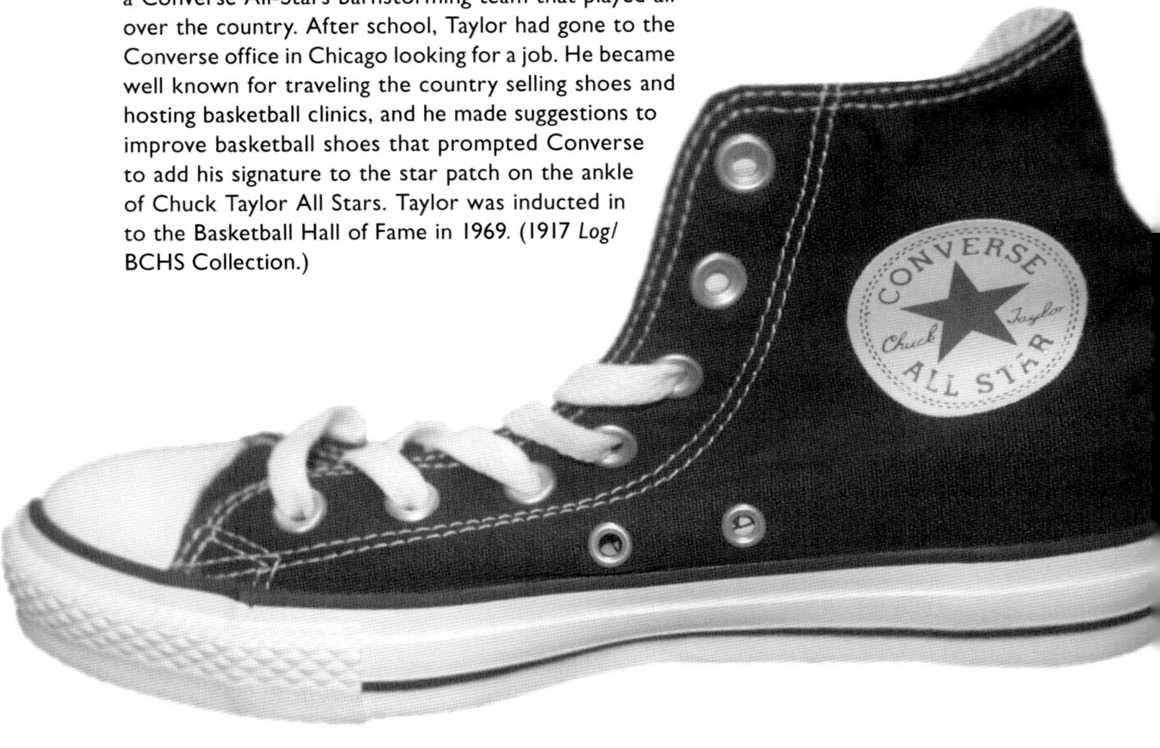

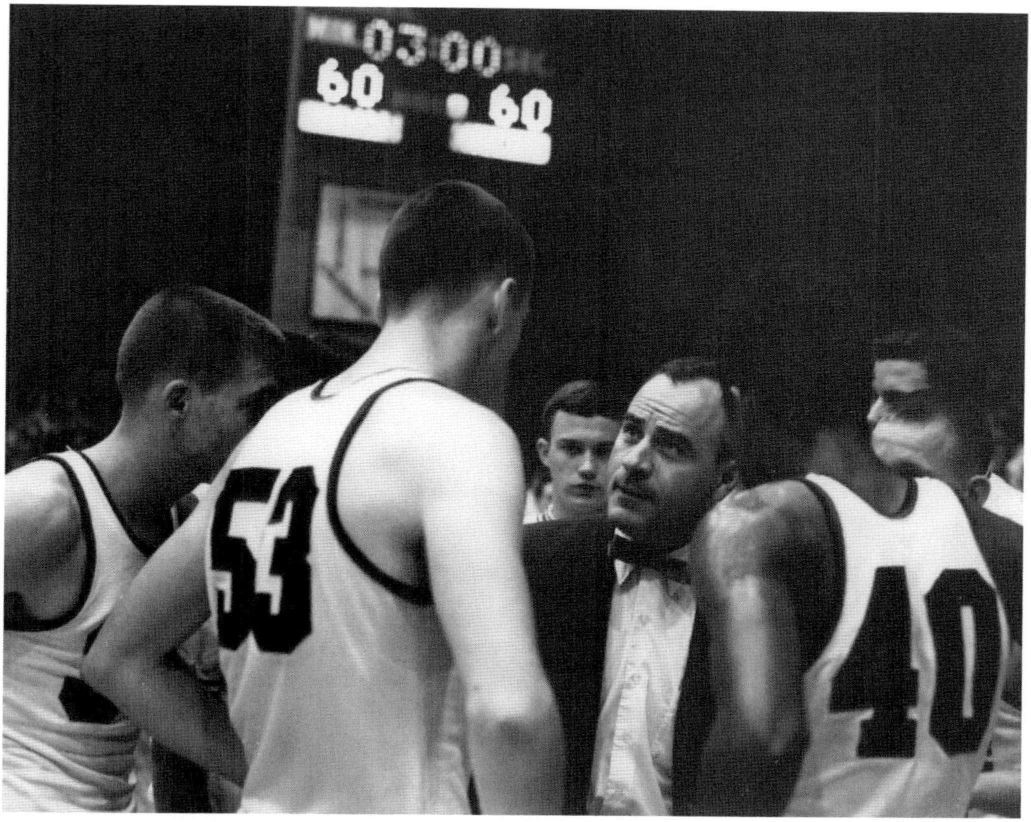

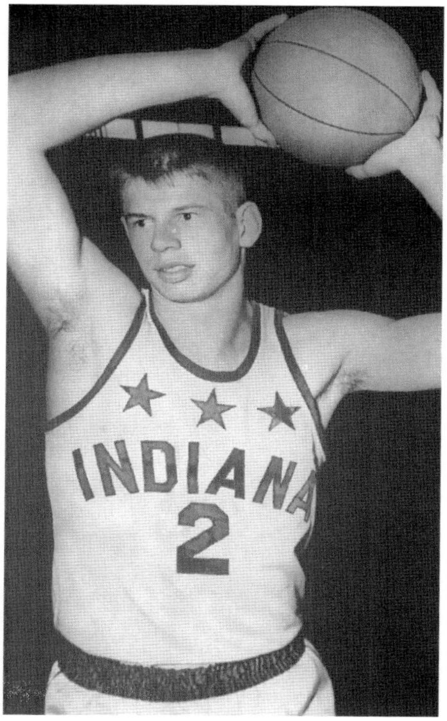

Bill Stearman

Bill Stearman had an impressive basketball career both as a player and coach. He graduated from Columbus High School in 1943 after being named MVP three of his four years. After college, he became a coach at his alma mater from 1952 to 1996. During that time, his teams won 714 games and earned 27 sectional titles, 12 regional titles, and 2 semi-state titles. He was inducted into the Indiana Basketball Hall of Fame in 1983. (BCHS Collection.)

Jerry Newsom

Jerry Newsom led the Columbus High School basketball team to the state finals in 1964. Newsom then went on to Indiana State University, where he led the Sycamores to three conference championships and to the 1968 NCAA Division II championship game, where he was named tourney MVP. He ended his college career as Indiana State's top career scorer, a record that stood until 1979, when it was broken by basketball star Larry Bird. (Courtesy of Columbus North High School.)

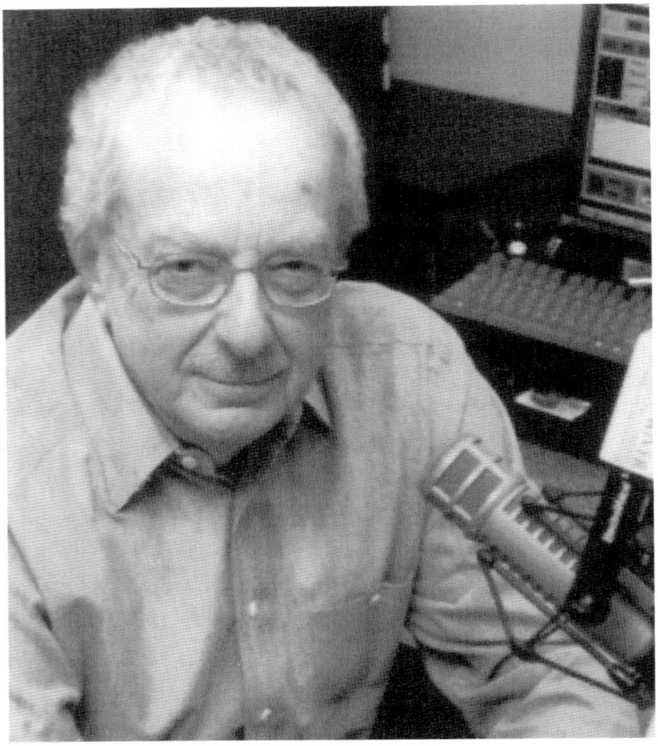

Sam Simmermaker

Sam Simmermaker has been a radio broadcaster for more than 50 years, with most of that time at WCSI in Columbus. Simmermaker spent 35 years covering news and sports but now focuses entirely on sports, especially local sports. He remembers the 1968 boys regional basketball championship, won by Columbus High School, as the most exciting game he has ever covered. Simmermaker is in both the Sportscasters Hall of Fame and the Indiana Basketball Hall of Fame. (Courtesy of Sam Simmermaker.)

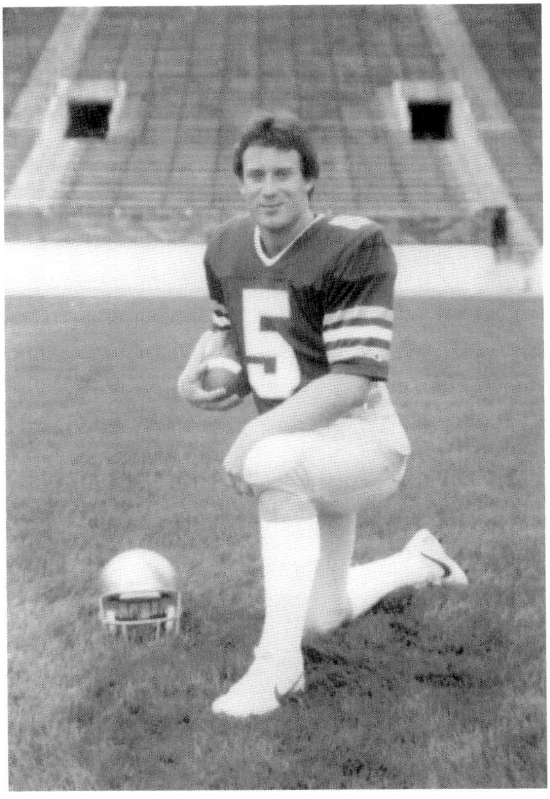

Blair Kiel

Blair Kiel was a three-sport star at Columbus East High School and led the football team to a state championship in 1979. He went on to Notre Dame, where he was a four-year starting quarterback and punter. He set a Notre Dame record for the longest pass in 1981 with a 96-yard throw. In 1984, he was drafted into the NFL where he played for seven years for the Buccaneers, Colts, and Packers and then one year in Canada before retiring in 1992. (Courtesy of the Kiel family.)

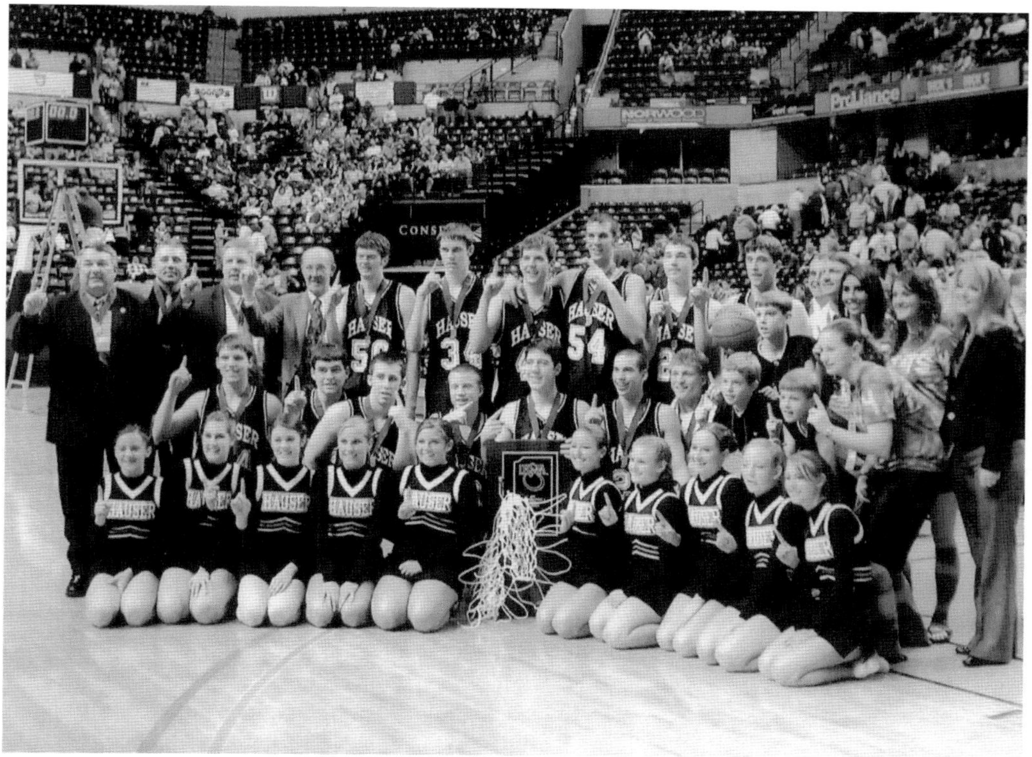

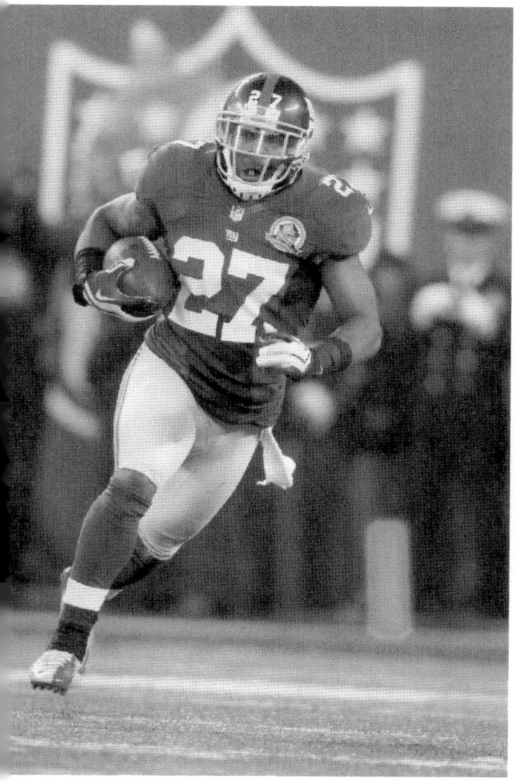

Hauser Boys Basketball 2006 Class 1A State Champs
During the 2005–2006 basketball season, the Hauser High School boys team united the town as it made its way through the state tournament. On many tournament game days, the town seemed deserted, as hundreds of fans followed the team to cheer them to victory. When Coach Bob Nobbe's team capped off the season with a win in the championship game, they boys were welcomed back to Hope with a parade and community pep rally. (Photograph by James Stafford.)

Stevie Brown
The 2012 NFL football season was a good one for New York Giants safety Stevie Brown, a Columbus East High School graduate. He played football for the University of Michigan, where he led the team in tackles and was named captain his senior year. Drafted in the seventh round of the 2010 draft, Brown did not join the Giants until 2012. That year, he set a Giants single-season record for interception return yards and was twice named NFC Defensive Player of the Week. (AP Photo/ Evan Pinkus)

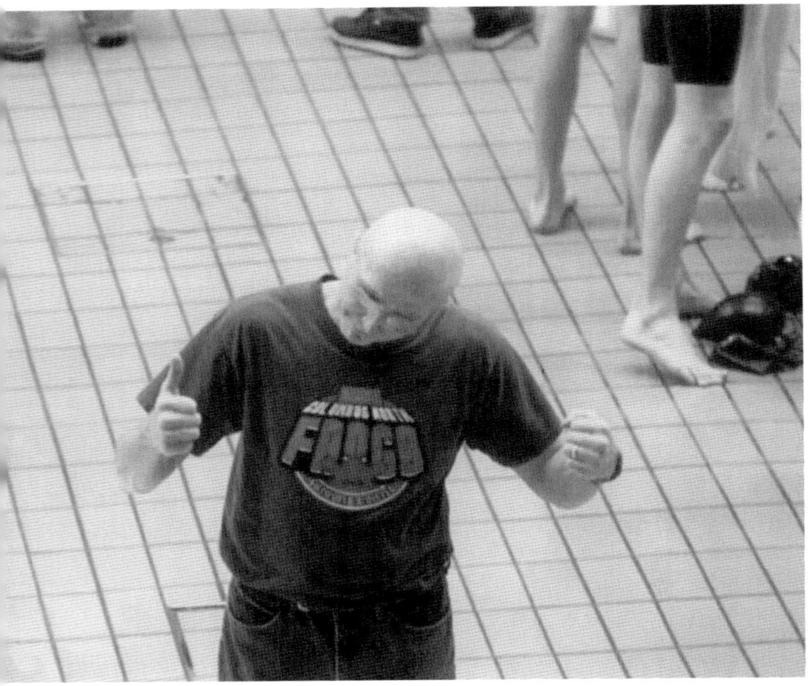

Jim Sheridan
Jim Sheridan has coached successful swimming programs at Columbus East (1980–1984), Clemson University (1991–1994), and Columbus North (since 1995). At North, he was named Indiana Swimming Coach of the Year 10 times—four for the boys team and six for the girls team. His East girls team won the state title in 1982 and his North boys teams won three consecutive titles from 1998 to 2000. Sheridan has also coached numerous individual state champions and many All-Americans. (Photograph by Meika Sheridan.)

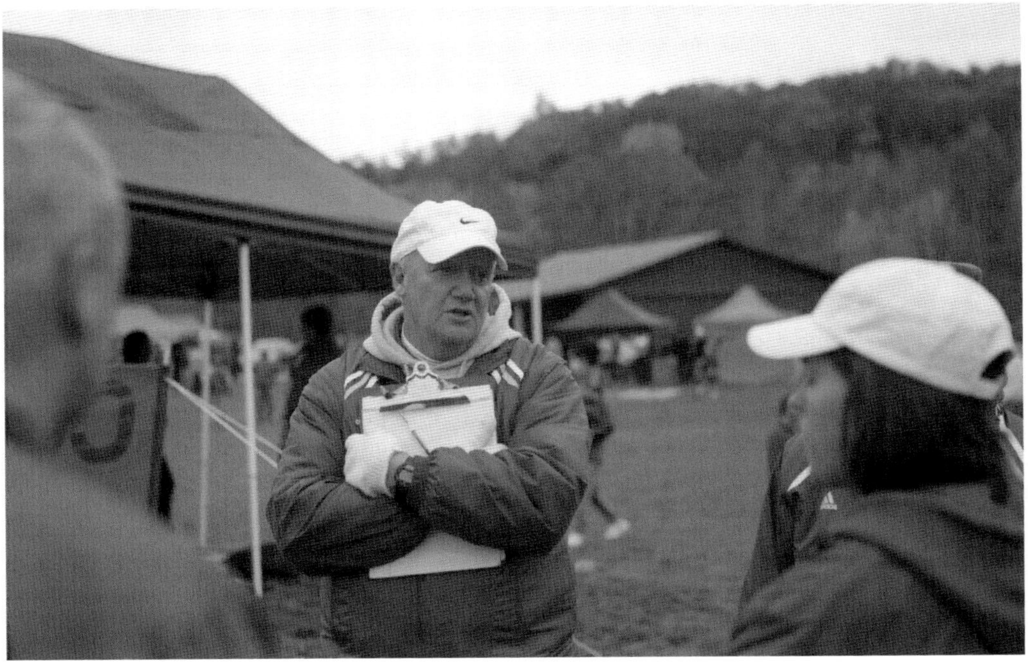

Rick Weinheimer
Among the most successful athletic programs in Columbus is the cross-country program at Columbus North, which has been coached by Rick Weinheimer for more than 35 years. The boys and girls teams have been to the state finals a total of 44 times and, in 2009, both teams won the state championship. Weinheimer uses his belief that one can learn important life lessons through running to develop successful student athletes who have life skills that carry them beyond high school. (Photograph by Greg Jones.)

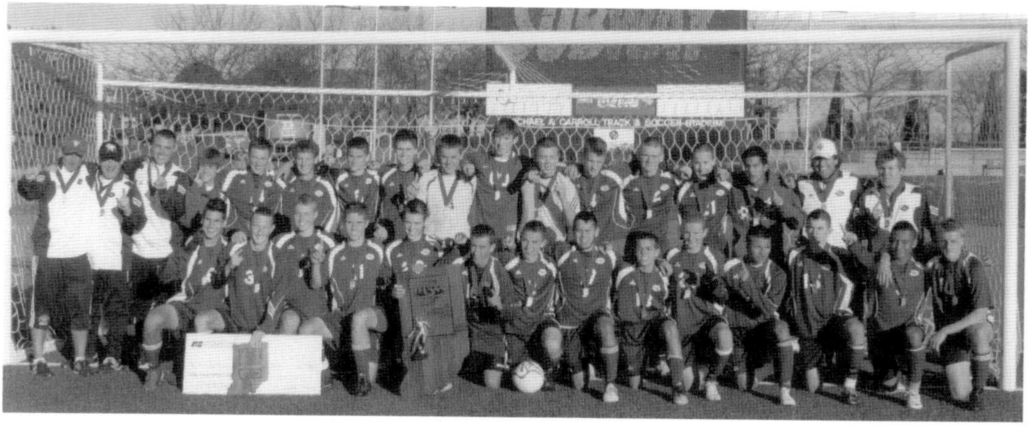

Columbus North Boys Soccer 2012 State Champs
In 2012, the Columbus North boys Bulldogs brought a state soccer championship home to Columbus after a stellar season that included a top 15 national ranking. Coached by Andy Glover, the team beat Warsaw 1-0 in the state finals, and Bulldog Brad Shaw (who scored the only goal of the final game) was named a soccer All-American. (Courtesy of Columbus North High School.)

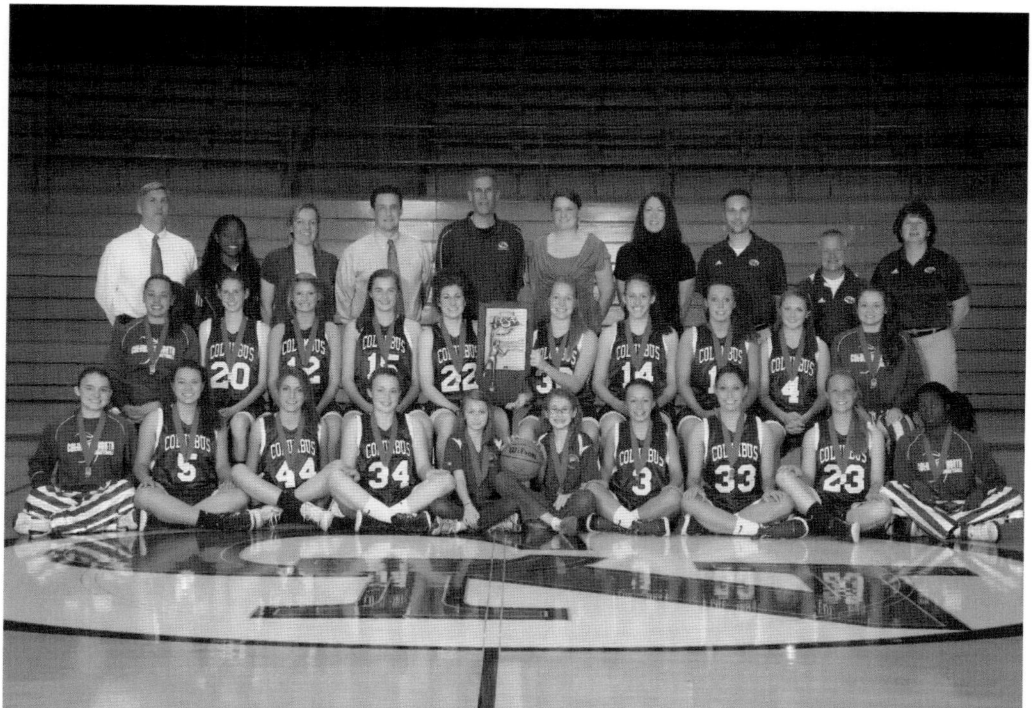

Columbus North Girls Basketball 2012 State Runners-Up
In 2012, the Columbus North High School girls basketball team capped an impressive season by becoming the Class 4A state runners-up. The team lost 50-48 in overtime to North Central High School, when their opponents sank two free throws with 0.8 seconds remaining on the clock. Although the game was played in Terre Haute, hundreds of Columbus residents traveled to support the Lady Bulldogs, who were coached by Pat McKee. (Photograph by Todd Voelz.)

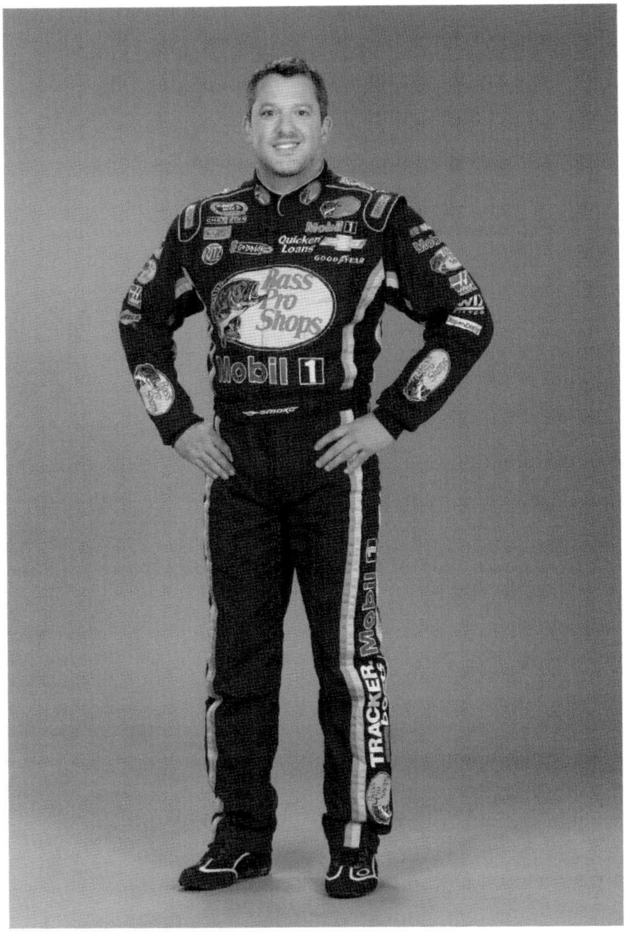

Tony Stewart

One of Columbus's most famous native sons is race car driver Tony Stewart, who was born in Columbus in 1971 and graduated from Columbus North High School in 1989. Even as a child, Stewart was interested in racing, starting in go-kart races. His first championship came at the Bartholomew County Fairgrounds, where he won a four-cycle rookie junior class championship at age eight. By the end of high school, Stewart was moving up through the ranks and becoming known all over the world of racing. In 1995, he was the first driver to win all three divisions of United States Auto Club (USAC)—Midget, Sprint, and Silver Crown—in a single year. He followed this up with an IRL Indy Car Series championship in 1997 before moving to NASCAR. Stewart also won the final IROC (International Race of Champions) series championship in 2006. Stewart's most widely acclaimed titles are his three NASCAR Sprint Cup Series championships in 2002, 2005, and 2011. As his fame has risen, Stewart has always felt at home in Columbus. In 1997, he bought the home in the heart of Columbus where he had grown up with his family. Today, he has a larger, more private property in the Columbus area where he enjoys spending free time when he is not racing. Sometimes during racing season, he will fly to Columbus after a Sunday race and spend a quiet Monday before rejoining his team and preparing for the next weekend's race. While there are many businesses around town that advertise support for Stewart, one fun place to visit is the downtown Dairy Queen, where a mural of Stewart (by artist Catherine Burris) graces one wall. Dairy Queen owner Bob Franke was an early sponsor of Stewart back when he raced go-karts. In addition to racing, Stewart has become known as a philanthropist, creating the Tony Stewart Foundation to support children and animal charities. (Courtesy of CIA Stock Photography.)

CHAPTER SEVEN

Contributing in Special Ways

To characterize the contributions of some people is easy. Teachers teach, artists entertain and inspire, businessmen and politicians lead, and so on. Others, however, make their marks in different ways. Columbus has been home to a wide array of interesting and notable individuals who have had an impact on the town or on the people in their lives. Jack Miller, popularly known as "Jack the Bum," is an example of that. Today, Miller would be called a hobo or vagabond, but in the mid-1900s, he was appreciated for his status as an unofficial lifeguard for local children playing in the swimming hole at the river. Enough people valued his contribution to the community that artist Catherine Burris was commissioned to paint a mural of Jack the Bum to hang in city hall.

Several women from Columbus have especially interesting stories. Beulah Brown Fletcher led a colorful life as a journalist in the early part of the 20th century, traveling all over and meeting famous actors and politicians of the time. She did not let her status as a female hinder her career dreams. Clementine Tangeman was born into a privileged life but also gave back to her community and world. During World War II, she volunteered for the Red Cross on the Italian Coast and, for the rest of her life, she was a great supporter and benefactor of the Girl Scouts. Prentess Smith was raised in a time of segregation and was the last living student who attended the all-black Booker T. Washington School in Columbus. She was a remarkable woman who lived to be 99 years old and spent much of that time volunteering in the community to help others.

Columbus is also full of many examples of ordinary people seeing a need and working to fill that need. Volunteers in Medicine Clinic, Freedom Field, kidscommons, and the Jolie Crider Skate Park are examples of community assets that came about from the grassroots efforts of local citizens.

Some extraordinary stories from Columbus have a tragic element as well. Jolie Crider's life was tragically cut short by sudden illness, and Abby Brinkman lost her life in a diving accident. Both girls, however, have had lasting impacts on countless others, as both families channeled their grief and created lasting memorials to give back to others and keep Jolie's and Abby's memories alive.

Although some stories may be hard to classify, their appeal and their importance to Columbus are clear.

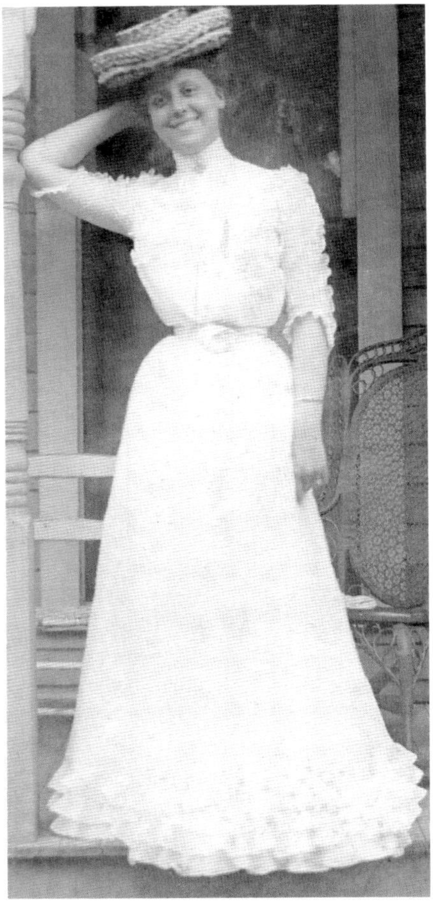

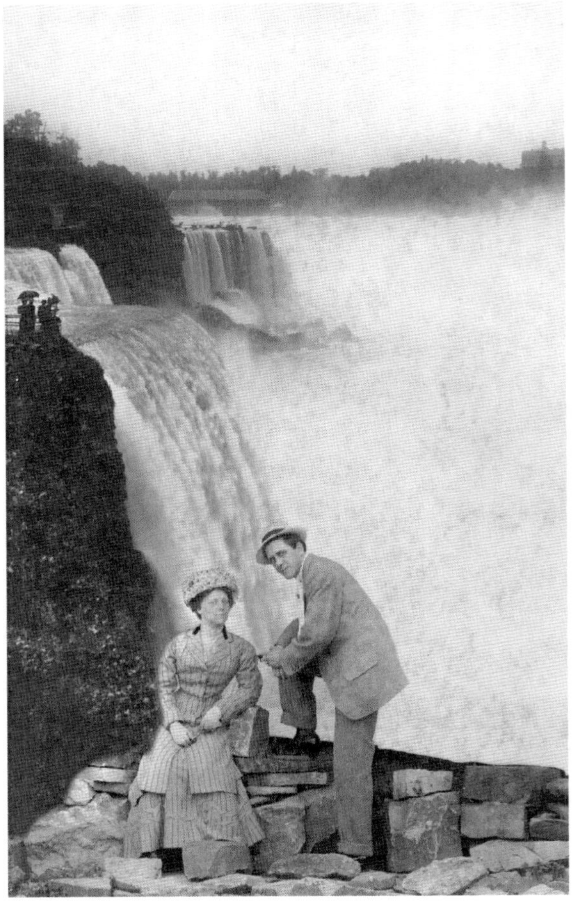

Beulah Brown Fletcher

In an age when many women did not pursue careers outside the home, Beulah Brown Fletcher led a colorful life. The daughter of Chalmers Brown, cofounder of the *Evening Republican*, she was born in Columbus and attended Columbus High School before establishing herself in the world of journalism. Fletcher began working as a society reporter for the local paper at age 15 but took advantage of an opportunity to show more serious journalistic skills five years later. While attending a dinner party, she learned of an interurban railroad crash north of Columbus and left the party in her long gown to go to the scene of the accident. After helping with the injured, she telephoned the story to the *Indianapolis Star*, boosting her young career. Fletcher went on to work at the *Cleveland Press*, where she frequently reported on the plight of the poor. Once, she spent several weeks living and working as a telephone operator in order to report about complaints with the local telephone service from the point of view of the operators. She also received national wire service exposure for an interview with John D. Rockefeller that required her to follow him on the golf course. Fletcher moved to San Francisco after marrying Montelle Fletcher (pictured with her at Niagara Falls) in 1909 but returned to the Midwest after Montelle's tragic death in an automobile accident in 1912. She worked again in Cleveland and then in St. Louis before becoming a theater press agent in New York City. In this role, Fletcher met and interviewed many famous people of the time, including Ethel Barrymore and Sarah Bernhardt, and became acquainted with author Somerset Maugham and several presidents. Because her fame was well known in certain circles, she gained exclusive interviews with many sought-after interviewees, including British suffragette Emma Pankhurst. After a successful career, Fletcher came back to Columbus where she lived a much quieter life until her death in 1949. (BCHS Collection.)

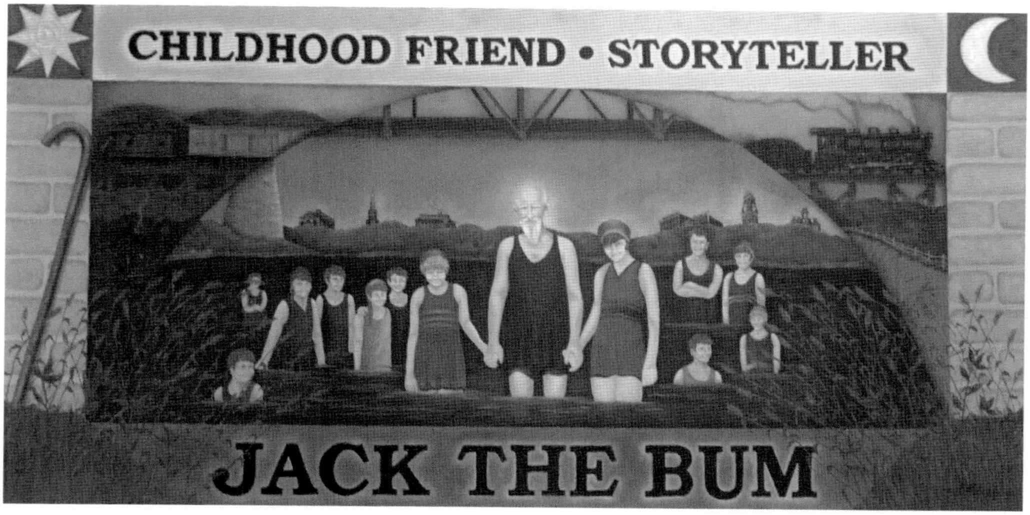

Jack the Bum

From the early to mid-20th century, Jack the Bum acted as a lifeguard to many children who enjoyed the swimming hole under the railroad bridge on Flatrock River. His real name was Jack Miller, but not much was known about his personal life. In 1999, a mural by local artist Catherine Burris was unveiled in city hall to celebrate a man who played a prominent role in the early lives of many Columbus children. (Painting by Catherine Burris.)

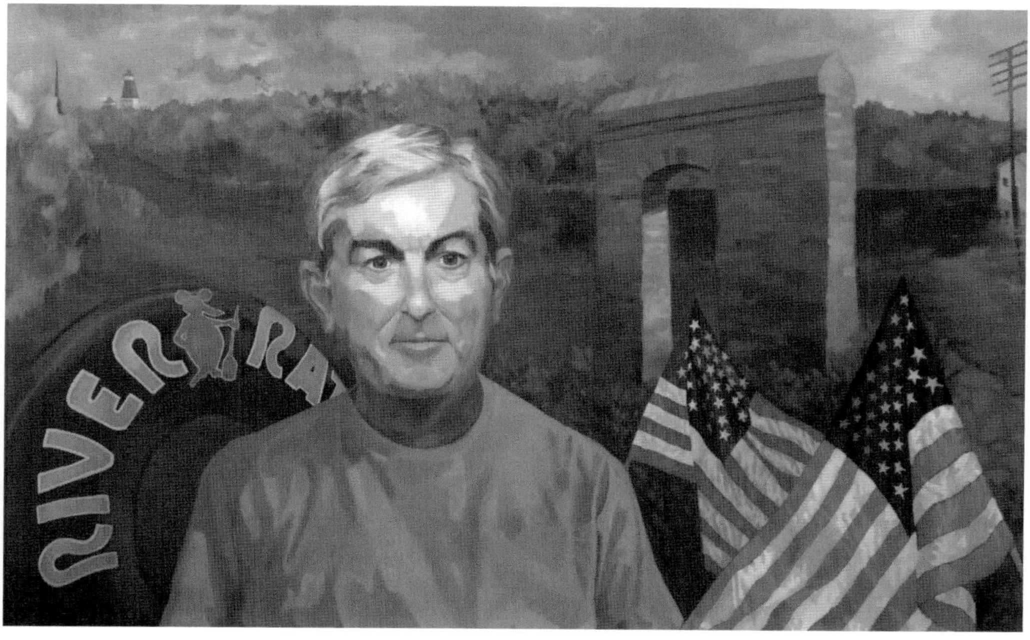

Carl Miske

Carl Miske was the leader of the River Rats, a grassroots group that led the cleanup of the area formerly known as Death Valley (for its penchant for flooding the ramshackle homes in the area) and its transition into Mill Race Park. For several decades, Miske continued to lead the Rats in fundraising for the park. Carl Miske Drive now winds its way through Mill Race Park in his honor, and a painting honoring Miske hangs in Columbus City Hall. (Painting by Lydia Burris.)

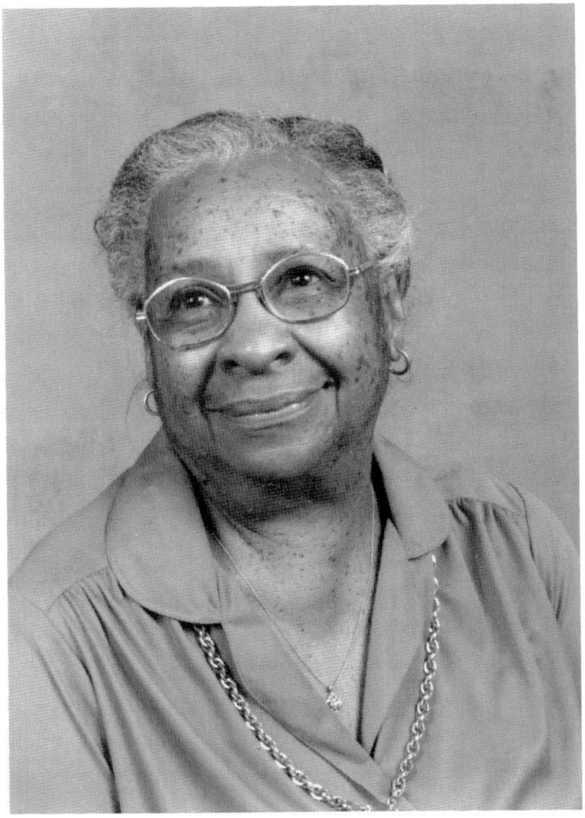

Prentess Smith

Prentess Smith led a very long and remarkable life. She was the youngest of five children born to parents of African and Cherokee descent, and her family was one of the first African American families to settle in Bartholomew County. Columbus schools were integrated between her seventh- and eighth-grade years, and she eventually became the last living student who had attended the segregated Booker T. Washington School at Fourteenth and Union Streets. Her father was one of the founders of Second Baptist Church, where Prentess played piano for more than 50 years and taught Sunday school even longer. Her musical talent was well known, and over her lifetime, Prentess sang in most every church in Columbus, and she had the honor of singing with the Billy Graham Crusade choir. Out of this honor came another—she and her husband, Bill, were invited to have dinner with First Lady Lady Bird Johnson when she came to Columbus. Prentess was a founder of the Ladies Bible Class in 1944 and was one of the first black citizens to own and drive a car in Columbus. She believed in the golden rule and spent much of her life helping others. An excellent cook, she prepared meals for the Ladies Bible Club for many years and had a gift for making meals for many out of what looked to be a small amount of food. She also volunteered at Columbus Regional Hospital for more than 35 years, assisted with Meals on Wheels, and served on the boards of the Salvation Army, Lincoln-Central Neighborhood Association, and family services. One of the first persons of color in the Ecumenical Assembly, Prentess served on the William Laws Foundation to help disadvantaged youth. She spent many years working for the Nichols, Miller, and Sweeney families, and Ninth Street Park in Columbus was dedicated to Prentess Smith and Clementine Tangeman. Known as "Mama Smith" to many, she was proud of all 10 of her kids and treated them all equally, including her stepchildren. She had strong opinions and taught her children to be true to themselves. Prentess made the most of her 99 years—bowling until age 96, playing piano until age 98, and enjoying her large family until the very end. (Courtesy of the Smith family.)

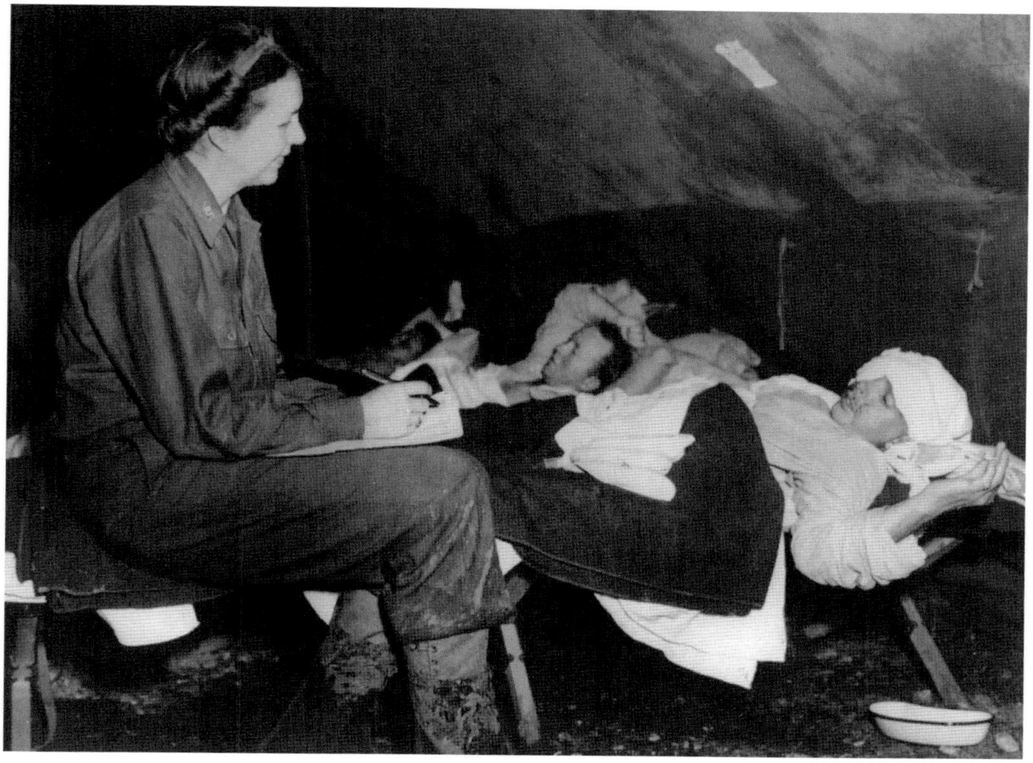

Clementine Miller Tangeman

Clementine Tangeman was the sister of J. Irwin Miller, the great-granddaughter of Joseph Irwin, and one of many philanthropists in the Irwin-Sweeney-Miller family. Tangeman graduated from Smith College in 1927 just before the Great Depression, when few jobs were available. Her parents encouraged her to look for work to be done that did not pay a salary, and she spent much of the rest of her life engaged in charitable endeavors. During World War II, she was a Red Cross volunteer and was sent to Italy, where she worked in a hospital on the Anzio beachhead, which was frequently under fire. She is pictured transcribing a letter from an injured soldier in the photograph above, which was printed in the *New York Times Magazine* in 1944. Tangeman had a lifelong passion for Girl Scouts, and she chaired the Board of World Foundation for Girl Guides and Girl Scouts and was a director of Girl Scouts of the United States. Tangeman was the last member of her family to live in the family's historic home on Fifth Street. (Above, reprinted by permission of the *New York Times Syndicate*; below, Irwin-Sweeney-Miller Family Collection, IHS.)

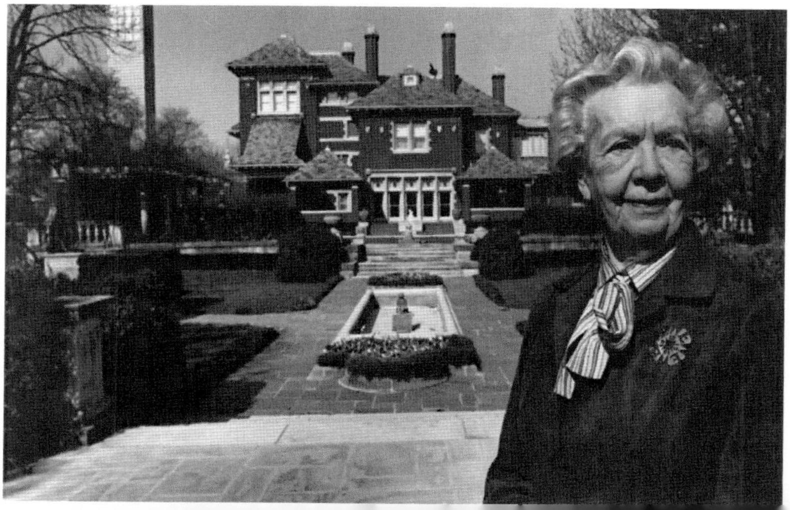

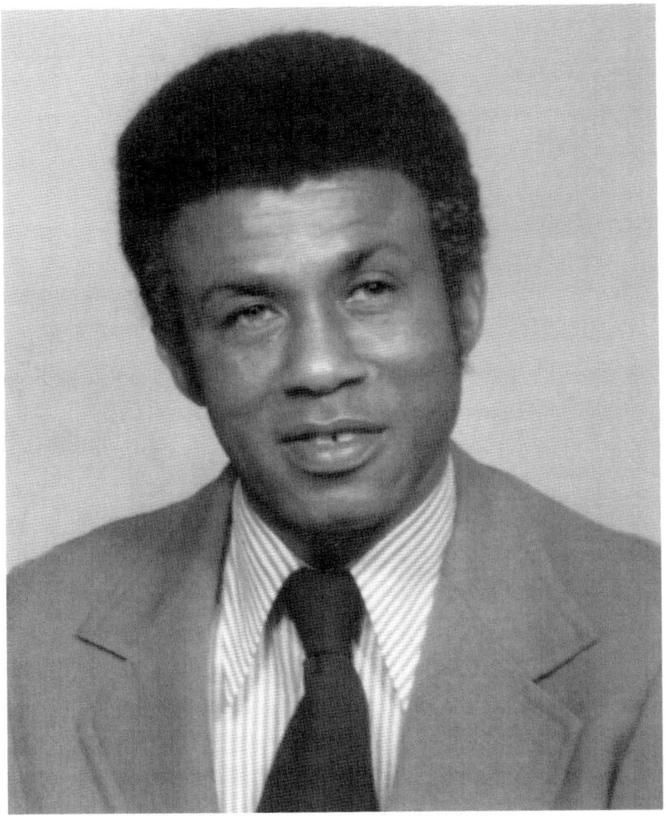

Benjamin "Mickey" King

When Benjamin "Mickey" King accepted a job as a microbiologist at Bartholomew County Hospital in 1958, Columbus was not a welcoming place for African Americans. Restaurants and movie theaters were still segregated, and black men had to leave town to get a haircut from an African American barber. Originally from South Carolina and a veteran of the Korean War, King met his wife, Ann, while he was stationed at Camp Atterbury. They married in 1953 and moved to Columbus permanently in 1958 after Mickey graduated from Purdue. Initially, they lived with Ann's parents because they could not find a realtor or landlord who would rent to them. Eventually, a local businessman rented them a house downtown where they lived for three years, at which time hospital administrator Olive Murphy offered to rent them a house on the north side of town on a bigger lot. The Kings were concerned and upset to learn that neighbors near their future home created a petition in an attempt to keep them out of the neighborhood, but they moved in anyway, and Mickey King became passionate about improving the housing situation in Columbus for all races. With Rev. Bill Laws, attorney Lee Hamilton, and businessman Owen Hungerford, King helped found the Human Rights Commission in 1962, which set as one of its goals a housing ordinance for the city. J. Irwin Miller and Cummins supported the objective by publicly stating that providing housing for all would help the entire city of Columbus by allowing Cummins to recruit talented workers of all races. During this time, King was also concerned that young blacks were not going to college, so he started a tutoring and scholarship program for young students. The program primarily served black students but welcomed all students regardless of race, and King was very proud of the program's success. In addition to his community involvement, he was very well respected as a microbiologist, and his services were very much in demand. He was a consultant at several hospitals outside Columbus and he started his own company, Columbus Biologicals. In 1974, Mickey King suffered a fatal heart attack while on a business trip at age 44. He left behind his wife, two children, and a town that became more welcoming for all, thanks to his efforts. (Courtesy of Ann King.)

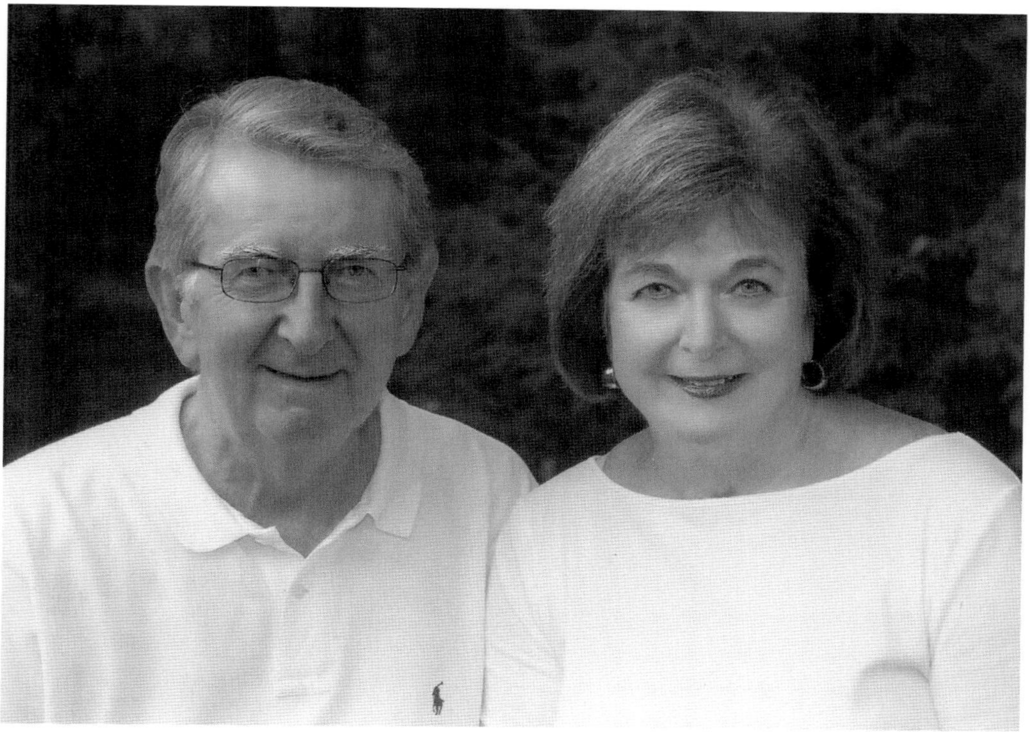

Dr. Sherm and Jacquie Franz

Both Dr. Sherm and Jacquie Franz have worked to improve the health and wellness of the citizens of Columbus. A psychiatrist, Sherm was involved in starting the local hospice program in the 1970s and in opening the first halfway house in Columbus for those recovering from mental illness. In the early 1990s, Sherm learned about an innovative free clinic in South Carolina staffed by physician volunteers and serving those without insurance. He knew many Columbus residents lacked access to health care and became the driving force to establish a similar clinic in Columbus. He brought speakers to town, polled the medical staff at the hospital about their willingness to staff such a clinic, and created a steering committee. Focus groups showed the overwhelming desire of those who were uninsured was the ability to obtain medical treatment with dignity and respect, and this became central to the mission statement for the clinic. After several years of reaching out to groups all over the community for support, the Volunteers in Medicine (VIM) Clinic opened in 1996. At the time, it was the second clinic using the VIM name and model of care in the country. (By 2013, more than 80 clinics followed this model.) At the same time that Sherm was working toward the creation of the VIM Clinic, Jacquie had left her job in academics to cofound the Healthy Communities Initiative for Bartholomew County with John McGinty, the hospital chief executive officer. Healthy Communities' goal was to improve the health and quality of life for community residents by promoting healthy lifestyles, healthy relationships, and access to health care for all members of the community. As a collaborative initiative, great overlap existed between the work to start VIM and Healthy Communities. Jacquie became the president of the Hospital Foundation, which still serves as the funding source for VIM. Healthy Communities required capital as well, and Jacquie continued to work with the organization until its $5-million endowment had been funded before retiring in 2000. Today, Healthy Communities continues to improve the health of the community through its coalitions, some of which provide education about tobacco cessation, domestic violence, Shaken Baby Syndrome, and assistance to Spanish-speaking patients and those who cannot afford medications. Volunteers in Medicine also continues to fill a need in the community as it serves more than 1,300 patients per year. Both Sherm and Jacquie continue to serve on the Healthy Communities Council, and Sherm continues to volunteer at VIM. (Courtesy of Sherm and Jacquie Franz.)

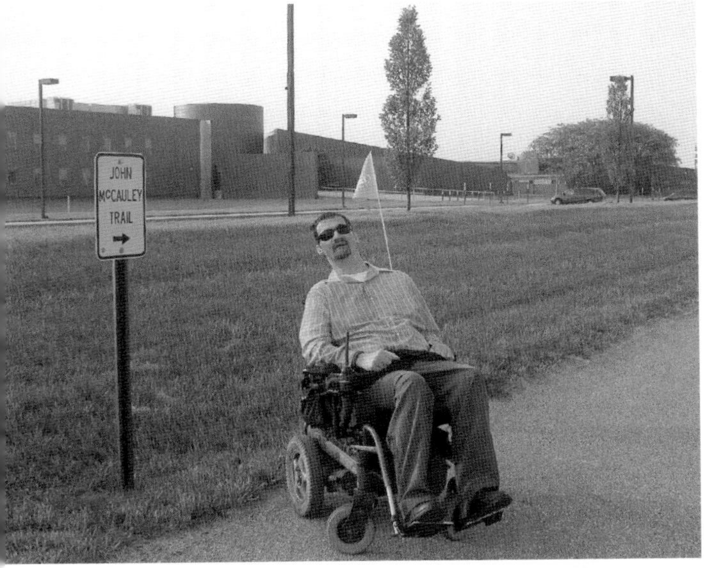

John McCauley

John McCauley never let his disability stop him from championing the causes he believed in. John had cerebral palsy and was confined to a wheelchair but was a staunch supporter of the People Trails and the city bus service, both of which he frequently utilized. As a member of the Columbus Transit Advisory Committee, he helped the city obtain new buses before his death in 2007. A portion of the People Trails is named after John McCauley. (Photograph by John Rhoades.)

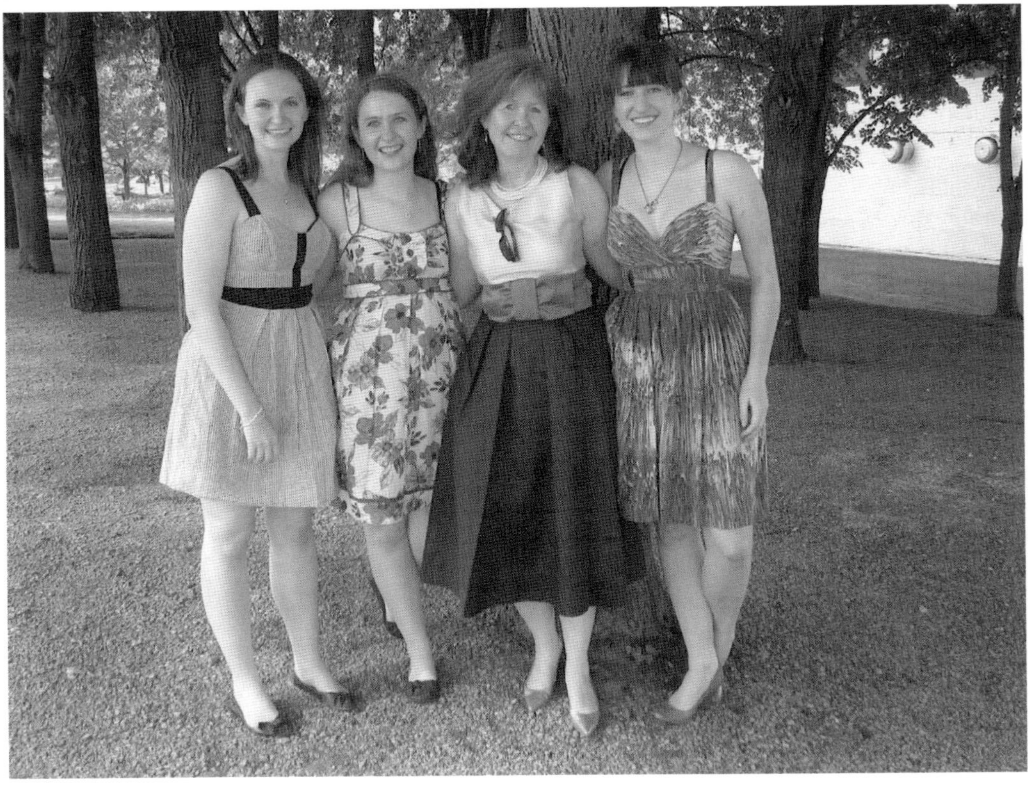

Lynne Maguire

In the mid-1990s, Lynne Maguire formed a committee to explore the idea of a children's museum in Columbus after discovering the joys of smaller children's museums on her travels with her three daughters (pictured with her in 2012). Although some doubted Columbus could support such a place, Maguire guided the group through extensive planning, then to a small pilot museum in 1998, and finally to the opening of the current kidscommons in 2005. (Courtesy of Lynne Maguire.)

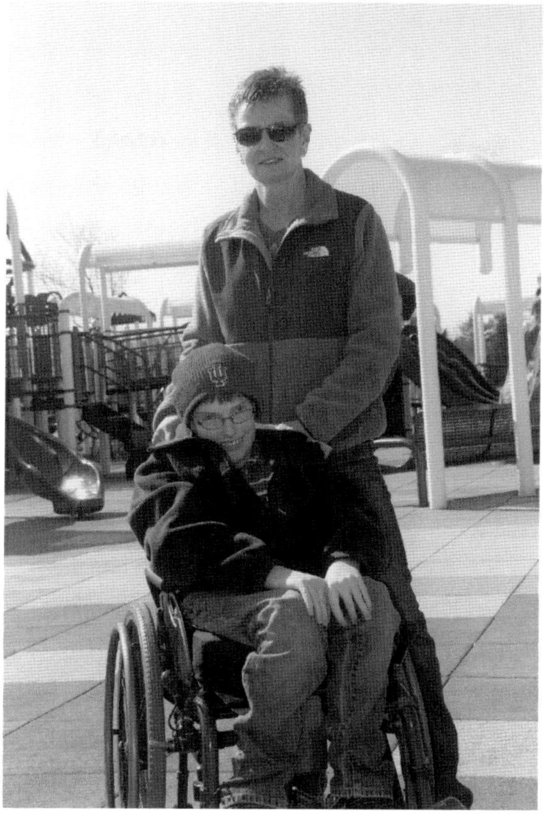

Laurie Booher

For most parents, taking their children to a playground is a simple and routine part of parenting. For parents of disabled children, it can be anything but simple. Laurie Booher remembers working hard to push her son Collin's wheelchair across the mulch at a playground in downtown Columbus one day in 2003, when the idea hit her and Collin's aunt Amy Lienhoop that there must be a better option. This started a three-year journey in which the two women spearheaded an effort that eventually included many individuals and businesses throughout the area to create Freedom Field, a playground accessible to all. Booher and Lienhoop visited 56 accessible playgrounds around the country, as far away as Florida and California. They researched the disabled population in Columbus in order to prove that there was a need and studied city bus routes in order to show that those who could most benefit from such a place would be able to get there. The two women also educated themselves about various playground structures and surfaces to make the area truly accessible and also maintainable. With such a large project, fundraising proved the biggest challenge. Booher made 196 presentations to civic and business groups to spread the word and try to secure the funds necessary to make such a large dream a reality. During the process, both Columbus high schools began fundraising for new artificial turf football fields, which almost derailed Freedom Field. Fortunately, Booher and Lienhoop were persistent, and Columbus stepped forward for such a worthy cause. Partnering with Columbus Service League and securing large donations from Cummins, Heritage Fund, and private donors—along with receiving many in kind donations from businesses who worked on the project—construction finally started after more than three years. In September 2006, Freedom Field, at the time the largest accessible playground in Indiana and fifth largest in the nation, opened at Blackwell Park with a grand celebration. Laurie (pictured with Collin at Freedom Field) was asked if she pursued the project for her son, and she answered "I did not do it for him. I did it because of him." All of Columbus has benefited, as children and adults of all ages and abilities have a fun, safe place to play and explore. (Photograph by author.)

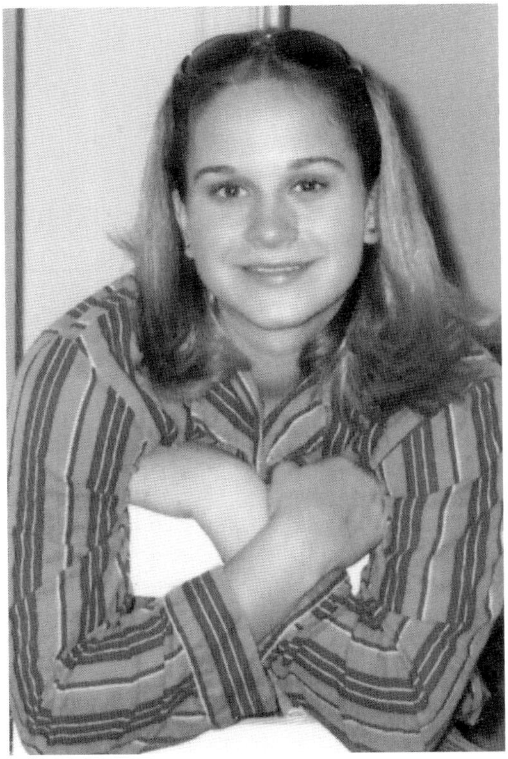

Jolie Crider

In 1998, Bob Crider and Shayla Holtkamp faced the greatest nightmare parents can face when their 14-year-old daughter Jolie died suddenly of meningitis. Jolie had been a bright, friendly, and athletic girl who played basketball, volleyball, and softball up until the day before she died. More importantly, Jolie had a gift for seeing beyond outward appearances and befriending people of all different ages, backgrounds, and interests. Numerous friends stood at Jolie's memorial service and gave testament to Jolie's loving heart when many of them remembered Jolie as their best friend. In addition, her parents remembered that Jolie was friendly with many of the youth who were skateboarders in Columbus, a group of which already had been working together at the time of her death to raise money and construct a skate park. When the skate park near East High School was opened in 1999, it was named the Jolie Crider Skate Park, both for the organizers' desire to honor their friend Jolie and for her parents' financial contributions to the park, including $25,000 given by the Jolie Crider Reach Out Fund that Bob Crider established. In their struggle to find meaning in their tragedy, Bob and Shayla looked for ways to honor Jolie's memory by honoring organizations that made a difference in Jolie's short life or that would have been important to Jolie. With donations to support the athletic programs at area schools, the Police Athletic League, the Foundation for Youth, and Columbus Parks and Recreation Department, to name a few, Bob and Shayla have created something positive out of their loss. Because grieving parents want to assure their child's memory lives on, the family has supported other gestures in Jolie's honor as well, including a trophy case at Columbus North High School and a sculpture at Columbus Regional Hospital by artist Linda Peterson, placed in a quiet outdoors spot with benches to allow patients or their families a moment of peaceful reflection. In addition, each year an eighth-grade female scholar-athlete is awarded the Jolie Crider Award at Central Middle School, one of Jolie's former schools. Jolie's parents learned later that days before her death Jolie commented to friends that she never wanted to be forgotten. Her parents have made every effort to ensure she is never forgotten by using their gifts to honor Jolie in many ways to make a difference in Columbus. (Courtesy of Bob Crider.)

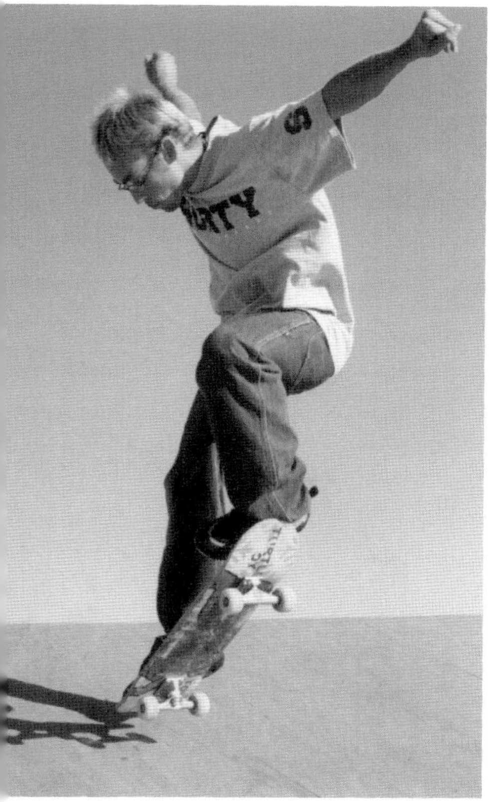

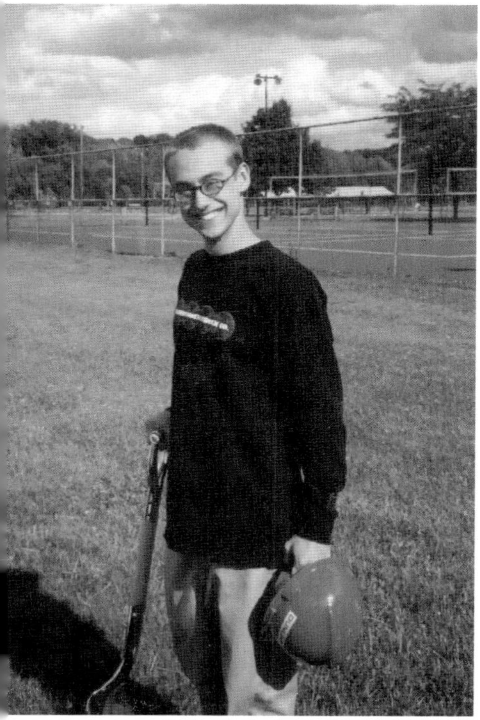

Joe Nierman

When high school student Joe Nierman spent Career Day with the Parks and Recreation director in 1997, it changed his life. Director Chuck Wilt asked Nierman what Columbus needed, and Nierman answered without hesitation "a skate park." An avid skateboarder, Nierman and his friends struggled to find places to skate around Columbus, with property owners and city officials often chasing them away. Nierman was quickly given a list of problems with this idea—including safety, location, and cost—and told if he could work these issues out he could talk to the parks board. The often-undeserved reputation the skaters had as troublemakers meant that no one took the idea seriously, but Nierman was determined. He and his friends started by designing a skate park that skaters would enjoy, even including some elements of Columbus's architecture in the design. They researched locations and found space near an existing park, which was safe from flooding and served by city buses. They then found two experts who promised to help them build their design if the project got that far. Although the teens' hard work eventually got the attention of the parks board, the $100,000 price tag remained an obstacle. What could have derailed the process completely instead spawned a creative idea for funding. Nierman and his friends decided to contact the businesses that had chased them away, guessing correctly that many of these business owners would contribute to a dedicated skate park. Many Columbus companies contributed materials as well. Midway through the two-year process, a friend of many of the skaters, Jolie Crider, passed away suddenly, and the group decided they wanted to name the park in her honor. Jolie's parents were so honored by the idea that they donated the remainder of the needed money to the project, which was then ready for construction. Ground-breaking occurred in May 1999, and the teens took turns sleeping in tents at the park during the next six weeks to protect the building materials. In August 1999, the Jolie Crider Memorial Skate Park opened, and Nierman has been proud of it ever since. In addition to receiving awards for his efforts, leading the creation of the skate park taught Nierman life lessons about working hard for one's goals. Years later, Nierman's career finds him working as a financial advisor, but he continues to enjoy skating whenever he can. (Courtesy of Joe Nierman; skating photograph by Phil Allen.)

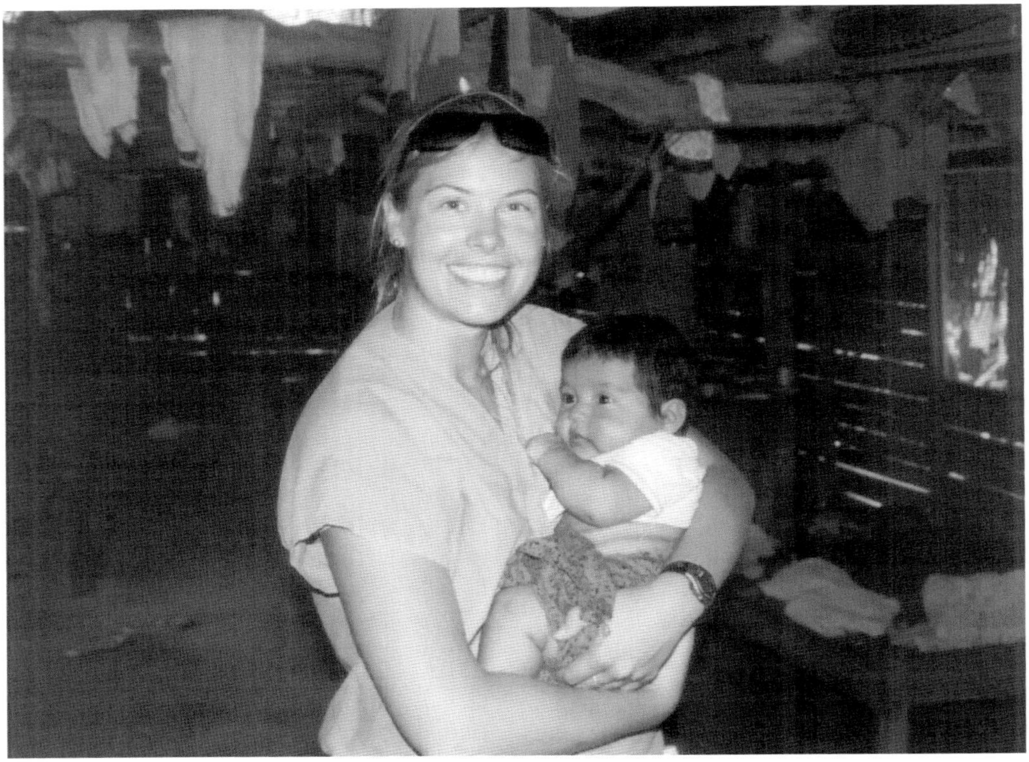

Abby Brinkman

When Abby Brinkman traveled to Belize in 2005 for a month-long tropical medicine rotation at Hillside Clinic, her family knew how much the trip meant for her. A fourth-year medical student, Abby had wanted to be a pediatrician since age 12 and had grown to love the country of Belize during an undergraduate study course there years earlier. In addition, the outgoing and adventurous woman loved diving, something for which Belize was well known. Abby celebrated her 28th birthday in Belize, and her family was lucky enough to spend a few short days with her, just two weeks before tragedy would strike. Just as Abby could work hard, she could let loose and relax, and so at the end of a long week of treating the many needy patients, Abby and a friend decided to take a break to go diving on Belize's storied barrier reef. With a group of several others, their boat set sail from the town of Placencia before running into engine trouble. The engine was restarted once but stalled again before the divers reached their destination. Abby and the others onboard realized they were being pulled out to sea and made the fateful decision to attempt to swim to safety. Soon separated by choppy seas, three divers survived and were rescued after more than two days in the water, but Abby's body was recovered more than 50 miles out to sea. Only recently returned to Columbus from their trip to visit their daughter, her family was consumed with grief. Initially unsure how they could go on without Abby, the Brinkmans found an outlet when organizers at Hillside Clinic asked them to help build a dormitory at the clinic that would increase the number of medical volunteers who could work there at any one time. After fundraising for over a year, Abby's House was dedicated in November 2008, and patient visits to the clinic doubled. Abby was passionate about caring for children and felt a calling to help children in the poor area where the clinic was located. Many of the children the medical volunteers cared for were infested with lice and scabies, but Abby was not deterred from holding or cuddling them. She picked up the baby in the picture and told a friend "I'm gonna take this one home as soon as I treat the scabies!" Several scholarships in Abby's name support other students following their dreams, and Abby's parents have honored her with their gift to the clinic where she felt so passionate about caring for others, allowing other volunteers to do so in her name. (Courtesy of Roger and Jan Brinkman.)

CHAPTER EIGHT

Preserving History

Columbus has a rich agricultural, industrial, and architectural history, and fortunately, many people have taken on the task of preserving this history. The Delaware Indians were long thought to be the earliest inhabitants of the area, and groups of Delaware reportedly still were living in Bartholomew County when the first white settlers arrived around 1819. In the 1970s, evidence of much earlier prehistoric people was found on Gene Wint's farm in Sandcreek Township. The Riverton Culture Indians were nomadic people who traveled seasonally, and archeologists and volunteers uncovered evidence of house patterns thought to have originated around 1450 BC.

With more than 100 volunteers and staff, the Bartholomew County Historical Society has championed area history since 1921, collecting and preserving the history of Columbus and towns throughout the county. The society shares its rich resources, collections, and knowledge of history with the public through its museum and the Henry Breeding Farm, programs for adults and children, exhibits, websites and publications. The society has benefited from various benefactors over the years. One of its founders, George Pence, was an early collector of Bartholomew County history and served as the first president. Henry and Blanche Breeding and Evelyn Seward left their homes and personal belongings to the historical society after their deaths.

Many local individuals in Columbus also collect history on a smaller scale. Jim Loesch has collected thousands of local history items; Bill Stahl collects vintage farm equipment and shares his expertise with vintage steam engines; Larry Ruble has amassed a large collection of Arvin radios and paper memorabilia from the company at which he worked for 40 years. A descendant of the owners of the Orinoco Furniture Company and the Lincoln Chair Company, Rhonda Bolner has collected many pieces of Orinoco furniture and company history and spearheaded the effort to place a state historic marker at the site of the Orinoco factory.

Lynne Bigley realized during her lifetime that the city's architectural heritage should be protected and led the way for the creation of the Columbus Indiana Architectural Archives. Others have purchased and restored historic buildings to protect them for the future.

Since 1981, Bartholomew County has had a county historian who has shared interesting stories about local history with others, primarily through newspaper columns. Ross Crump served from 1981 to 1985, and then Susie Jones took over until her death in September 1993. Jones combined her love of history with a love of learning and a love of writing. She relished poring over old records and tramping through fields and down railroad tracks looking for disappearing clues to people, buildings, and anything related to the history of the area. Since 1993, Harry McCawley has held the position.

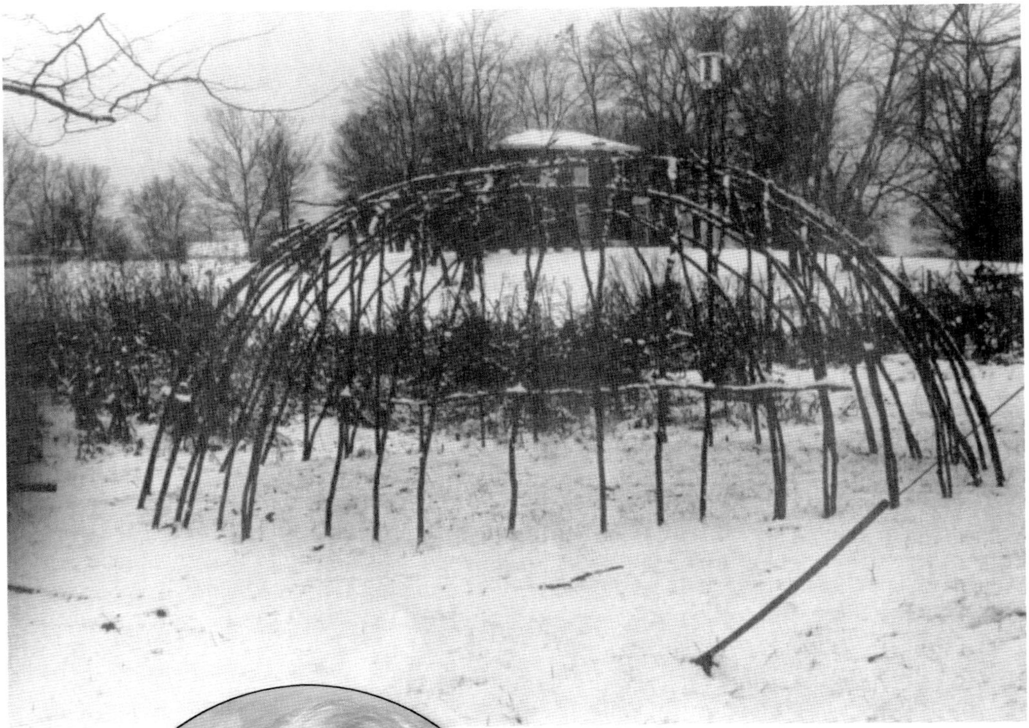

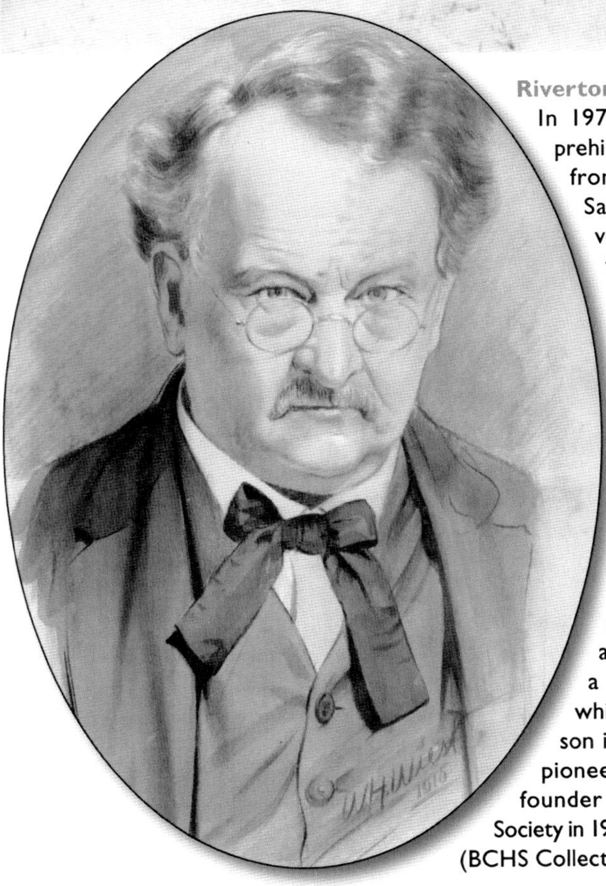

Riverton Culture Indians

In 1979, archeologists found evidence of a prehistoric Riverton Culture Indian community from approximately 1450 BC on a farm in Sandcreek Township. Archeologists and volunteers uncovered soil stains of posts from three houses with an overlapping circular shape (pictured reconstructed), along with fire pits and small bird points or arrowheads. These are thought to be evidence of the oldest houses in Indiana. (Courtesy of Candy Carr.)

George Pence

George Pence was born in Columbus in 1852 and began collecting the early history of the area as a young man. He spent much of his life writing and speaking about history and acquired for the county a portrait of Gen. Joseph Bartholomew, which was in the possession of Bartholomew's son in Wisconsin, and portraits of other early pioneers. Perhaps most importantly, he was a founder of the Bartholomew County Historical Society in 1921 and was the organization's first president. (BCHS Collection.)

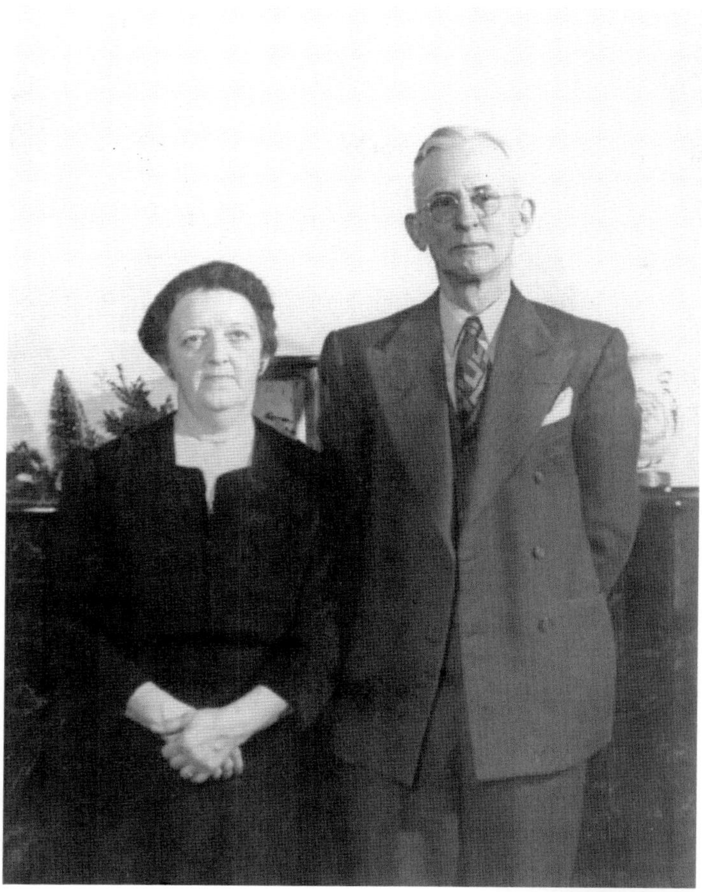

Henry Breeding
In 1916, Henry Breeding bought the stately farmhouse built by his grandmother in 1871 north of Columbus. He and his wife, Blanche, restored and remodeled the house over the years, including moving the kitchen from the basement to the first floor and enclosing a large side porch. The property was willed to the BCHS after Henry's death in 1982, and the farm, along with the Henry Breeding family collection, is an important part of the BCHS. (BCHS Collection.)

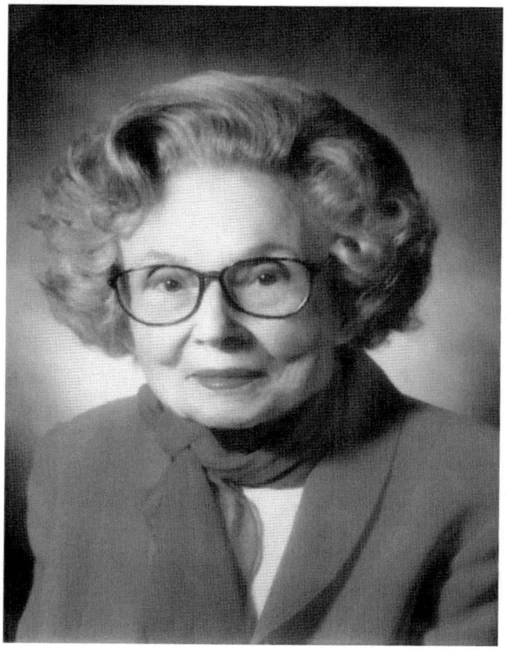

Millie Reeves
Millie Reeves created the Reeves Foundation in 1997 to honor her late husband, Carl Reeves. Because both she and her brother suffered from macular degeneration, she stipulated that half of the grant money awarded go to macular degeneration research and the other half to organizations in Columbus. Reeves also left a $5-million gift to Heritage Fund upon her death in 1999 to support Youth Camp, First Presbyterian Church, and the Bartholomew County Historical Society. (Courtesy of Heritage Fund.)

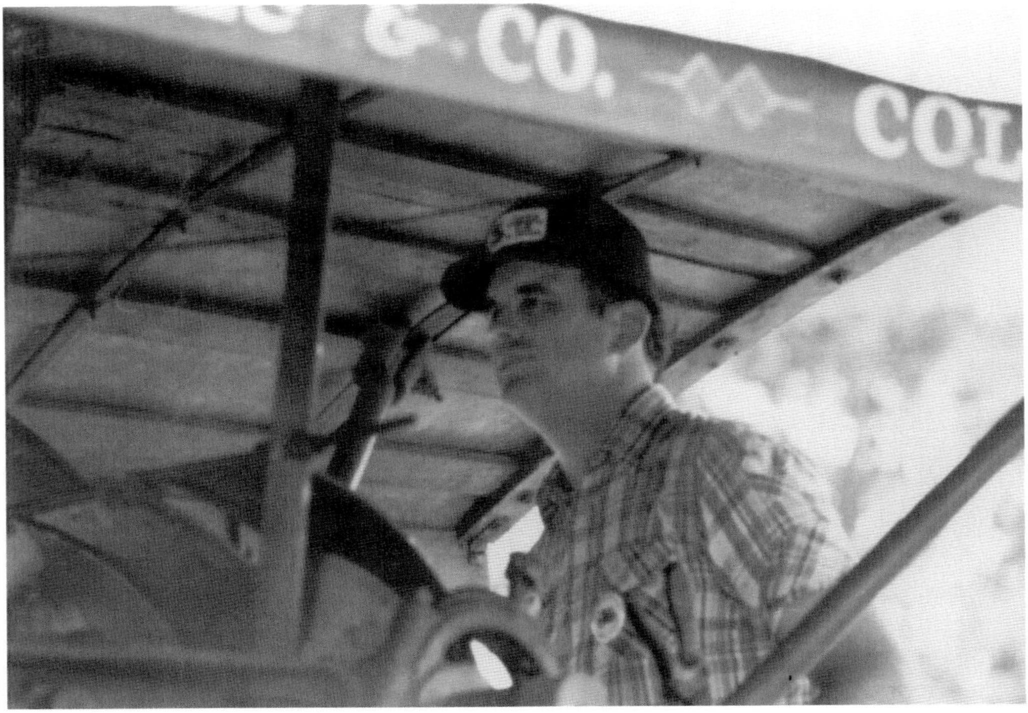

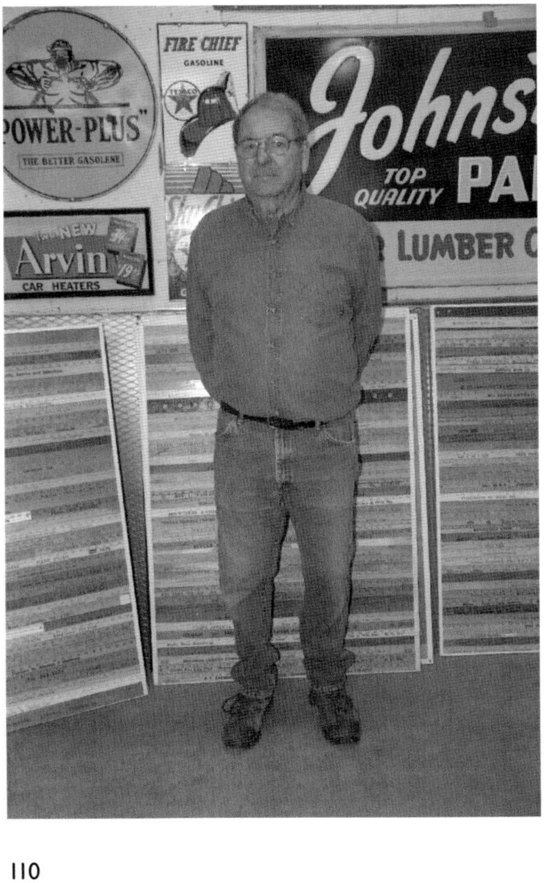

Bill Stahl

Bill Stahl can literally make history come alive. A collector of antique farm equipment with an interest in old steam engines, Stahl has restored numerous engines and operates the historical society's two Reeves engines. Stahl has fired up the engines on numerous occasions for festivals and school groups to demonstrate how the engines worked. He has also taught "steam school" at the Breeding Farm. (Courtesy of Bill Stahl.)

Jim Loesch

When the BCHS needs an item for an exhibit or special event, it calls Jim Loesch, who has collected thousands of objects including license plates, oil and gas cans, gas engines, tractors, and more. Loesch (standing in front of a wall with Columbus yardsticks and advertising signs) is particularly interested in anything related to Columbus or Reeves history and displays many of his finds in the family business, Loesch Heating & Air Conditioning, now run by the fifth generation of the family. (Photograph by author.)

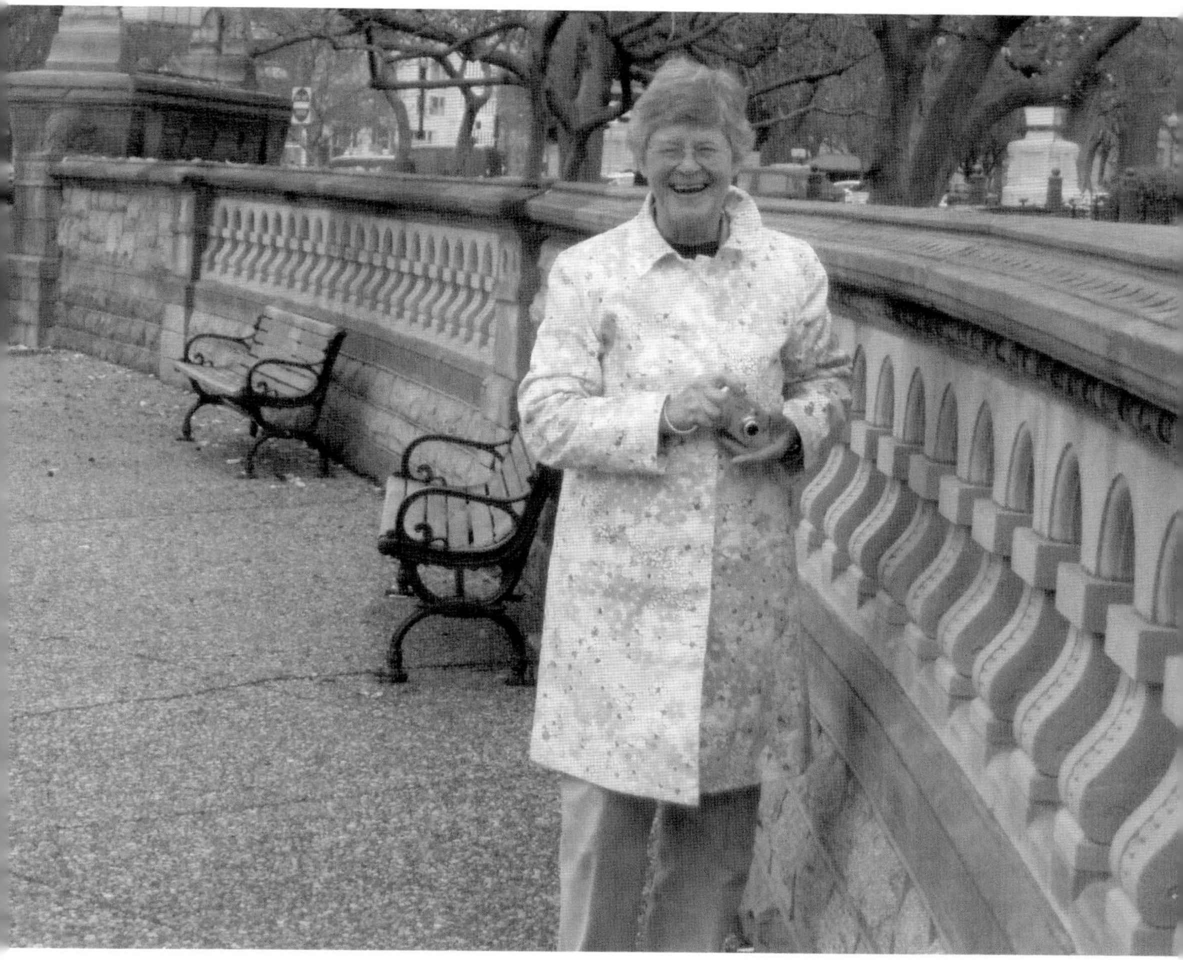

Lynn Bigley

Lynn Bigley's extensive community involvement included the creation of the Columbus Indiana Architectural Archives (CIAA), an idea that came to her after visiting many historically significant buildings in Washington, DC. Bigley realized that architectural archives would be an important part of preserving Columbus's architectural heritage; and she led the fund drive at the CIAA's inception, helped collect the documents and artifacts for the collection, and served as the organization's president. She was also a longtime tour guide for and board member of the Columbus Area Visitors Center and served on the boards of numerous other local groups, including the Columbus Human Rights Commission and the Foundation for Youth. Politically, Bigley was also very active, serving three terms on the city council and as state chair for the League of Women Voters. Together, Bigley and her husband, Tom, created Leadership Bartholomew County, a program designed to foster leadership qualities in local individuals. (Photograph by Sue Wilgus; courtesy of Rhonda Bolner.)

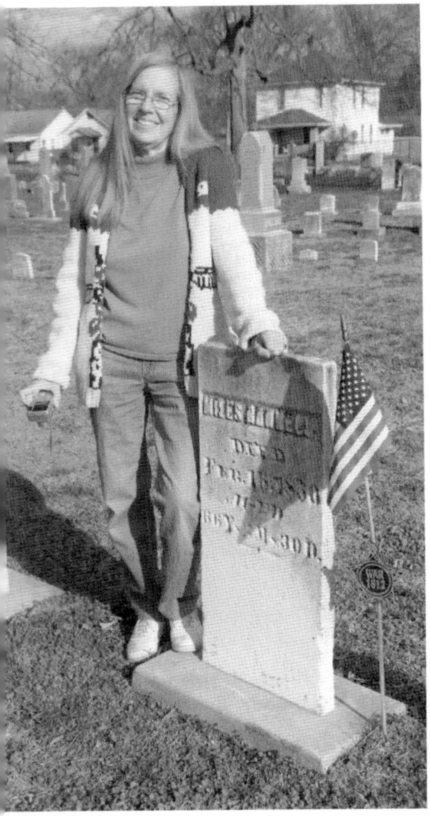

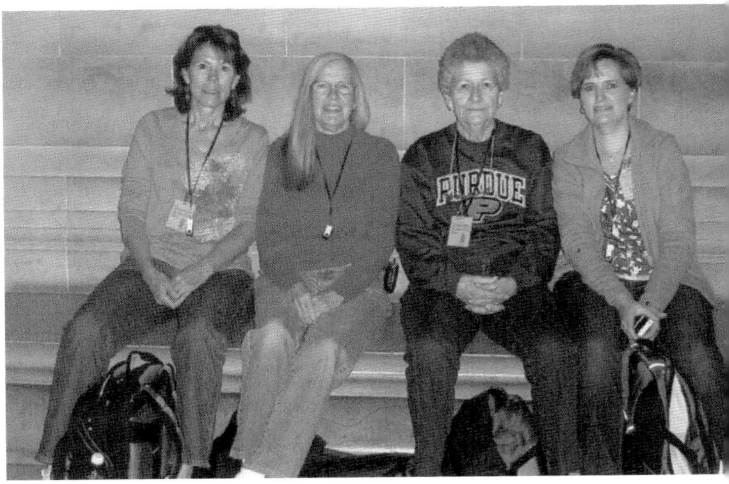

Genealogy Ladies

Four Bartholomew County Genealogical Society members, (from left to right) Kim Ray, Donna Kuhlman, Frances Land, and Rebecca Speaker, traveled to the National Archives in Washington, DC, as part of a project to identify veterans of the War of 1812 who were buried in Bartholomew County. More than 100 veterans have been identified, and 40 verified graves have been marked with War of 1812 flag stands. Kuhlman has also spent countless hours recording data about area cemeteries into the online database findagrave.com. (Left, photograph by author; above, courtesy of Donna Kuhlman.)

Susie Jones

Former county historian Susie Jones started writing stories as a child but grew to love history as she discovered the best stories are true stories. Raised on the East Coast in a family that valued travel, genealogy, education, and books, Jones embraced her new hometown and its history after moving to Columbus. She wrote often for the newspaper and authored *It Began With Bartholomew*, a collection of stories about the county's early history designed for fourth graders. (Courtesy of Meg Baker.)

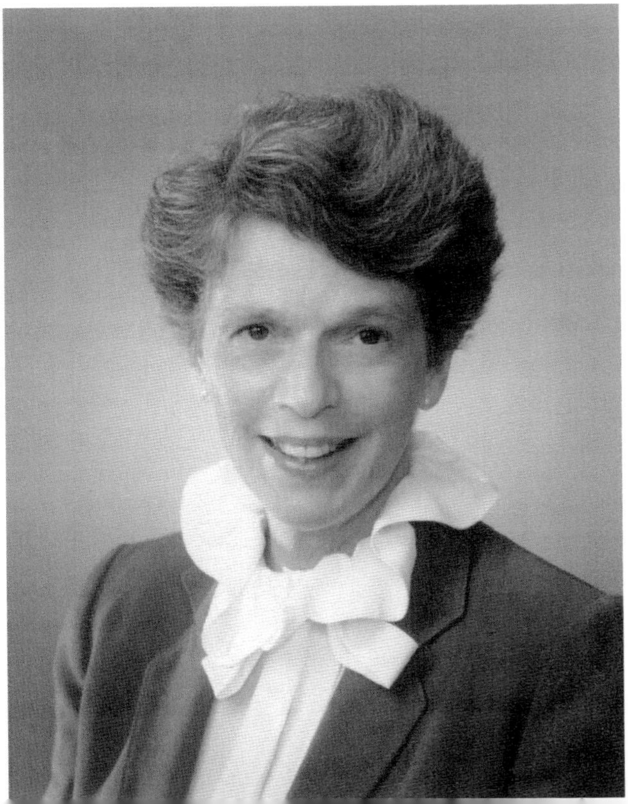

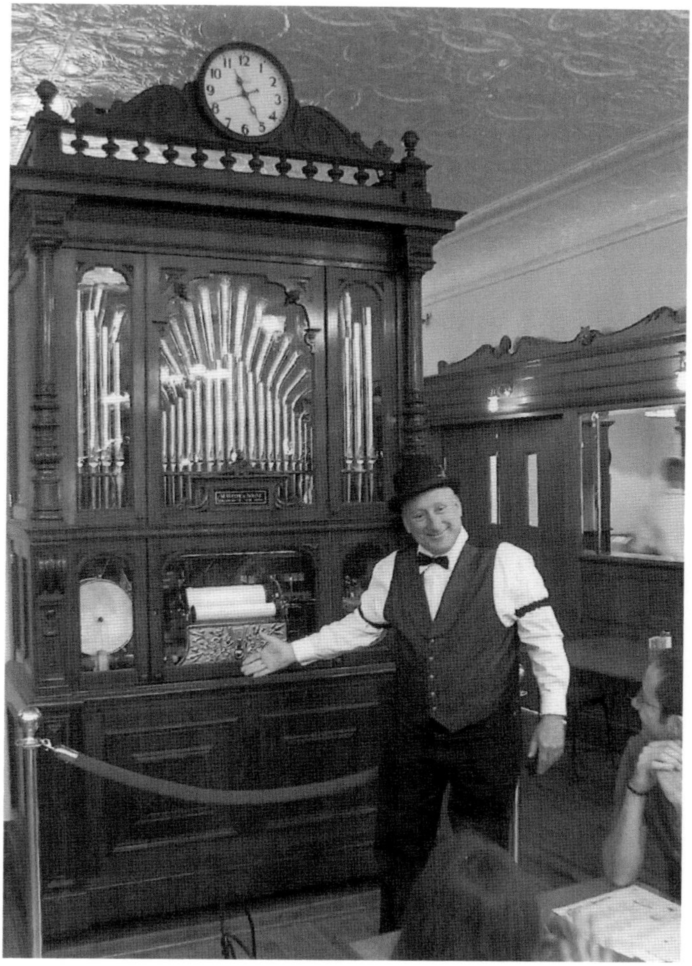

Tony Moravec

Zaharakos has been an institution in downtown Columbus for more than 100 years. Founded by the Zaharako brothers in 1900, the business started as a candy store and then became an ice cream parlor and soda fountain. For more than 100 years, members of the Zaharako family owned and managed the business, which was well known for its antique soda fountain and its German player organ. When the last of the Zaharako family to run the business passed away, the business closed in 2006. After 106 years serving generations of Columbus residents, much of the town mourned this closing, but soon local businessman and entrepreneur Tony Moravec, who owns Blairex Laboratories in Columbus, purchased the building. Moravec wanted to make an investment in the future of his community, and from 2007 to 2009, he carefully restored Zaharakos to its former glory, along with a soda fountain museum next door. The restoration included work on the original woodwork and onyx soda fountain, but for many locals, one of the best aspects of the refurbished restaurant was the reappearance of the German Welte orchestrion (a self-playing pipe organ that sounds like a full orchestra), which had been prominently featured at Zaharakos from 1908 to 2006, when it was sold to a collector. Moravec tracked it down, purchased it, refurbished it, and returned it to its home. Since its reopening, Zaharakos has been featured in numerous national stories about Columbus. While Moravec has supported other important causes, including helping found a scholarship fund for aspiring technology and manufacturing students at the local community college, it was his dedication to preserving an important part of local downtown history that helps draw visitors from all over to this restored Columbus landmark. (Courtesy of Zaharakos.)

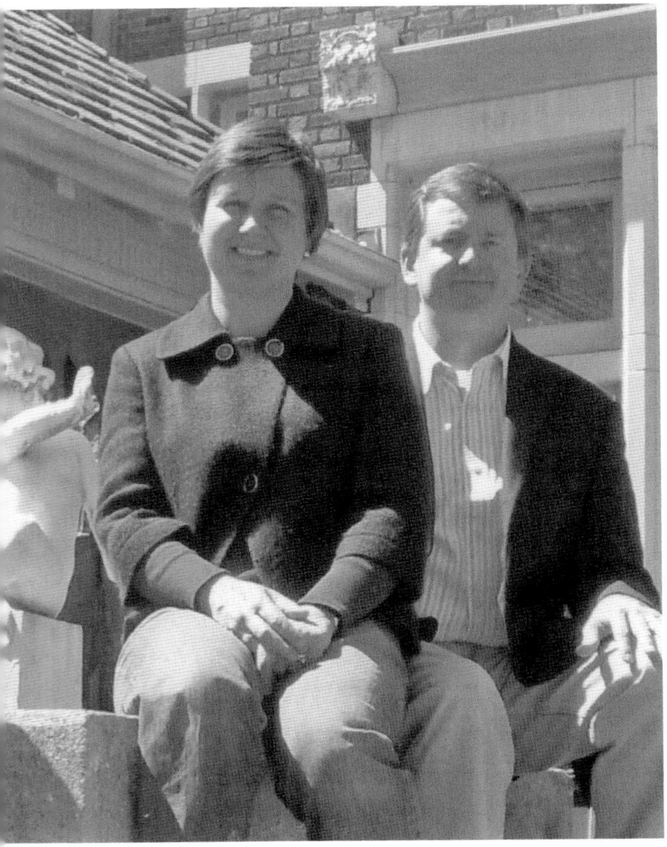

Chris and Jessica Stevens

The Irwin House on Fifth Street had been a landmark in downtown Columbus for more than 140 years when the Miller family put the home up for sale. Local couple Dr. Chris and Jessica Stevens felt passionate about protecting this community asset. Fueled by their love of old homes and entrepreneurial spirit, they purchased the home and its furnishings in 2010, opening the Inn at Irwin Gardens as a bed-and-breakfast and small event space. (Courtesy of Chris and Jessica Stevens.)

Larry Ruble

Larry Ruble has spent years preserving the history of Arvin, a company that no longer exists but was known throughout much of the 20th century for automotive components and household goods. A third-generation Arvin employee, Larry began collecting his almost 400 Arvin radios during his 40 years at the company. A plan to turn an old firehouse into an Arvin museum never materialized, and Larry has created a mini-museum of Arvin radios in his home instead. (Photograph by author.)

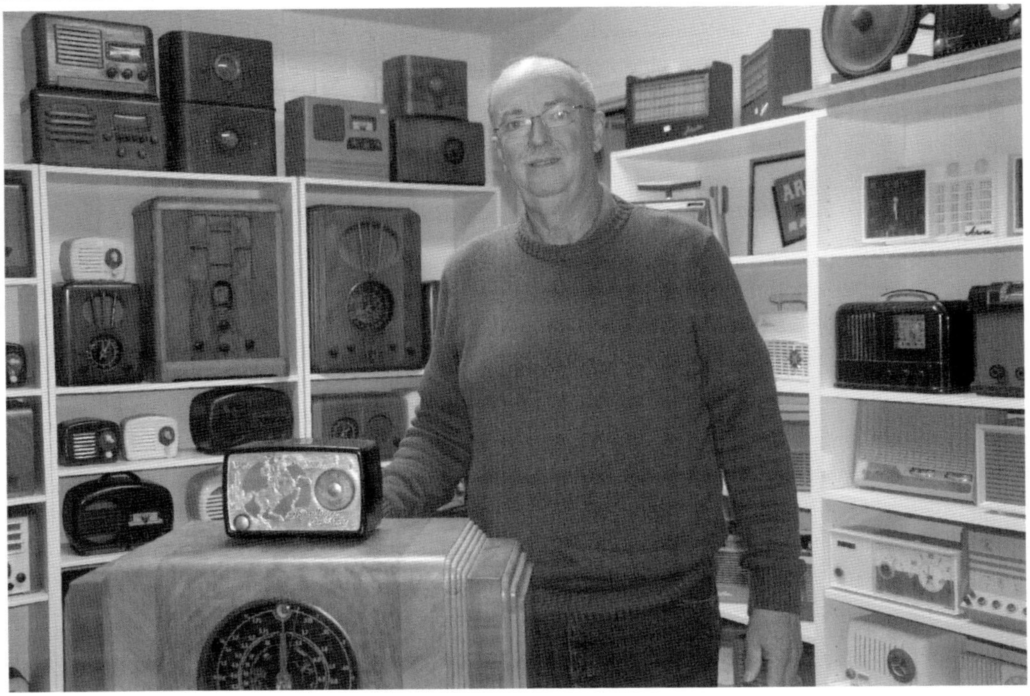

CHAPTER NINE

Exploring the County

Bartholomew County has a rich history outside the city of Columbus as well. Beginning with Joseph and Mary Cox, who, in 1819, settled in the Haw Patch near Haw Creek, many pioneer families settled on farms around the county. Quakers, who were known for their antislavery views, organized Sandcreek Township in May 1821, and the area was later home to several stops on the Underground Railroad. Escaped slaves entered Indiana by crossing the Ohio River and proceeded north to southern Bartholomew County. Underground Railroad conductors allowed the escapees to hide in their fields, outbuildings, or sometimes in hidden spaces in their homes, often without asking the runaways' names, so they could honestly report they had not seen a particular person if the slave catchers came looking.

Hope was settled in 1829 when Martin Hauser and his famil115y, along with several other Moravian families from North Carolina, arrived in the area to start a new Moravian community. The first Moravian church was built the next year. Since that time, Hope has been important in the history of the US Postal Service and home to many colorful individuals. Dr. Eugene Regennas was truly a man of varied talents, serving as dentist, physician, carpenter, and church organist for more than 50 years. Photographer J.T. Schaub took photographs of Hope and Columbus in the late 19th century. He also photographed many Hope citizens, although no known photographs of Schaub or his family survive. At a time when few in town owned automobiles, Elda Spaugh opened a filling station in Hope in 1915 but needed more customers. He came up with a unique plan to paint yellow stripes around fence posts and telephone poles along the roads leading into town and advertised "Spaugh's Garage, the Home of the Yellow Trail." The history museum in Hope takes its name from this. Former teacher Barbara Johnson has helped keep history alive in Hope for many years. She sponsored history clubs at the elementary, middle, and high school levels and serves on the Yellow Trail Museum Board today.

Other small towns out in the county have their own stories, including Hartsville. Bishop Milton Wright, father of aviation pioneers Orville and Wilbur, lived and taught here for a time, and Hartsville is the final resting place for Civil War veteran Barton Mitchell, who played a large role in events that led to the Battle of Antietam and indirectly to the end of the war. Hartsville was also home to Hartsville College, a well-respected institute of higher learning in the second half of the 19th century.

Some county towns were not so lucky and did not survive. Cormantown in Flatrock Township was once thriving but disappeared after the railroad chose instead to go through Clifford. Likewise, Nortonburg was a bustling stop on the railroad in the 19th century, but today all that remains is a railroad sign with the name. In Ninevah Township, the town of Kansas disappeared after the government took over land in northwest Bartholomew County and built Camp Atterbury in 1942.

Many early pioneer families established farms around the county beginning in the first half of the 19th century. Some of these families still own their original farms and have been awarded Hoosier Homestead awards for more than 100 years of family ownership. Other families remain in the area but no longer own any or all of their family's original land. In 1900, the Marr family had the unique distinction of owning land in Eastern Bartholomew County that included the geographic center of population of the United States at that time.

Although the city of Columbus has had its share of legendary locals, other areas of Bartholomew County have been home to many interesting individuals as well.

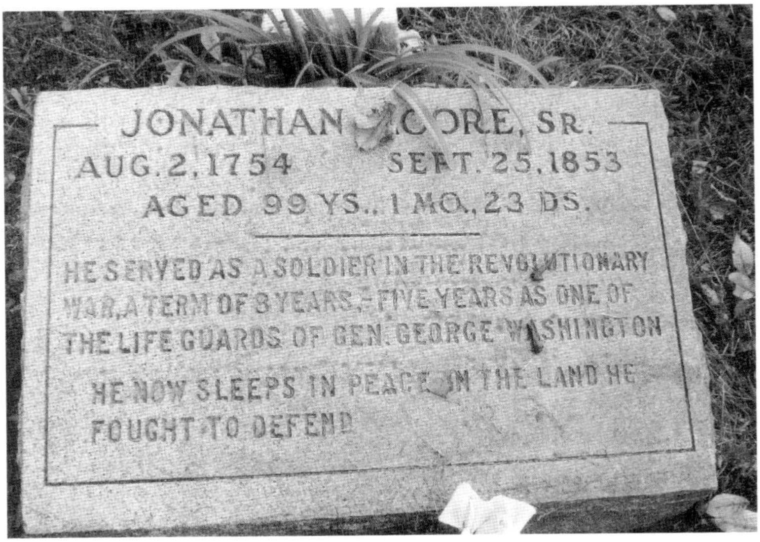

Jonathan Moore
Sharon Cemetery in Clay Township is home to the grave of Revolutionary War veteran Jonathan Moore, who served five years as one of George Washington's lifeguards, or personal bodyguards. He served with Washington in several important battles, including the Battle of Yorktown. After the war, Moore eventually moved to Bartholomew County, where he died in 1853 at 99 years of age. State Road 46 west of downtown is named after Moore. (Photograph by Candy Carr.)

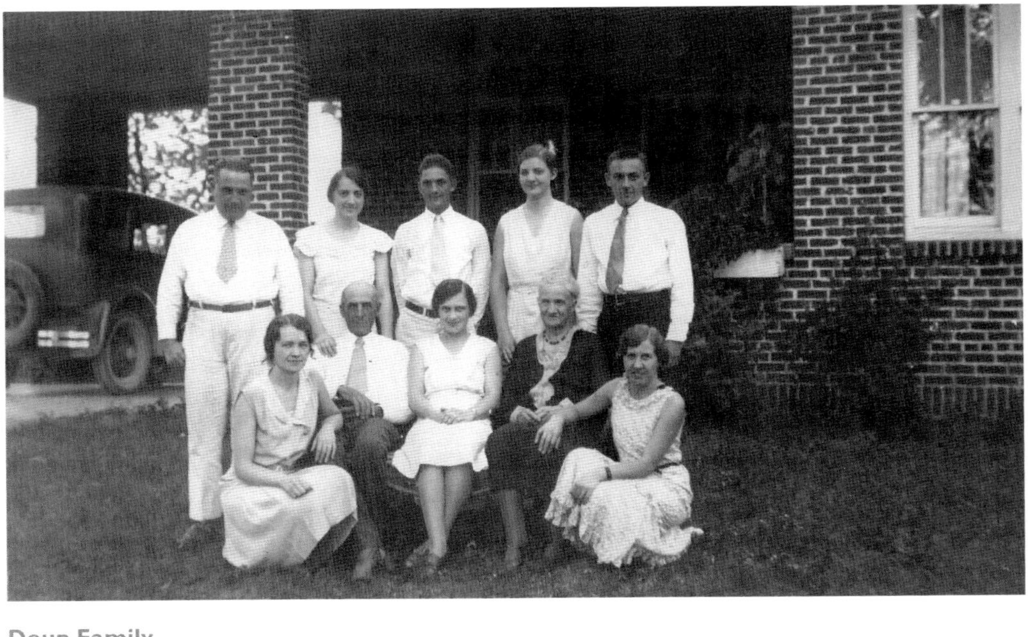

Doup Family
George Doup was one of Bartholomew County's original settlers, arriving around 1821 and settling in the Haw Patch. His great-grandson Clarence Doup and his wife, Mary, had eight children (pictured around 1932). Oldest sibling Scott (standing at left) was a colorful storyteller who led unofficial tours of Columbus after his retirement. Brothers George (standing at center) and Perry (standing at right) were the last of the Doups to farm the land, some of which remains in the family. (Courtesy of the Doup family.)

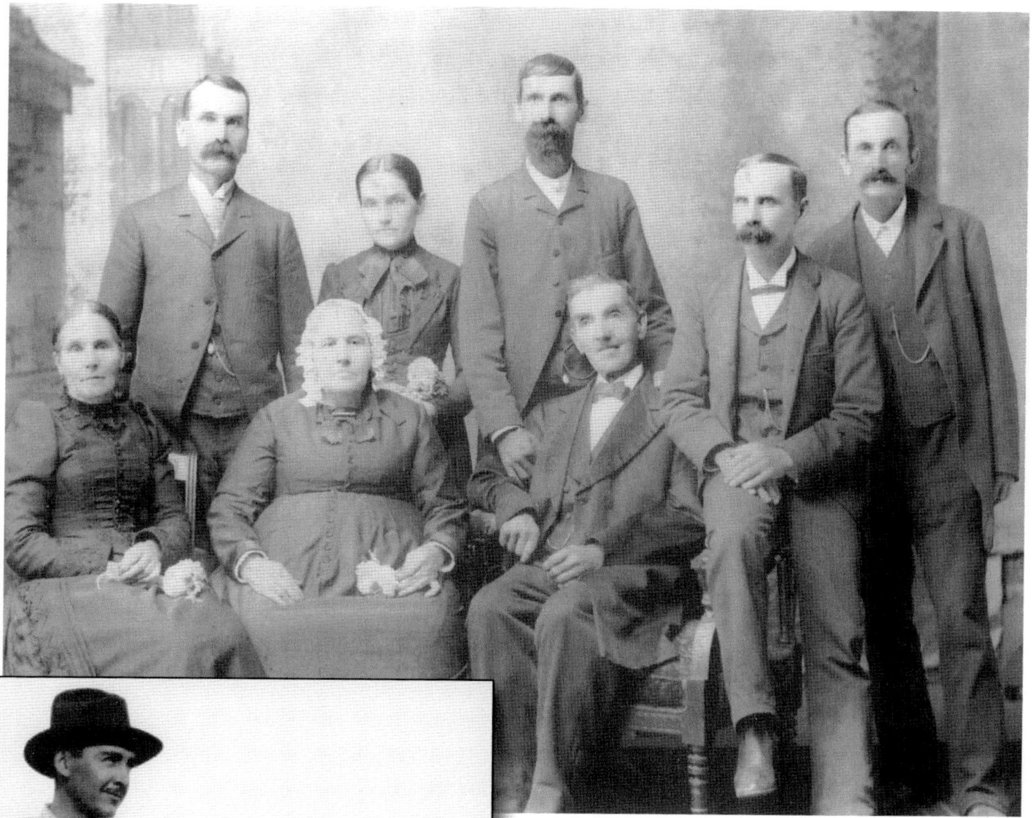

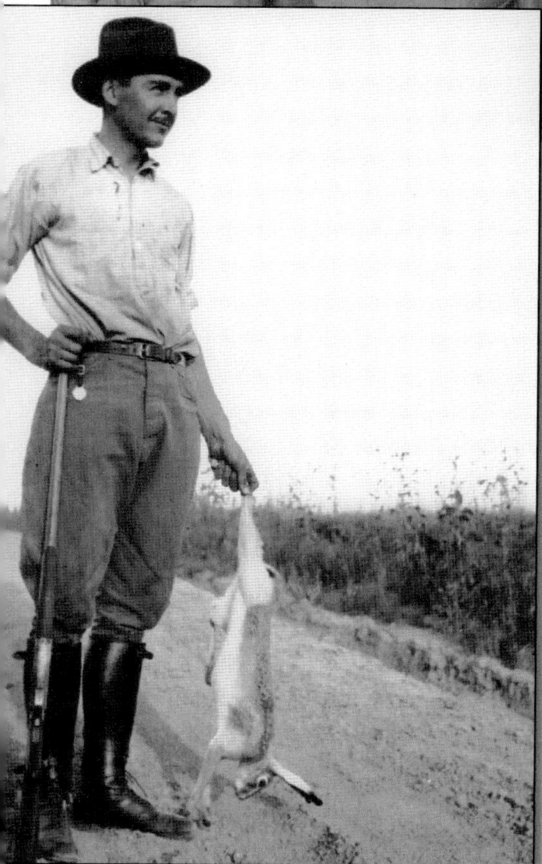

Joseph and Delilah Glick

Joseph and Delilah Glick came to Bartholomew County with their family in 1854. Their farmhouse in Clifty Township was one of the first brick homes in the county. They also built a Lutheran church but could not find a Lutheran minister who would travel to the country church, so they became Methodists. As per a custom of the time, upon Joseph's death in 1895, they called a photographer to photograph the family (above) before his burial. (Courtesy of Linda Glick Forster.)

Lloyd Henry Glick

Lloyd Glick was a Purdue-educated teacher who went into farming after World War II. He started a seed corn business on three acres given to him by his father, and all work initially was done by hand. Today, Lloyd's great-grandsons Trevor and Brett Glick are the fourth generation to run the family business, which is now called L&M Glick Seed. (Courtesy of Linda Glick Forster.)

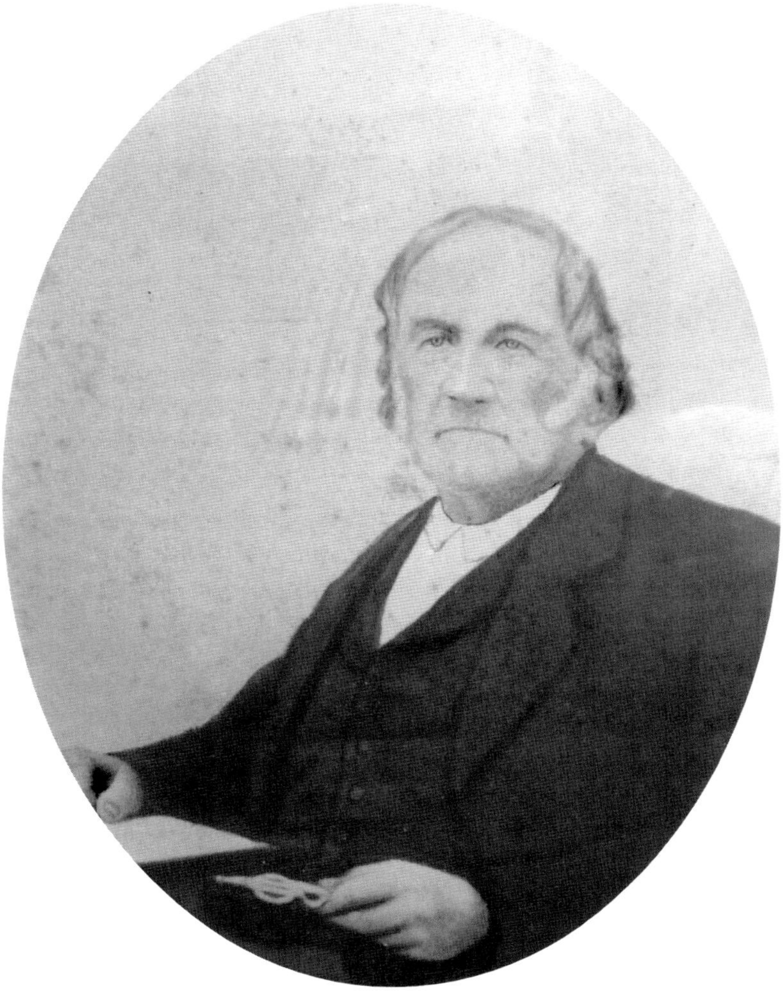

Martin Hauser

In 1829, Martin Hauser and his family, along with a small group of other Moravian settlers, chose to move west from Salem, North Carolina, to Indiana, where Hauser's brother Jacob had settled earlier. Martin Hauser was a self-taught minister of the Moravian church and convinced church officials that he could start a new town and new church in Indiana. Jacob had settled in what was known as the Haw Patch in northern Bartholomew County, but Martin settled east of there and founded Hope (originally called Goshen), Indiana. Martin Hauser and his family moved into their newly completed cabin in March 1830, and church services were held at their home until the first church building was complete in June of that year. Today, the Hope Moravian Church is the only Moravian church remaining in Indiana. One of the oldest denominations in the world, the Moravians were known for their support of education for all, including girls and young women. In the 1860s, the Moravian Female Seminary for Young Ladies was started in Hope to educate girls from all over the Midwest. The school closed in 1881 for financial reasons, and the buildings were later used for a teacher-training school. The Moravians are also known for using music in their worship service and for starting the tradition of an Easter sunrise service. Martin Hauser eventually moved on to start another Moravian community in West Salem, Illinois, and that church also survives today. His wife, Susannah, died in West Salem in 1868, and Hauser returned to Hope to be close to friends and family. Hauser died in 1875 while still in Hope but is buried in Illinois next to Susannah. (Courtesy of Hope Moravian Church.)

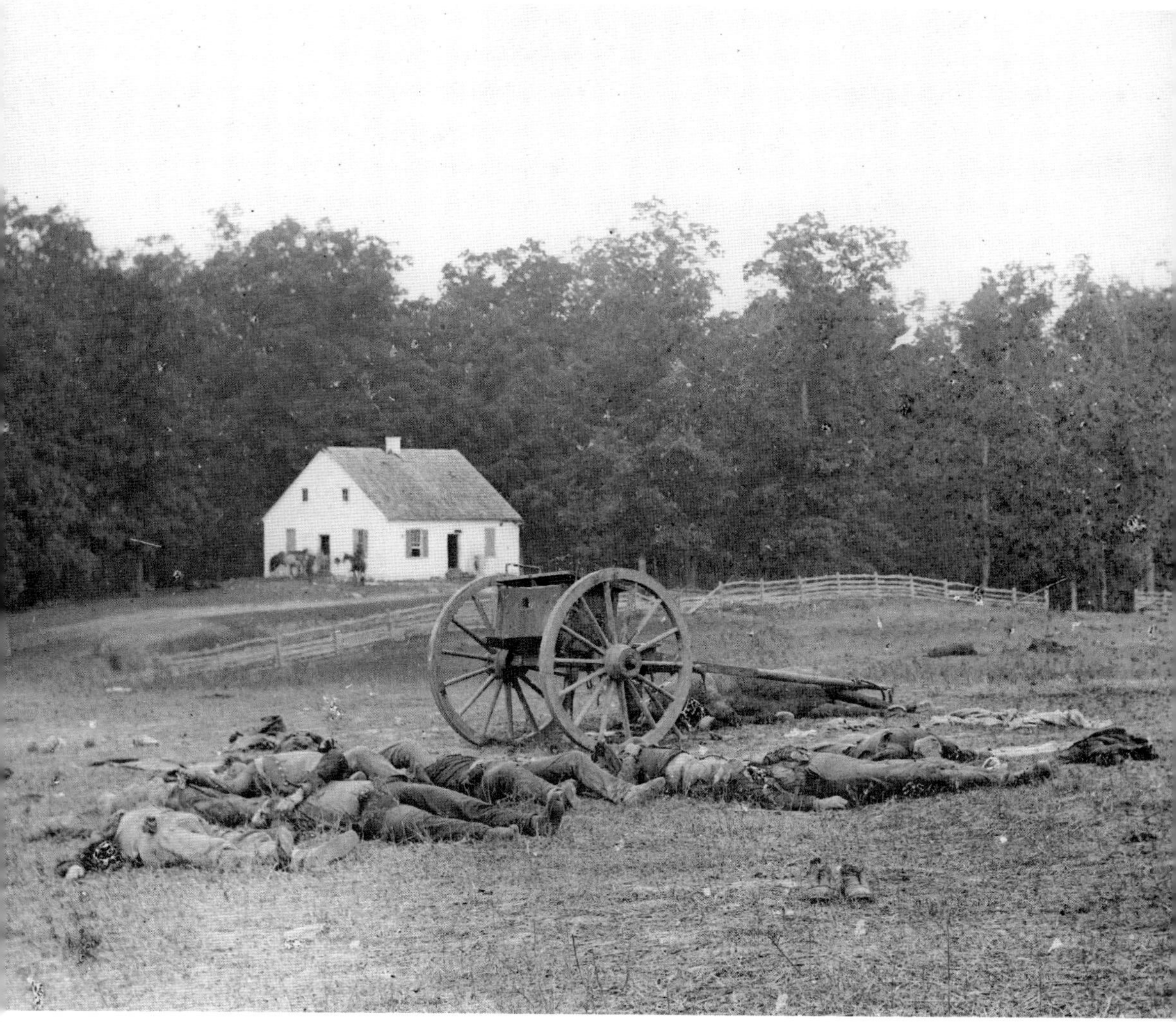

Barton Mitchell

In September 1862, a future Bartholomew County resident, Pvt. Baron Mitchell, was resting with a fellow soldier in Maryland early in the Civil War. Mitchell came across something that would turn the tide of the war to the benefit of the Union but with devastating consequences. Wrapped up with three cigars, the men found what appeared to be lost orders from Confederate general Robert E. Lee, revealing a plan to invade Maryland. The men passed the orders to their superiors, who, upon learning of Lee's plans, chose to engage him early instead. The result was the Battle of Antietam on September 17, 1862. This was the first battle fought on Union soil and the single bloodiest day of the Civil War, with 23,000 Union and Confederate casualties. The Confederate losses forced Lee to withdraw to Virginia. Although it was not a decisive win for the North, it prompted Pres. Abraham Lincoln to release the Emancipation Proclamation, which discouraged British or French recognition of or aid to the Confederacy, something Northerners had feared could propel the South to victory. After the war, Barton Mitchell retired to Bartholomew County, where he died three years later. He is buried in Hartsville, where a plaque in the town square commemorates his important role in the Civil War. (Library of Congress.)

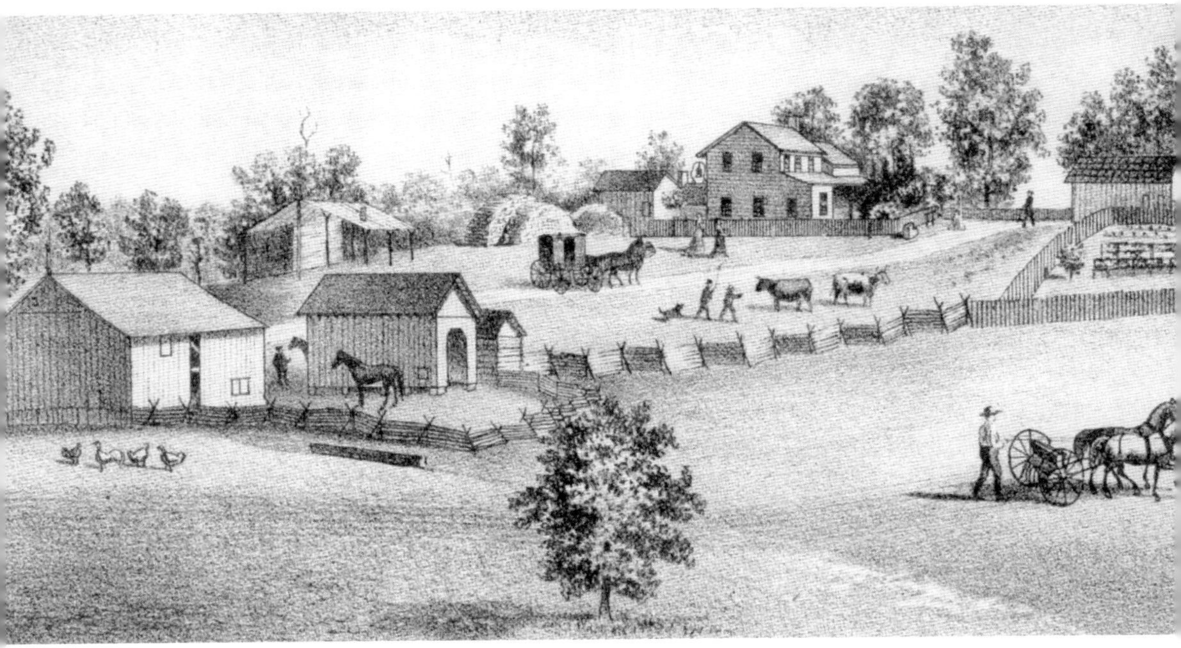

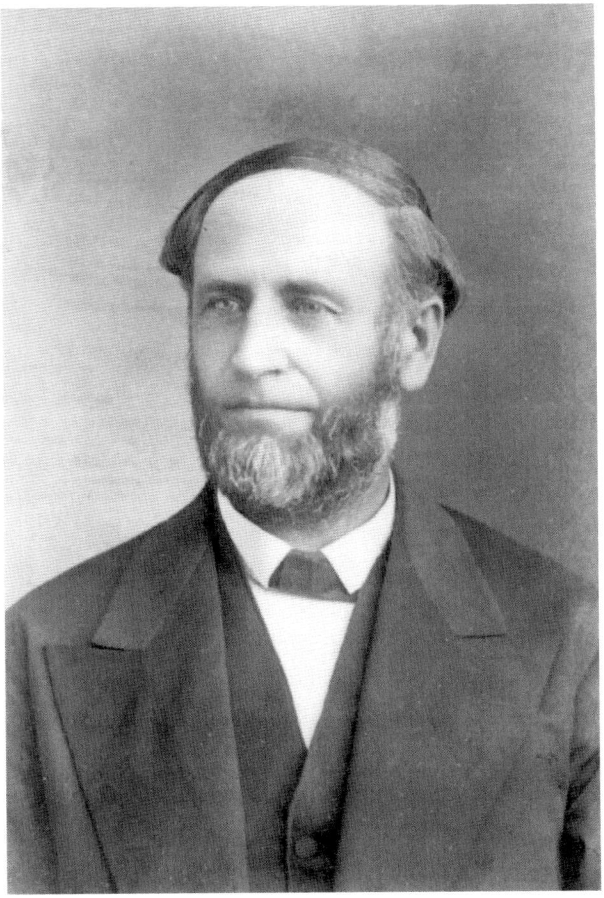

John Hall
In the 1800s, Sandcreek Township was an important stop for escaped slaves on the Underground Railroad. Quakers did not believe in war or slavery, and John Hall and his neighbor John Thomas were conductors on the Underground Railroad and allowed former slaves to hide on their farms. Because Kentucky was a slave state, the Underground Railroad started for many escaped slaves as soon as they crossed the Ohio River into Indiana. (Author's collection.)

Bishop Milton Wright
The father of Orville and Wilbur Wright, Bishop Milton Wright met his future wife, Susan, at Hartsville College in Bartholomew County. A pastor, Wright moved his family 12 times among various towns in Indiana before settling in Dayton, Ohio. Between 1868 and 1869, the Wright family (including toddler Wilbur) lived in Hartsville while the elder Wright taught theology at Hartsville College. (Courtesy of Special Collections and Archives, Wright State University.)

Dr. Eugene Regennas

Dr. Eugene Regennas was a Hope dentist, physician, poet, architect, and musician. A member of the Moravian church, Regennas served as organist for more than 50 years (1877–1932). He was a talented wood-carver and poet, and samples of his carvings and his books of poetry are on display in the Yellow Trail Museum in Hope. In 1915, Regennas designed the original town square bandstand, a replica of which still stands today. (Yellow Trail Museum Collection.)

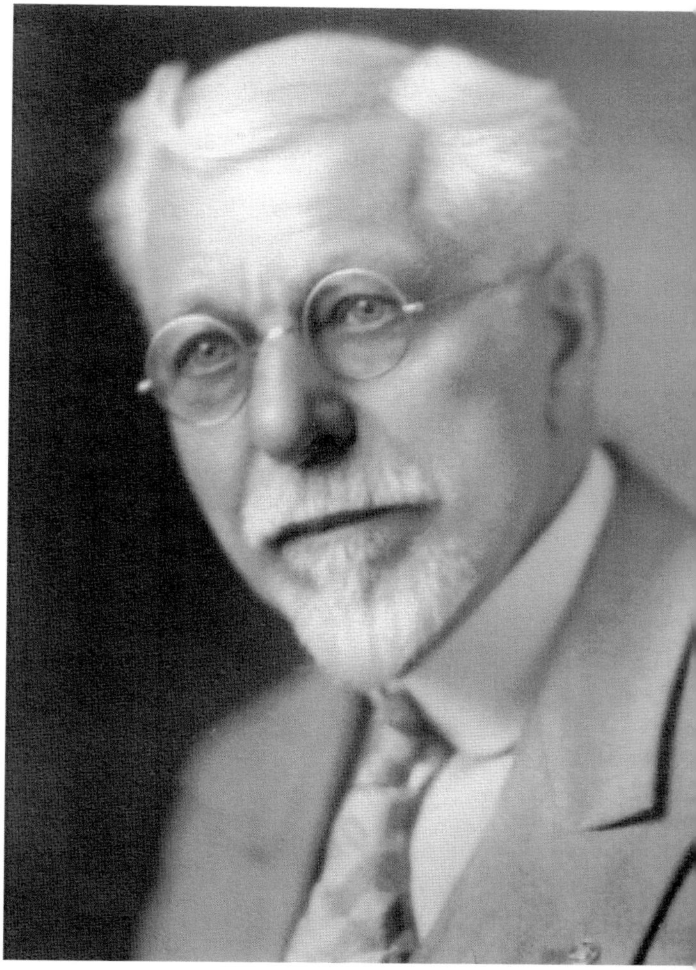

Hope Rural Mail Carriers

In 1896, the US postmaster general chose Hope as one of the first experimental sites for rural mail delivery. Prior to this, citizens traveled to the post office to pick up their own mail. The photograph shows Hope's rural mail carriers about to leave on their route in 1903. From left to right are Joe Clouse, M. Rominger, Albert Hitchcock, John Moore, and Frank Rominger. Today, Hope is home to the Rural Letter Carriers Museum. (Yellow Trail Museum Collection.)

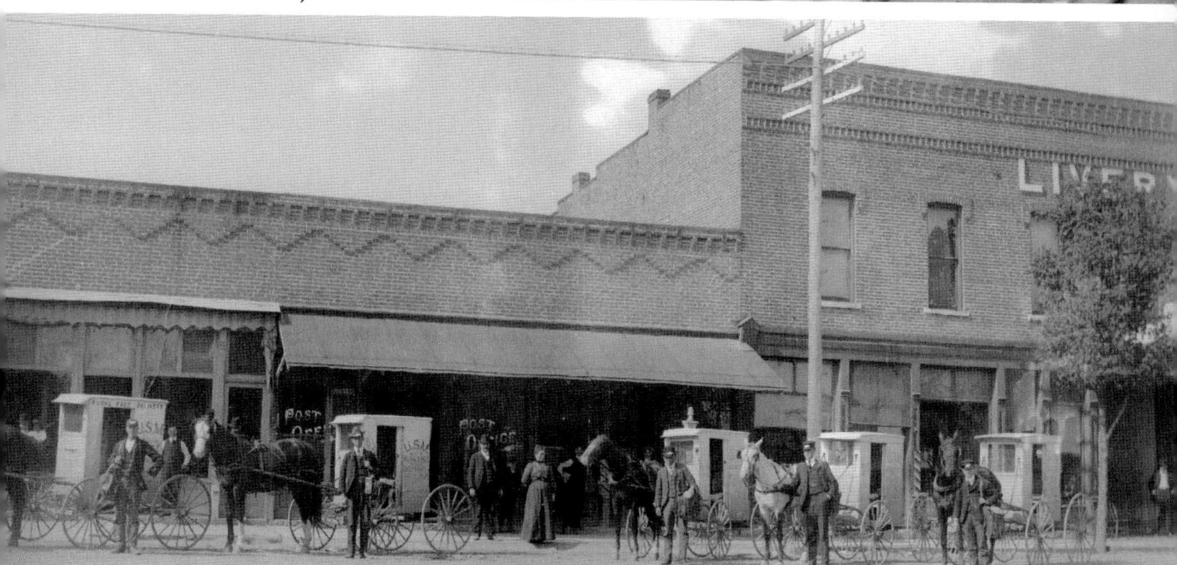

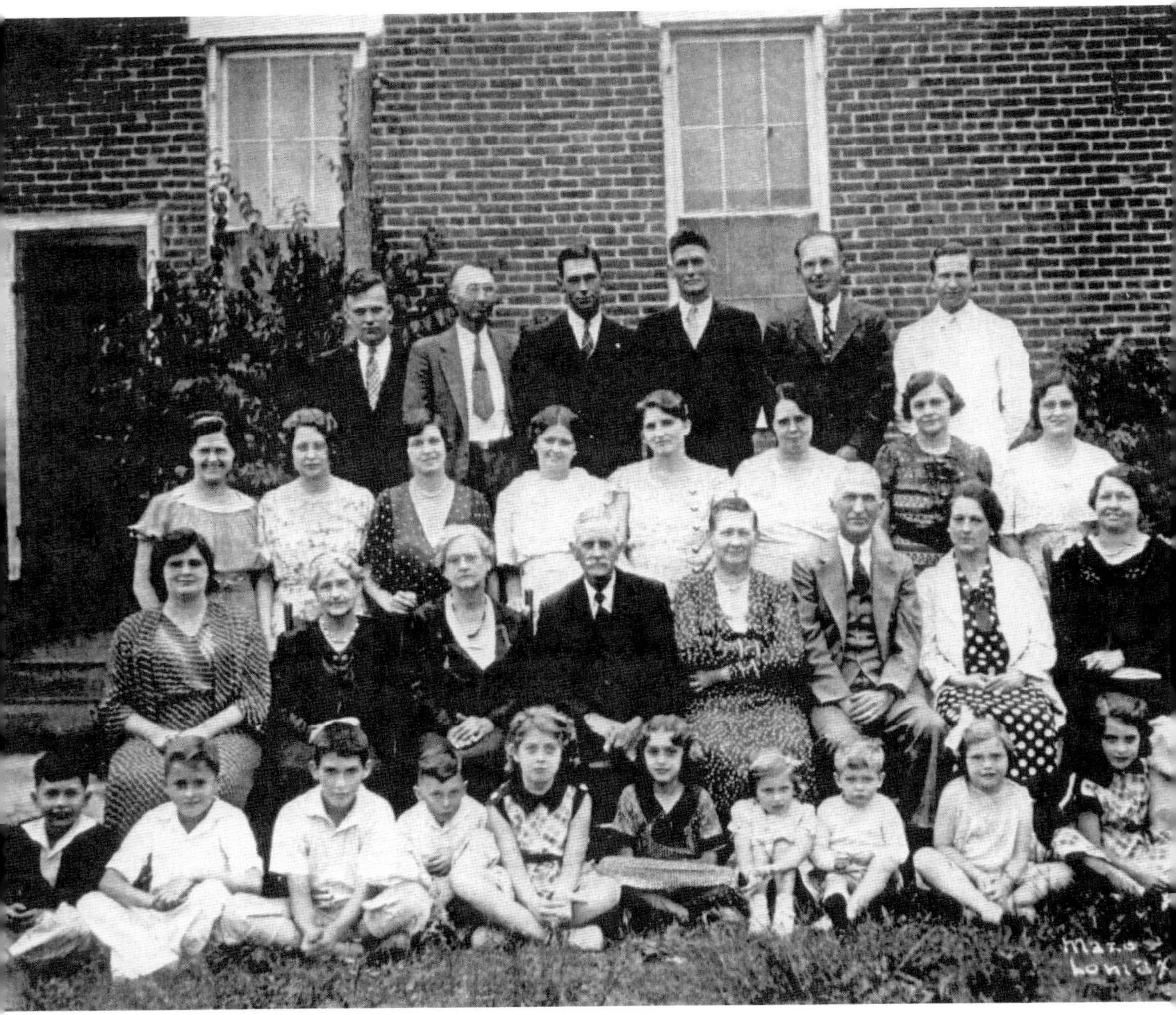

Fodrea Family

The Fodrea family lived and farmed near Azalia across the road from a one-room schoolhouse, which they bought and turned into their home after their house burned to the ground. After finishing eighth grade, the children could go to Columbus High School if they could get there via the interurban trolley, which traveled to Columbus several miles away. Later, older sisters Grace and Bess lived in town and housed any of their siblings who wanted to attend high school. Every Sunday, the extended family gathered at the family home for dinner and music, with the adults gathering around the piano and pump organ to sing together. The musical talent carried on to following generations, as Maude Fodrea Barbour (third row, third from left) was the mother of Don and Ross Barbour, two of the founding members of the Four Freshmen (page 78). Nelle Fodrea Flanigan (third row, far right) was the mother of Bob Flanigan, another member of the Freshmen. (Courtesy of Ivadel Simpson Hannah.)

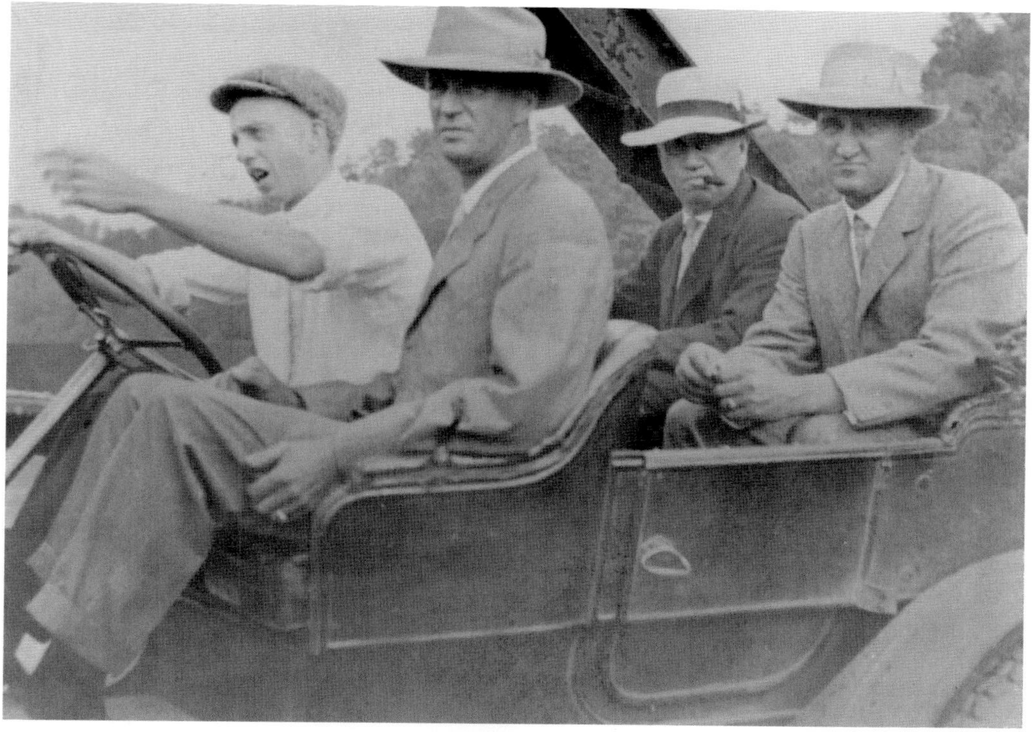

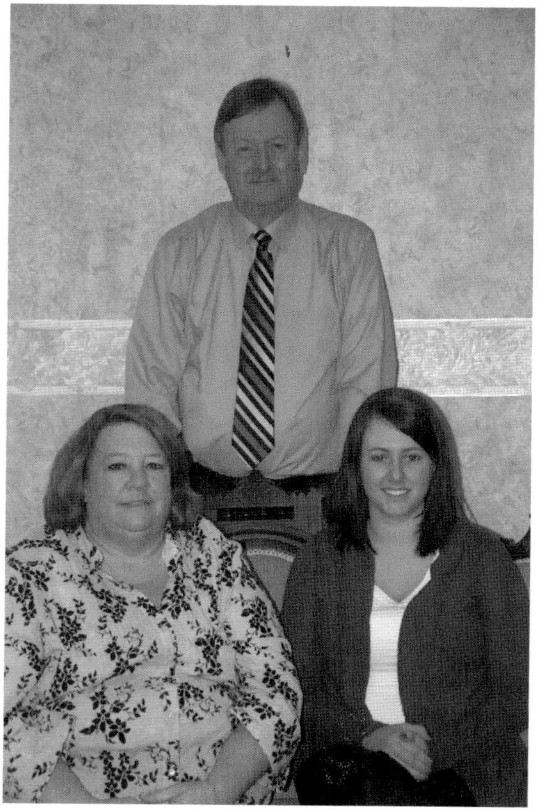

Marr Family

James Marr settled in German Township around 1820 before later moving to Iowa Territory in 1842. His grandson, (also named James Marr) had three sons, Edd (far right), William (second from right), and Henry (sitting in front with William's son David). Edd farmed the original Marr farm northeast of town on Marr Road, and Henry farmed near Elizabethtown on a farm that was the US center of population in 1900. (Courtesy of Lou Marr.)

Norman Family

Norman Funeral Home is the oldest business in Hope run by the same family and one of the oldest businesses in Bartholomew County. The business was established in 1880 by father and son George and E.A. Norman and, in 1901, moved to its current location on the town square. John Norman was the fourth generation of Normans to run the business, and prior to his death in 2013, he and his wife, Suzie, began training their daughter, Ashley, (pictured with her parents) to take over the funeral home. (Photograph by author.)

Glen Keller

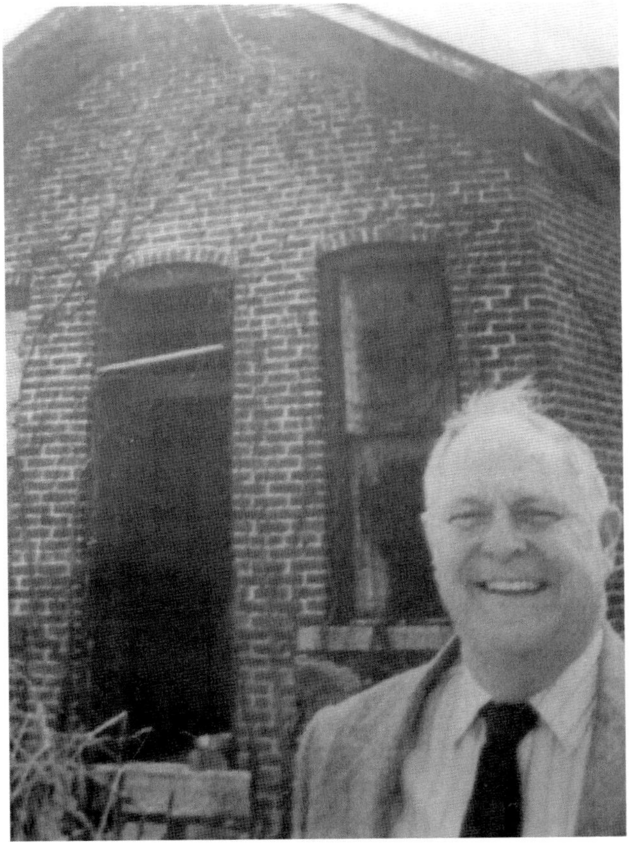

Over the past two decades, approximately 50,000 elementary students have learned firsthand about attending a one-room schoolhouse at Simmons School in Hope thanks to an ambitious plan led by Glen Keller. Keller grew up in Hope and was a longtime educator and principal who spearheaded the effort to bring an old one-room schoolhouse to the Hope Elementary School grounds. Fundraising commenced in 1988 and took over four years. The plan was to transport the derelict building, which had been used as a school from 1879 to 1907, from the Simmons family land to the new location. In 1989, the school was moved slowly through town to its new home in a flurry of excitement and publicity, and in September 1992, the Simmons School was dedicated. Since then, students come from up to 80 miles away for field trips to learn about the past with trained "school marms" teaching them. (Right, courtesy of Glen Keller; below, photograph by author.)

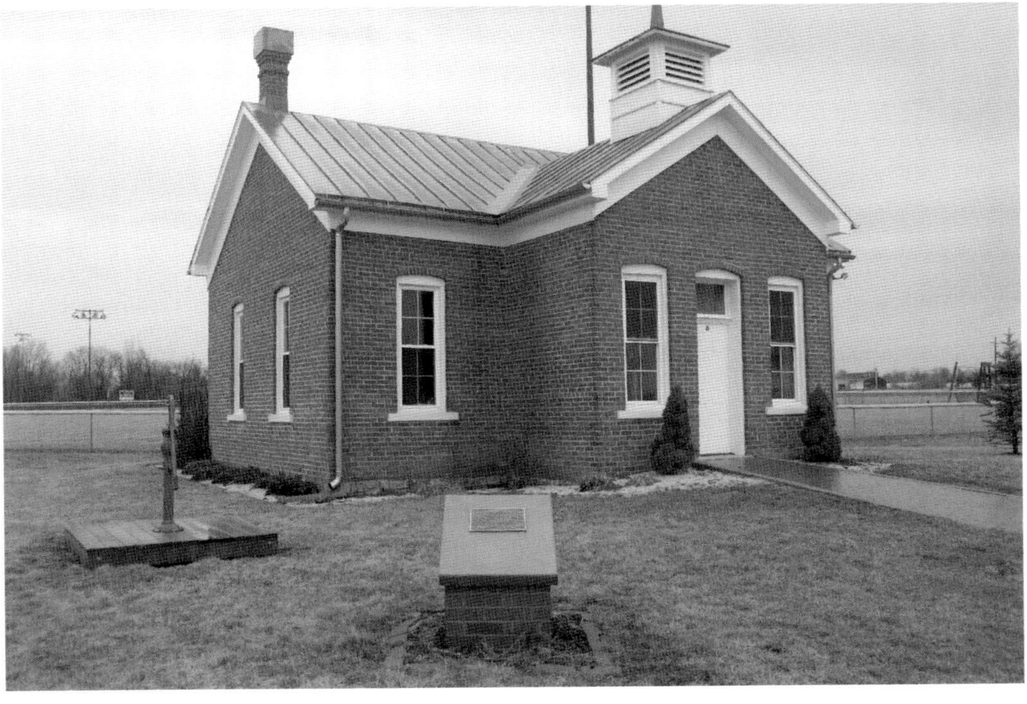

Merrill Clouse

Merrill Clouse always felt a strong connection to the community in which he was born and where he spent most of his life. He married his childhood sweetheart, Norma Gilliland, before leaving Hope to serve in the Army in 1942. When he returned to town after the war, he joined his father to expand the family business, a grocery and meat locker on the town square that later included a slaughterhouse and smokehouse. Eventually, Merrill became owner of the business, which he continued to run into his seventies. Along the way, he was head of the Hope Business Association and, in 1967, he spearheaded the first Hope Heritage Days, an annual festival to celebrate community history. Initially including period costumes and historic demonstrations, the festival later expanded to several days and continues today as a much-anticipated community event. Clouse worked with Dorotha and J. Bill Heilman during the early years of Heritage Days to encourage all businesses on the town square to display antiques during the festival in their front windows. Soon, the need for a place permanently to display and store the artifacts became apparent. In 1975, the upstairs of a building on the square owned by the Clouses became available, and he offered the space free of rent for use as a history museum. The Clouses and Heilmans visited other local history museums in Indiana to get ideas for the Yellow Trail Museum. When the downstairs of the building later became available, Merrill allowed the museum to expand into that space, eventually selling the building to the museum for a nominal fee. Over the years, Merrill addressed other community needs as well, including serving in Hope's volunteer fire department. When the fire siren would sound, Clouse and other volunteers would leave their homes or businesses, race to the fire station, and travel to the fire. When he was asked to serve as chief due to his years of experience, Clouse accepted the job and kept it for more than 36 years. Later in his career, Clouse and several friends in the American Legion decided that Hope's veterans deserved recognition and raised money for a veteran's memorial, which was placed at the edge of the Moravian Church Cemetery in 1990. (Courtesy of the Clouse family.)

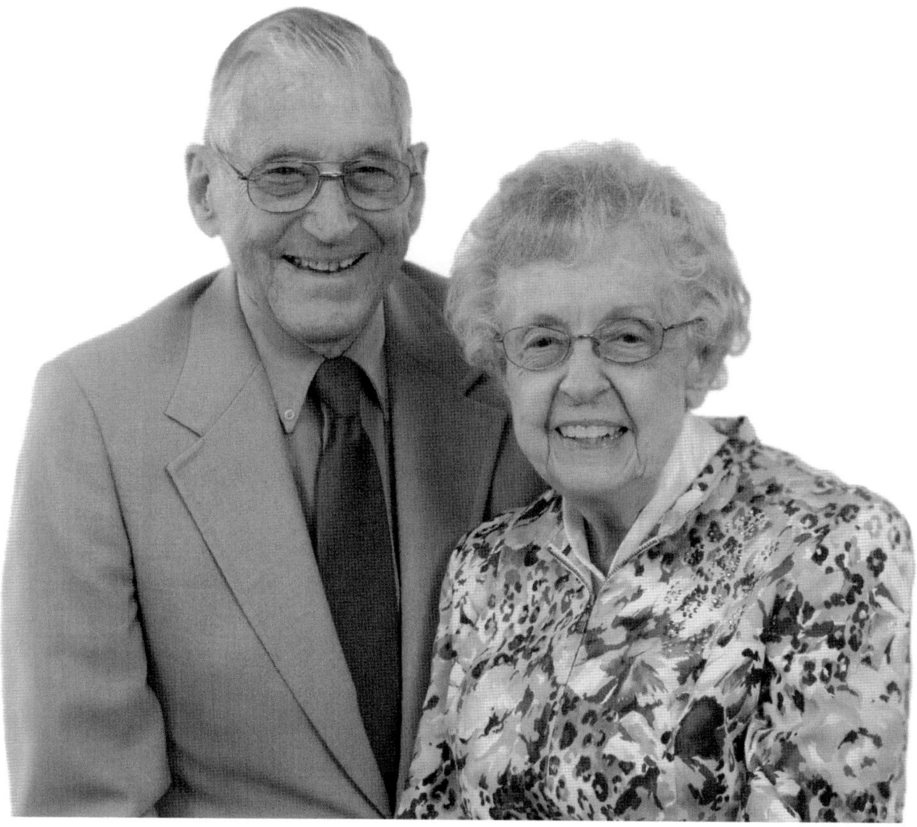

INDEX